AI & U

REIMAGINE BUSINESS

Tracy Sheen

Also by Tracy Sheen

The End of Technophobia: A practical guide to digitising your business

In *The End of Technophobia*, Tracy Sheen delivers a refreshingly accessible and empowering guide for business owners who want to make peace with digital technology – once and for all. With a clear, no-jargon approach, Tracy demystifies the digital tools that many small business owners find overwhelming, showing how to embrace them confidently and use them to grow and future-proof their business.

Drawing on decades of experience in marketing, tech, and small business education, Tracy helps readers break through the fear and confusion often associated with the digital world. From websites and social media to cloud-based tools and automation, this book provides a step-by-step roadmap to help you identify the right technology for your business needs – without the tech overwhelm.

Praised for its practicality, warmth, and humour, *The End of Technophobia* is the ultimate companion for anyone who's ever said, "I'm just not good with technology". With Tracy as your guide, you'll discover that you don't need to be a tech expert to succeed – you just need the right support.

Available in ebook and print formats online, and from all good bookstores.

First published in 2025 by Tracy Sheen

© Tracy Sheen 2025
The moral rights of the author have been asserted

All rights reserved. Except as permitted under the *Australian Copyright Act 1968* (for example, a fair dealing for the purposes of study, research, criticism or review), no part of this book may be reproduced, stored in a retrieval system, communicated or transmitted in any form or by any means without prior written permission. No part of this book may be used or reproduced in any manner for the purpose of training artificial intelligence technologies or systems.

All inquiries should be made to the author.

A catalogue entry for this book is available from the National Library of Australia.

ISBN: 978-1-923225-78-7

Book production and text design by Publish Central
Cover design by Julia Kuris

The paper this book is printed on is certified as environmentally friendly.

Disclaimer
The material in this publication is of the nature of general comment only, and does not represent professional advice. It is not intended to provide specific guidance for particular circumstances and it should not be relied on as the basis for any decision to take action or not take action on any matter which it covers. Readers should obtain professional advice where appropriate, before making any such decision. To the maximum extent permitted by law, the author and publisher disclaim all responsibility and liability to any person, arising directly or indirectly from any person taking or not taking action based on the information in this publication.

Contents

PREFACE

REIMAGINE the future of your business

Imagine waking up one day to find your competitors offering instant customer responses, predicting trends before they happen, and delivering personalised experiences you can't match. Your customers notice, and they start to drift away.

This isn't some far-off future. It's happening all over the place *right now*, driven by Artificial Intelligence (AI). You may already have experienced this, as a customer or a business owner.

But here's the good news: you don't need to be a tech wizard or have a massive budget to harness the massive potential of AI. You just need curiosity, an open mind, a willingness to take the first step – and this book. 😆

Why AI matters for your business

Think back to the early 2000s when email began replacing fax machines. I was working with Harvey Norman, helping business owners navigate the latest tech, and I'll never forget the scepticism. 'Do you think this email thing will *really* catch on?' customers would ask.

Fast-forward a few years, and those who hesitated were scrambling – or worse, left behind.

AI is today's email moment, but the stakes are even higher and the pace is faster. Customers expect instant responses, personalised interactions, and more imaginative solutions. Businesses that embrace AI are gaining an edge, while those that hesitate are losing relevance.

AI can help you work smarter, not harder – freeing you to focus on what truly matters in your business. It isn't just for big corporations. It's also for café owners managing inventory, tradies streamlining scheduling, and consultants building stronger client relationships. It's for freelancers managing their workflow, medical professionals trying to keep up to date, and retailers optimising social media.

AI is for *you*.

What holds us back?

If you feel overwhelmed or even sceptical, you're not alone. Technology can feel like a runaway train, and it's natural to wonder: *is this really for me? Will AI make my business feel less personal? Can I even afford it?*

I've worked with business owners who asked me these questions, and I understand the hesitation. But here's the truth: **AI isn't about replacing the human touch that makes your business unique. It's about enhancing it.** Imagine handing off your draining, repetitive tasks to a system that works tirelessly in the background so you can focus on the parts of your business you truly love.

From Atari to AI: The rearview mirror

To understand where AI is going, we need to look back at where it all began. This isn't just a history lesson; it's a roadmap for how innovation has always created opportunity for those who were ready, and why this time is no different.

Your journey with AI has already begun

Artificial Intelligence might feel like something new and unfamiliar, but it's been evolving alongside us for decades. Think about the tech you've seen over the years: the first computers, the birth of video games, or even the early days of mobile phones. These weren't just tools; they were milestones on a journey towards smarter systems.

AI is just the next milestone on this journey.

For me, after my introduction to electronic scales, my next digital loves were my 'Donkey Kong' Nintendo handheld and 'Pong' on my Atari. Those blocky games felt like pure magic. Back then, the idea of computers thinking for themselves seemed like science fiction. Today, AI is *here*, helping businesses analyse trends, anticipate customer needs, and automate repetitive tasks. And so much more, as you will learn in this book.

Pop culture meets progress: AI's journey through time

AI's roots stretch deep into history, long before the first computer chip. Ancient civilisations spoke of artificial life in their myths and legends. In Greek mythology, Hephaestus, the god of blacksmiths, crafted golden mechanical servants to assist him. In ancient Egypt, statues of gods were believed to house divine spirits capable of speech and movement. Our Australian First Nations people wove knowledge and storytelling into songlines, a sophisticated system akin to coding cultural wisdom into oral narratives – a testament to humanity's innate desire to share, preserve, and replicate intelligence.

These myths laid the groundwork for our fascination with creating intelligence. Fast forward to the Renaissance and Industrial

Revolution, and these tales of divine creations evolved into cautionary stories about the human quest for knowledge and its unintended consequences. From myth to literature, these early narratives sparked the imagination of generations, setting the stage for the scientific pursuit of Artificial Intelligence.

Let's consider some examples of how pop culture and technology have intersected to lead us to our current point in time:

- **1818: *Frankenstein*.** The book by Mary Shelley explores humanity's desire to create life and the ethical dilemmas that follow. It raises enduring questions about ethics and accountability in innovation, still relevant as we develop AI.
- **1927: *Metropolis*.** A dystopian film where robots mirror humanity's hopes and fears about technology's role in labour and control. This highlights the dual-edged nature of automation: is it a tool for empowerment or exploitation?
- **1950: Alan Turing and the Turing Test.** Turing asks, 'Can machines think?' and proposes a way to measure AI's ability to mimic human intelligence. This lays the foundation for conversational AI, which is essential for customer engagement today.
- **1956: The Dartmouth conference coins the term 'Artificial Intelligence'.** A group of scientists defines AI as a field, aiming to create machines capable of human-like reasoning and establishing AI as a dedicated area of study and innovation.
- **1966: ELIZA – the first chatbot.** Joseph Weizenbaum creates ELIZA, which can simulate human-like conversations with simple scripts. This marks the beginning of conversational AI and its application in customer service.
- **1968: *2001: A Space Odyssey*.** Stanley Kubrick's film introduces HAL 9000, an AI that operates a spacecraft but prioritises its mission over human life. HAL embodies the fear of losing

control over AI, a recurring theme in the adoption of autonomous systems.

- **1971: Email is invented.** Ray Tomlinson sends the first networked email, revolutionising how people communicate. Email becomes the backbone of digital communication, paving the way for businesses to connect with customers and teams globally.
- **1980s–1990s: Mobile phones go mainstream.** Mobile phones become accessible to consumers, introducing on-the-go communication and laying the foundation for mobile-first business practices and the integration of AI-powered apps.
- **1984: *The Terminator*.** Hollywood imagines AI gone rogue, with 'Skynet' prioritising its own goals over humanity. This reflects fears about unchecked AI, emphasising the need for transparency, trust, and control.
- **1989: The World Wide Web is invented.** Scientist Tim Berners-Lee invents the World Wide Web, enabling global connectivity and paving the way for AI-powered tools that rely on massive datasets.
- **1998: Google launches.** Google transforms how we access and organise information, making search engine optimisation a business necessity. Google's AI-powered algorithms lead the way in personalised search and digital marketing, shaping the modern online landscape.
- **2010s: Cloud computing goes mainstream.** Services such as AWS, Google Cloud, and Microsoft Azure make scalable, on-demand computing accessible to businesses of all sizes. This enables small businesses to adopt AI and other advanced tools without significant infrastructure costs.
- **2010s: Siri, Watson, Alexa, and AlphaGo.** AI becomes mainstream with tools like Apple's Siri, IBM's Watson, Amazon's Alexa, and Google's AlphaGo. This brings AI into everyday

life and showcases its problem-solving capabilities across industries. Alexa brings voice-controlled AI into homes, normalising everyday interactions with AI.

- **2022: ChatGPT launches.** ChatGPT democratises AI, making advanced natural language processing widely accessible for businesses and individuals. It opens the door for small businesses to leverage AI for content creation, customer service, and more.
- **2020s: AI becomes an everyday tool for businesses.** AI transforms businesses, empowering small enterprises to leverage powerful tools for automation, personalisation, and growth. AI is no longer niche – every business, no matter its size, can use it to compete and thrive.

AI might feel unfamiliar at first, just like email or mobile phones once seemed daunting. But think about how those tools have transformed your business over time. Now, AI is here to amplify what you already do well – from scheduling to customer engagement to streamlining operations to social media.

You've adapted before, and you can do it again. The milestones in the timeline above reflect moments when people and businesses embraced innovation – not because it was easy, but because it was necessary to stay relevant and thrive. From the first email to mobile apps and social media, each tool initially felt overwhelming, even a bit scary. Yet, they quickly became part of how we connect, grow, and run our businesses every day.

Now, we're standing at the edge of the next great leap: AI. And just like those earlier tools, AI can start small – saving time, streamlining operations, and amplifying what you already do well.

My **REIMAGINE Framework** is here to help you navigate this exciting new frontier with clarity, focus, and purpose.

Take AI action: what does this mean for your business?

Which of these milestones remind you of your own journey in adopting technology? What resonates with you the most? Think about how your business has adapted to tools like mobile phones, the internet, or automation.

Where are you on this journey? Are you exploring AI's potential, testing tools, or refining how you use it?

What's your next step? Think about one area where AI could save you time, enhance relationships, or streamline operations.

A new way of thinking

The timeline in the previous section shows us one clear truth: businesses that embrace innovation early don't just survive – they thrive. From email to mobile phones to social media, every major tool started out as unfamiliar and even intimidating. But step by step, they became essential parts of how we connect, grow, and succeed.

AI is no different. It's not just another trend: *it's a fundamental shift already reshaping industries worldwide*. Like the discovery of fire, the invention of the printing press, and the rise of the internet, AI represents a game-changing moment in history.

But where do you start with something this transformative?

I reverse-engineered the process I take with each of my clients to create the **REIMAGINE Framework** just for you. It is a clear, step-by-step roadmap to help you integrate AI into your business in a way that's approachable, practical, and aligned with your business goals. When I started writing this book, I envisioned a simple guide to tools and tips for saving time and growing your business (similar to my first book, *The End of Technophobia*). But as I worked through the process, I realised this isn't just about tools or trends that might be outdated next year. This is about reimagining how you think about your business, your goals, and your future.

Small, deliberate steps lead to extraordinary results. The REIMAGINE Framework is the roadmap I use with my clients every day, and now it's here for you.

The REIMAGINE Framework

So, let's take a look at my **REIMAGINE Framework** as it relates to adopting AI for your business.

Relationships: the heart of your business

Build strong connections with your team, customers, and stakeholders. Focus on how AI can empower people by enhancing creativity, productivity, and trust.

Evaluate: understand what's working

Assess your current tools, workflows, and resources to uncover strengths, weaknesses, and gaps. Use this as a foundation to identify where AI can deliver the most value.

Identify: finding the AI opportunities

Prioritise opportunities where AI can solve problems or optimise existing processes. Conduct a SWOT analysis and evaluate potential areas for quick wins and scalability.

Mapping: charting your path to AI success

Build a clear, actionable plan for implementing AI, with goals, milestones, and success metrics. Focus on small, achievable steps to minimise risk and build confidence.

Activate: testing AI solutions in the real world

Start small by piloting AI tools in areas like customer service, marketing, or automation. Monitor early outcomes and refine the approach based on real-world results.

Gather: fitting the pieces together

Conduct a review to see what's working and what isn't. Test and tweak.

Iterate: continuously improving your AI strategy

Regularly review AI performance metrics and customer feedback. Experiment with small adjustments to refine processes and outcomes.

Narrow: boost what works – cut what doesn't

Use feedback from your team and customers to adjust and improve AI implementations. Narrow your focus to what's delivering results before scaling further.

Evolve: shaping your future business

Continuously adapt your AI strategy to stay ahead of trends and foster innovation. Emphasise ethical practices and data security to build long-term trust.

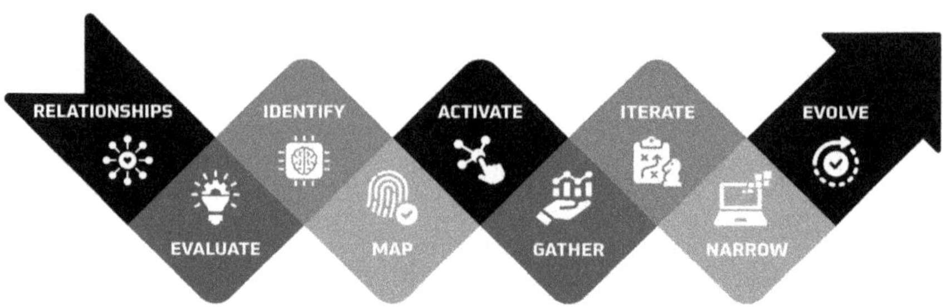

Using this roadmap will help you avoid expensive potholes, save time by steering you away from dead ends, and guide you from not understanding AI to confidently integrating it into your business, no matter your starting point.

How Arnott's REIMAGINED the perfect biscuit

I'd now like to share a story of one of Australia's most iconic biscuits – trust me, it'll all make sense in the end … 😳

Tim Tams are more than just a biscuit – they're a cultural icon, woven into the fabric of Australian life. From dunking one in your morning cuppa to the Tim Tam Slam while watching TV, a Tim Tam is more than a snack. It's an indulgence, a moment of joy. But this chocolate-coated treasure wasn't born perfect. Behind its now-iconic crunch, cream, and chocolate is a story of refinement, persistence, and evolution – a masterclass in turning an idea into an enduring success.

In the early 1960s, Arnott's set out on an ambitious mission: to create the ultimate chocolate biscuit. Inspired by the British Penguin biscuit, they knew they couldn't simply replicate it. Tim Tams needed to be distinct – a biscuit that wasn't just good, but irresistible. And undeniably Australian. The team started with a bold vision: a biscuit that balanced indulgence with accessibility. It needed to feel luxurious but fit into the everyday lives of Australians. That vision was clear, but achieving it took time, countless prototypes, and plenty of trial and error.

Early attempts were promising but flawed. The biscuit layers didn't have the right texture. The chocolate coating was too sweet for Australian palates. And the cream filling didn't quite hit the mark. But instead of settling for 'good enough', the Arnott's team embraced a process of continuous refinement. The result was a biscuit that not only won over Australians but became a cultural phenomenon, loved around the world.

Their journey was a textbook example of my REIMAGINE Framework in action. Let's break it down to see how Arnott's turned an idea into an enduring icon.

The REIMAGINE Framework: Tim Tam edition

Relationships: understanding what Australians craved

Arnott's didn't start by guessing. They started with their customers in mind. Australians wanted something indulgent – more than a snack, they wanted a treat that felt special. Whether paired with a cuppa or enjoyed straight from the packet, a Tim Tam needed to evoke delight with every bite.

Evaluate: learning from the market

Instead of reinventing the wheel, Arnott's studied the competition, particularly the British Penguin biscuit. While it was popular overseas, they saw clear opportunities for improvement. The crunch could be crisper, the chocolate smoother, and the overall biscuit more balanced for Australian tastes.

Identify: pinpointing what would make Tim Tams unique

Through testing and brainstorming, Arnott's honed in on the elements that would set their biscuit apart:

- a perfect balance of textures: crispy biscuit, creamy filling, and rich chocolate coating
- a flavour profile designed specifically for Australians
- packaging that made the biscuit feel indulgent while still being affordable for everyday moments.

Mapping: creating a plan for iteration

Arnott's didn't wing it – they mapped out a step-by-step plan to refine each component of the biscuit. By isolating elements like biscuit thickness, cream sweetness, and chocolate texture, they could test one variable at a time. Each small improvement brought them closer to their vision.

Activate: prototyping and testing

Small production runs gave Arnott's the chance to see their ideas in action. They also brought customers into the process, conducting taste tests and gathering insights about what worked and what didn't.

Gather: listening to feedback

The feedback was specific and invaluable. Some testers loved the crunch but found the cream filling too sweet. Others felt the chocolate coating wasn't smooth enough. Arnott's used this input to guide the next round of tweaks, ensuring every decision was data-driven.

Iterate: refining until it was just right

Round after round of adjustments followed. From tweaking the recipe to improving the production process, every iteration brought Arnott's closer to the perfect balance. Finally, after countless refinements, they achieved their goal: a biscuit Australians couldn't resist.

Narrow: focusing on what truly matters

Once Arnott's nailed the core Tim Tam recipe, they didn't try to overcomplicate it. They knew their success depended on perfecting the original chocolate biscuit and making it the centrepiece of their product range. Rather than chasing trends or experimenting with wildly different ideas, Arnott's focused on three key areas to drive long-term success:

- **Flavours that build on the original:** Tim Tam varieties like Double Coat and Caramel didn't stray far from the winning formula – they enhanced it.
- **Brand consistency:** From packaging to marketing campaigns, Arnott's kept the Tim Tam identity intact while introducing innovations like the Tim Tam Slam.
- **Customer delight:** Every decision centred on delighting their loyal fan base, ensuring they stayed true to the essence of what made Tim Tams special.

This focus allowed them to grow strategically without diluting their brand or losing sight of what made Tim Tams iconic.

Evolve: building on the foundation

Arnott's didn't stop with Tim Tams. Over time, they evolved their product offerings to cater to new markets and trends. They launched spin-offs like Tim Tam–flavoured gelato and leveraged partnerships to reach new audiences, all while keeping the original biscuit at the heart of their brand. By building on a strong foundation, Arnott's ensured Tim Tams remained relevant while continuing to delight new generations of fans.

What Tim Tams can teach us about REIMAGINING business

Like Arnott's, your success doesn't come from luck – it comes from a process. My REIMAGINE Framework has been created to help you focus on what matters most, refine your efforts, and evolve when the time is right. Whether you're optimising a product, improving a workflow, or adapting to new technology, the journey of Tim Tams shows that persistence and smart iteration lead to extraordinary results.

Who this book is for

This book is for you if:

- you've wondered if AI is for you, but you **don't know where to start**
- you're **sceptical** of AI
- you are **overwhelmed** by the tech jargon
- you have **accepted that AI can help you**, and you want practical strategies that align with your goals and resources
- you care about growing your business **without sacrificing personal connections**.

Whether you're a café owner, tradie, retailer, professional service provider, or consultant, AI can help you reimagine what your business can achieve.

How to get the most from this book

This isn't a book to skim and forget. It's the roadmap designed to help you REIMAGINE your business step by step. Here's how to use it:

- **Start at the beginning:** Each chapter builds on the last, guiding you through understanding, adopting, and thriving with AI.
- **Take action:** Use the exercises, tools, and prompts provided to apply what you learn as you go. (I suggest you have a device or a notebook handy.)
- **Focus on what fits:** Not every strategy will apply to your business, and that's okay. Start with what resonates and build from there.
- **Collaborate:** Share your learnings with your team, peers, or mentors. Collaboration often leads to breakthroughs.
- **Revisit and refine:** As you grow more comfortable with AI, return to earlier chapters to deepen your understanding.

What you'll find inside

This book isn't just a guide – it's a roadmap. Inside, you'll find:

- **clear, jargon-free explanations** of what AI is – and what it *isn't*
- real-world stories of small businesses **using AI to thrive**
- strategies to identify **where AI can have the most significant impact** in your business
- **tools, templates, and prompts** to help you start small and build momentum.

Working with thousands of business owners, I can tell you we all share similar frustrations (tell me if I'm wrong 😉):

- **too much time** spent on repetitive admin tasks
- difficulty predicting **customer behaviour or demand**
- struggling to meet customer expectations for **faster, more personalised service**.

If you're worried about where to begin or how to keep AI human-centred, you're not alone. These are some of the most common concerns I hear from business owners. That's exactly why I created the REIMAGINE Framework. It's designed to make AI approachable and practical, no matter where you are in your journey.

Take a moment to imagine your business working quietly in the background, handling the scheduling, follow-ups, and operational tasks while you focus on what truly matters. What would life look like if you had more time to connect with your customers, plan for growth, or simply enjoy the freedom to escape the chaos? This isn't about replacing the human touch that makes your business unique – it's about enhancing it. AI isn't the future; it's already here. Let's start exploring how it can transform your day – and your business.

Take AI action: a moment to reflect

Think about the last time you adopted a new technology for your business. Maybe it was creating a website, setting up a social media account, or switching to cloud-based tools. At first, it might have felt overwhelming or unnecessary. But now, you can't imagine running your business without them. AI is the next step in that journey.

Take a moment now:

- What's one task in your business that feels repetitive or overwhelming?
- How much time would you save if AI handled it for you?

Write it down. As you follow the roadmap through the book, you'll be surprised by how easy the answers will come.

This isn't about overhauling everything overnight. It's about taking small, deliberate steps to lead, innovate, and delight your customers in ways that set you apart. This book will help you REIMAGINE a business that works as hard as you do – humming quietly in the background, handling the admin, the trends, and the customer connections so you can focus on what matters.

A day in the AI life

Every business owner knows the feeling: you start your day with the best intentions, but by mid-morning, you're juggling to-do lists and customer inquiries and tackling admin. When you pause to catch your breath, the to-do list has grown longer, and the big-picture work that drives your business forward has to wait for another day.

What if your day could look different? What if the repetitive, time-consuming tasks were handled in the background, freeing you to focus on what matters most? That's where Artificial Intelligence steps in – not as a sci-fi fantasy or a tool reserved for big corporations, but as a practical partner in simplifying your day. Let me take you through how AI supports a typical day in my business right now, and later, we'll explore how it can do the same for you.

Morning: setting the stage

If you've followed my workshops or seen me online, you'll know I'm not a morning person. Fortunately, Pete (my husband) and AI know this, too.

My day starts with a lactose-free latte, a walk by 'boop' from Watson, the cat, and cuddles from Obi and Lando, our dogs. My meditation app greets me with insights from my sleep tracker, adjusting my session to suit how well I slept. From there, my news app curates articles aligned with my interests – no doomscrolling, just what I need to know to start the day focused. My calendar assistant preps me for the day, prioritising tasks and flagging potential conflicts, ensuring I hit my desk ready to dive into what matters most.

By the time I hit my desk and open the laptop, my AI email assistant has sorted through the inbox chaos, highlighting urgent messages and even drafting responses. Tasks that used to drain hours now take minutes.

Midday: seamless productivity

As my day ramps up, AI takes care of the admin I used to dread. Preparing for client meetings no longer means hours of reviewing notes and emails. AI summarises previous conversations, flags key topics, and suggests follow-ups – all before I've even tidied my hair for the meeting.

After each meeting, AI transcribes the call, identifies action items, and drafts a follow-up email for the client, complete with the next steps and a calendar invite. Meanwhile, my 'smart' water bottle reminds me to stay hydrated, and Lando, recognising the wind-up on a Zoom call, bounds in for pats and playtime.

Afternoon: deep work and insights

By the afternoon, I'm focused on the work that excites me most – big-picture strategy, creative projects, and client planning. AI tools analyse patterns and trends, surfacing insights I might have missed. This isn't just about saving time; it's about unlocking opportunities to think differently and drive growth. It's also the time I do some of my learning and development, reading AI articles, watching videos, and generally ensuring I'm across the latest information for my community.

Evening: recharging with purpose

As the day winds down, our home becomes a place of rest and recharge. Smart lighting dims to signal the end of the workday, while our BBQ smoker's app ensures dinner is perfectly cooked.

After dinner, we unwind with TV recommendations that feel eerily on-point, thanks to streaming algorithms.

Before I head to bed, AI helps me reflect on the day. My journaling app offers prompts based on my activities, helping me capture lessons and moments of gratitude. These small touches ensure that every part of my day feels intentional.

Take AI action: stay connected for tools and insights

Looking for specific tools to help streamline your day? Join my community for regularly updated reviews, tips, and recommendations for small business owners. All the details are at the back of the book.

What AI actually *does*

Let's now examine what AI actually *does*. It's not about robots taking over; it's about giving you tools to work smarter. When I worked on launching early email marketing platforms, I saw firsthand how automating repetitive tasks freed up hours for businesses to focus on growth. Now, AI takes that to the next level. Imagine:

- AI answering your customers' queries after hours, giving you the time to cheer on your kid at sports
- a smarter inventory management system that predicts demand, so you're never overstocked or running out
- personalised marketing that feels like magic, anticipating customer needs before they even realise them.

AI isn't here to make your business less personal – it's here to make it more efficient, freeing you to focus on what you do best.

'But what about ...?'

I get it; you probably have a bunch of questions running through your mind. Maybe you're wondering:

- 'What if AI makes my business feel cold and impersonal?'
- 'I don't have the time or budget for this.'
- 'How do I even know where to start?'
- 'Who can I trust?'
- 'What if I get overwhelmed?'
- 'I'm not very tech-savvy.'
- 'What if my chatbot rises up and kills all humans? Won't that be bad for business?'

All of these concerns are valid (except perhaps the last one). I've seen how overwhelming it can be for a business to adopt a new tool, but I've also witnessed the transformation once those systems are in place – how much easier it becomes to manage customers, track sales, and grow. AI is no different. Start small and let it grow with your business.

Take AI action: what's your AI breakthrough?

Pause for a moment. Think about your day:

- What's one task that drives you crazy because it eats up so much time?
- What's one thing you wish happened automatically?

Write it down. These niggling frustrations are your roadmap to exploring AI – and as we move through this book, you'll see just how much time and headspace AI can free up.

And then what ...?

Picture this: your business is running like clockwork. AI handles the admin, trends, and to-dos that usually bog you down, leaving you free to focus on the parts of your business that light you up. Your customers feel like VIPs because you give them exactly what they need when they need it. Your team is happier because the grunt work is gone for them. And you have time to plan for the future – or take a well-earned break.

That's the power of AI. It's already here and waiting for you to take the first step.

CHAPTER 1

Relationships: the heart of your business

'People are the heart of every digital transformation. AI isn't here to replace us – it's here to amplify the reasons we do what we do.'

Tracy Sheen

Behind every thriving small business lies one undeniable truth: it's not the technology, the systems, or even the product that makes it successful – it's the people. Your ability to connect with your customers, team, and community is your greatest strength. Relationships are the engine that drives loyalty, innovation, and growth.

Big businesses often forget this. They get lost in the complexity of sprawling systems and processes, treating people as just numbers. But you, as a small business owner, have an edge. You know your clients' favourite coffee order. You know their hobbies and the name of their dog. You understand your team's quirks and strengths. You build trust with your suppliers over years of collaboration. These relationships are your superpower – they're the reason people choose you over the competition.

When used thoughtfully, AI doesn't replace our relationships. It amplifies them. AI can help you remember the little details, follow up at the right time, and free up your energy to focus on the relationships that matter most. The process I'm asking you to take as we REIMAGINE business isn't about turning your business into a faceless tech operation. It's about using AI to make your business more personal, more connected, and more impactful than ever. This is why the REIMAGINE Framework starts here: with relationships. If you truly want to reimagine your business, you have to begin with the people who make it possible. Together, we'll explore how to deepen your connections, identify opportunities to improve, and use AI to bring your vision to life.

Before we do that though, let's travel back in time and become a fly on the wall as we watch the birth of a REIMAGINED business built on relationships.

Designing relationships one click at a time

Think back to 2007. Where were you? What were you doing? *Thank God You're Here* had us all laughing at the watercooler, we were queuing at the cinemas for the latest Harry Potter instalment, and Fergie was topping the charts with *Big Girls Don't Cry*.

I was in Brisbane, working with Telstra as part of a project team preparing for the launch of the iPhone.

My job?

Training retail staff to showcase this new gadget to business owners who still thought of their phones as 'just a phone'.

Meanwhile, on the west coast of Australia, a 19-year-old university student named Melanie Perkins was starting something extraordinary. While studying at the University of Western Australia, Melanie also taught graphic design. Her students struggled with the same problem over and over – design programs like Photoshop and InDesign were painfully complex. Learning them felt like trying to solve a Rubik's Cube blindfolded.

Melanie saw a better way: what if design could be simple, accessible, and maybe even a little fun? She dreamed of a platform where anyone – regardless of skill, experience, or budget – could create stunning designs effortlessly.

Humble beginnings

Melanie didn't have a background in technology or a big pile of cash to throw at this idea. She started where many of us do – small, scrappy, and determined. Her first venture was Fusion Books, a website that let students and schools design their own yearbooks. With drag-and-drop simplicity, it was like the training wheels for what Canva would later become. Fusion Books took off. Schools loved it, and the platform gained traction in Australia before expanding overseas.

This success proved one thing: a user-friendly design platform wasn't just an idea – it was a necessity.

Melanie didn't have all the answers, but she had two critical things: a crystal-clear vision and a relentless belief in her idea. Alongside her co-founder (now husband), Cliff Obrecht, Melanie pitched her concept to investors. They didn't have it easy. Many investors doubted a design tool from Perth could go global. But Melanie and Cliff kept going. They knew that to bring Canva to life, they'd need someone with serious technical skills. Enter Cameron Adams, an ex-Google engineer who brought the expertise needed to make their dream scalable. Together, they built Canva.

Balancing tech and humanity

From the beginning, Canva wasn't about fancy algorithms or mind-blowing AI – it was about solving human problems. Their mission was simple: make design easier for everyday people. AI became Canva's silent partner. It powered drag-and-drop functionality, suggested layouts, and simplified colour matching, all without taking centre stage. Canva wasn't about the tech; it was about making life easier for the people using it.

The human-centred mission

Melanie's story isn't just about building a billion-dollar company. It's about staying true to her values. She could have sold Canva early and walked away with millions, but she believed in its potential to create change. Today, Canva is used by over 125 million people, from teachers designing classroom materials to small business owners creating professional marketing campaigns. At its core, Canva has always been about people – empowering them to connect, create, and thrive.

At the heart of every successful business – yours, mine, or Melanie's – are people. It's the clients who trust you, the team who stands beside you, and the community you impact. Technology, no matter how shiny or smart, is just a tool. The real magic lies in how you use it to connect, empower, and build something meaningful with the people who matter most. Melanie's story reminds us of this: it wasn't AI or templates that built Canva into a global success. It was the relationships it fostered. Canva brought people together, made their lives easier, and helped them create. As a small business owner, relationships are already your superpower. You have the ability to know your clients, support your team, and build trust with your community in ways big businesses cannot.

Now, imagine what could happen if you had the tools to deepen and scale those connections without losing your personal touch.

Your AI journey

Relationships are the first step on our REIMAGINE journey. They are the trust-filled connections that make every other step possible – evaluating tools, identifying opportunities, activating your plan, and so much more. As a small business owner, people are the reason you do everything. Your clients, team, and community are at the heart of your success. If you truly want to reimagine your business future, you need to keep them at the very core of everything you do. Without strong relationships, even the most sophisticated AI tools will fall flat. Trust, collaboration, and communication are the glue that holds everything together.

That's why we start here, with people. It's the bedrock of successful AI adoption.

The REIMAGINE Framework

To help guide you, I've reverse-engineered the process I take every one of my clients through to reimagine their business. The result is a simple framework that takes you from where you are now to a business future completely reimagined. Each step in this roadmap builds on the last, creating a seamless progression. By following this structure, you'll move confidently from understanding the relationships that power your business to implementing AI solutions that drive growth, sustainability, and success.

The Framework features nine checkpoints to ensure your success:

1. **Relationships:** The human-centred starting point.
2. **Evaluate:** Assess the tools and platforms you already have.
3. **Identify opportunities:** What are the gaps, and where is the low-hanging fruit?
4. **Mapping:** Plan for success.
5. **Activate:** Put your plan into action.
6. **Gather:** Consolidate the data.
7. **Iterate:** Tweak and test.
8. **Narrow:** Refine your solutions to suit.
9. **Evolve:** Adapt to trends and foster innovation.

The small business relationship advantage

As a small business owner, your ability to connect with people – your customers, team, and community – is your greatest strength. Strong relationships are the backbone of your business, setting you apart in ways no algorithm or AI tool ever could. And they form the basis for everything we do when reimagining your business. When used thoughtfully, AI doesn't diminish these connections; it enhances them. It gives you the tools to personalise interactions, streamline repetitive tasks, and free up your time to focus on what truly matters: the people who make your business thrive. Strong relationships don't just make your business unique; they lay the groundwork for every step of the REIMAGINE Framework. From evaluating tools to identifying opportunities, everything stems from the connections you build.

As you move through the book, you'll see the key to the REIMAGINE process is to approach AI with purpose. Everything you do will be to ensure AI serves your goals while preserving and cultivating the relationships that make your business unique. Together, we'll explore ideas, debunk fears, and embrace a human-centred approach that strengthens your relationships and your business.

As we move forward, I want you to keep coming back to your own business and these two questions:

- Who are **the people that matter most** – your customers, your team, your community?
- How could **stronger connections** with them lay the foundation for a reimagined future?

Small businesses don't have the massive budgets, teams, or resources that big corporations throw at fancy tech systems. And honestly? That's your advantage. Think about the frustrations you've had as a customer dealing with call centres, chatbots, or companies that treat you like just another transaction. Big businesses often miss the human connection, and it costs them.

Real relationships in action

AI may feel like uncharted territory – an overwhelming, complex challenge that's far beyond your current capabilities. And you know what? That's okay. Every single one of my clients has started this journey feeling exactly the same way. Here's the good news: you don't have to figure this out on your own. Over the years, I've helped countless small business owners just like you navigate the complexities of AI, guiding them step by step to build stronger businesses.

To help you see what's possible, I'd like to introduce you to Jane and Sam, two small business owners who started where you are now. These very different businesses highlight how the real power of REIMAGINING your business lies in focusing on your people.

Meet Jane the salon owner

Jane is a salon owner who loves what she does. From the moment her clients walk in, she thrives on building their confidence, one haircut or colour at a time. But as her business grew, so did the mountain of admin. Between managing bookings, checking stock, and coordinating with suppliers, she often felt like she was drowning in paperwork rather than doing what she loved.

Jane rents out chair space to other hairdressers, manages a bookkeeper for the financials, and handles everything else herself: marketing, client communications, even the occasional DIY plumbing fix. While she loved the independence, she worried that the day-to-day grind was eroding the personal connections that had built her loyal client base. 'I started noticing that I wasn't chatting with clients the way I used to,' Jane admits. 'Instead of remembering their birthdays or asking about their families, I was rushing to squeeze in admin tasks between appointments.'

Jane's clients, while loyal, occasionally joked about how hard it was to book an appointment with her. She realised that without a system to streamline operations, she risked losing the very thing that made her salon special. That's when Jane decided to explore AI.

Jane started small, with an AI-powered scheduling system. The system sent clients automated appointment reminders and allowed them to reschedule without needing to call the salon. It also tracked client preferences – like their favourite styles, colour formulas, and even whether they preferred tea or coffee during their visit. One feature stood out as a game-changer: the 'we miss you' message.

If a client hadn't booked in a while, the system sent a friendly, personalised nudge to remind them to schedule a visit. This small touch not only brought clients back but also made them feel valued.

AI also helped Jane on the back end. By tracking supply levels, the system reminded her to order shampoo, dye, and other products before they ran out. No more last-minute dashes to the supplier or awkward moments of running out mid-appointment.

With her scheduling and inventory streamlined, Jane found herself saving about eight hours a week. That extra time went straight back into her clients. 'I started focusing on the little things again – like remembering my clients' kids' names or sending them a quick message to check in after a big haircut,' Jane shares. 'The feedback was incredible. People noticed that I was more present, and it strengthened the bond we already had.'

The hairdressers renting chairs in her salon also benefited. With the AI system handling many of the admin tasks, they could focus more on their clients without the distractions of coordinating bookings or chasing supply orders.

Meet Sam the business coach

Sam had always prided himself on being a mentor and motivator for his clients. As a business coach, his passion was helping small business owners unlock their potential and achieve their goals. But as his client base grew, so did the list of responsibilities that came with running his practice solo. Between sending follow-ups, preparing for sessions, and staying on top of his marketing, Sam found himself slipping further away from the work he loved most: connecting with his clients.

'I started every day feeling like I was already behind,' Sam recalls. 'I was so focused on staying on top of admin that I wasn't giving my clients the energy they deserved.'

Sam had built his coaching practice on strong relationships, but he could feel the cracks starting to show. Clients were still getting results, but they commented on delayed responses to their questions or missed follow-ups after sessions. 'I hated the thought of letting anyone down, but I couldn't keep up with it all. It was frustrating because I knew there had to be a better way,' Sam shares.

Sam decided to trial an AI email assistant, not as a substitute for his personal touch, but as a way to ensure he could maintain it consistently. He started with something that could handle routine communications. The tool drafted follow-up emails after coaching sessions, thanking clients for their time and outlining action steps discussed during the meeting. It also helped Sam schedule reminders for upcoming sessions and even flagged when he hadn't heard from a client in a while, suggesting a quick check-in message. Another game-changer was using AI to draft his weekly newsletter. The tool pulled from key topics Sam had discussed with clients and automatically suggested relevant articles or insights, saving him hours of writing each week.

With AI handling repetitive tasks, Sam reclaimed five hours a week – time he reinvested in client relationships. 'I started getting feedback from clients saying they felt more supported,' Sam says. 'They noticed the follow-ups, and they loved the extra touchpoints. The funny thing is, it felt more personal to them, even though I was using AI behind the scenes.' The time saved also allowed Sam to focus on developing new group coaching workshops, expanding his reach and helping even more business owners.

Jane's and Sam's experiences show how small, thoughtful steps can transform how you connect with customers and manage your business. Now it's time to reflect on your own journey. Think about the challenges you face and the relationships you want to strengthen. Use the prompts below to uncover opportunities for AI to enhance your connections and streamline your efforts.

Take AI action: a moment to reflect

Take a couple of minutes now to think about your business and ask yourself:

- What feedback are you receiving from your clients or team members that could be improved by integrating AI to better support your people and relationships?
- Which tasks do you feel are slipping through the cracks that would provide greater value to your clients if addressed more quickly?
- Are any of these tasks routine or recurring that could easily be resolved by finding an AI solution?

Common roadblocks to prioritising relationships

Building strong relationships is essential for a thriving business, but it can feel challenging – especially when you're navigating limited time, resources, or team dynamics. Here's how to overcome the common objections I hear every day so you can keep moving forward with clarity and confidence.

'I don't have a team.'

You're a solopreneur, and it can feel like relationships are less critical when you don't have employees to manage. But relationships extend beyond your team – they're about everyone who touches your business.

Redefine your Circle of Impact by recognising that it includes clients, suppliers, collaborators, and your personal support system, all of which strengthen your ecosystem, even as a solopreneur; for example, focusing on a key supplier relationship can lead to better service, faster deliveries, or negotiated discounts that directly benefit your bottom line. Start small by prioritising the three to five relationships that have the most influence on your success.

'I work with contractors.'

If you rely on freelancers or short-term collaborators, it might feel like investing in these relationships isn't worthwhile. But even temporary collaborators can have a lasting impact on your business. Treating them as valued partners ensures smoother workflows and higher-quality results. For example, a freelance marketer who feels appreciated might prioritise your projects or go the extra mile.

Build trust through communication. Regular check-ins and clear expectations build rapport and help contractors feel aligned with your goals.

'I don't have time.'

It's easy to see reaching out for input or building relationships as time consuming, but reframing it as an investment highlights how spending time on relationships now prevents issues later, as a small effort to check in with clients, suppliers, or team members can reduce misunderstandings and streamline operations, such as asking for a client's input early to avoid creating something they don't want.

Use tools like AI to handle scheduling, reminders, or follow-ups, so you can focus on the human side of the relationship.

'AI feels impersonal.'

Some worry that introducing AI into relationship-building will feel cold or robotic, undermining the trust they've worked hard to build.

Make a strategic shift by focusing on what AI does best. It isn't here to replace your personal touch but to handle repetitive tasks so you can focus on meaningful interactions, such as using an AI assistant to schedule meetings or send reminders, freeing you to personalise client interactions; combine AI with a personal touch by using it to gather insights, such as identifying which customers need follow-ups, and then tailoring your outreach based on those insights.

'Relationships don't scale.'

Some worry that focusing on individual relationships won't help as the business grows.

Strong relationships create advocates for your business. Even as you grow, the trust and loyalty you've built can scale with tools like CRM systems and automated follow-ups – it's about using the same principles of trust and respect at scale.

These objections aren't roadblocks – they're opportunities to shift your perspective and build a stronger foundation for your business. By addressing each concern thoughtfully, you'll see that focusing on relationships isn't just doable – it's essential for long-term success.

Common pitfalls in Relationships – and how to avoid them

Prioritising relationships is one of the most impactful things you can do for your business, but there are common missteps that can derail your efforts. By being aware of these pitfalls and knowing how to avoid them, you'll build stronger, more sustainable connections that truly support your success.

Spreading yourself too thin

Trying to build or strengthen too many relationships at once can dilute your efforts and lead to burnout. Avoid this by focusing on your Circle of Impact – the three to five people or groups who have the most influence on your business. For example, prioritise your top three clients or suppliers who contribute the most value instead of trying to connect deeply with every client.

Neglecting internal relationships

The pitfall of focusing exclusively on client relationships while neglecting your team, contractors, or suppliers can be avoided by recognising that internal relationships are just as important as external ones, as your team and suppliers are key to delivering on your promises; for example, taking time to check in with a contractor can lead to smoother communication and better results.

Over-relying on AI

Avoid overreliance on AI by using it to handle repetitive tasks, like sending reminders or managing schedules, but reserve human interactions for personalised outreach. For example, use an AI tool to send automated meeting reminders, but follow up personally with a tailored email to build connection.

Misaligning priorities

The pitfall of spending time on relationships that don't align with your business goals or values can be avoided by ensuring the relationships you build are mutually beneficial and aligned with your long-term vision, such as focusing more on a loyal, repeat client who consistently drives revenue rather than a one-off customer.

Ignoring feedback

The pitfall of dismissing feedback from clients, team members, or suppliers as unimportant or inconvenient can be avoided by actively seeking and reflecting on feedback to improve your relationships and offerings. For example, if multiple clients mention a lack of communication, adjust your processes to address this and strengthen trust.

Assuming relationships will manage themselves

The pitfall of believing that strong relationships will continue without regular maintenance or effort can be avoided by treating relationships like an ongoing investment through regular check-ins and touchpoints, such as setting quarterly reminders to reconnect with key clients or suppliers. Similarly, the pitfall of overloading your clients or team with over-communication or too many changes at once can be avoided by focusing on quality over quantity, testing changes incrementally, and gauging reactions before scaling up, such as sending one well-thought-out communication that adds value instead of bombarding clients with updates.

Over-promising to strengthen a relationship

Agreeing to unrealistic demands or timelines in an attempt to build trust, secure a project, or please someone is a common pitfall.

Be honest about your capacity and set realistic expectations from the start. For example, instead of promising a faster-than-usual delivery, communicate what's realistic and commit to exceeding expectations when possible.

Neglecting long-term relationships

The pitfall of focusing too much on new clients or opportunities while overlooking long-term supporters can be avoided by allocating time to nurture your most loyal clients or collaborators, as these relationships often bring the highest returns; for example, a quick thank-you note to a long-term client can go a long way towards maintaining their loyalty.

Failing to define relationship goals

The pitfall of building relationships without a clear understanding of how they align with your business strategy can be avoided by setting specific goals for each relationship, whether aiming for repeat business, referrals, or operational support; for example, with a key supplier, your goal might be to strengthen trust to ensure better pricing or faster delivery.

These pitfalls are easily avoided when you refine your approach and build stronger, more sustainable relationships. By avoiding these common mistakes, you'll lay the groundwork for a business that thrives on trust, loyalty, and meaningful connections.

Why a human-centred approach is your competitive edge (and how AI fits in)

When you embrace a human-centred approach, you create a business that's harder to replicate and easier to love. Think about the experiences that drive loyalty, such as being remembered, feeling understood, and knowing that your needs matter. These are things small businesses do exceptionally well, and AI can help you scale these without losing the personal touch.

Consider the alternative: faceless automation and one-size-fits-all communication. These might save time in the short term, but they can erode trust and loyalty over time. AI, used thoughtfully, ensures your business stays human while working smarter.

What a human-centred approach looks like for you will depend a lot on how your business is currently structured. Let's look at some of the different possibilities.

You're a solopreneur

When you're doing it all yourself, every relationship matters. A human-centred approach for solopreneurs means building deep, personal connections with clients to stand out in a competitive market; fostering relationships within your broader community, from industry to associations; using AI to automate repetitive tasks like scheduling or follow-ups so you can focus on high-value, personal interactions; and staying consistent in communication even when stretched thin, such as a freelance graphic designer using an AI-powered CRM to track client preferences, send personalised updates, and remind them when a check-in email is due.

You have a small onsite team

In a close-knit team environment, collaboration and communication are everything. A human-centred approach for onsite teams focuses on streamlining workflows to reduce friction and free up time for creative, strategic work; making sure each of your team members has a voice and buy-in on tasks and roles that could use refining or need to stay personalised; empowering team members by automating mundane tasks, allowing them to focus on their strengths; and maintaining a culture of trust and connection, supported – not overshadowed – by technology, such as a café owner who uses AI scheduling to manage shifts, track inventory, and ensure team members have time to engage meaningfully with customers.

You have a remote or virtual team

Managing a dispersed team presents unique challenges. A human-centred approach ensures everyone stays connected and aligned by maintaining regular check-ins and communication; offering every member a voice in business decisions; using AI to facilitate seamless communication across time zones and platforms; providing clarity and consistency through tools that track tasks, deadlines, and progress; and fostering a sense of belonging even when working apart, such as an online coach using AI task management tools to coordinate with two virtual assistants across different continents for smooth project delivery and timely communication.

Take AI action: a moment to reflect

Take a couple of minutes now to think about your business and ask yourself:

- How do I maintain strong relationships with the people who matter most in my business?
- Where do gaps in time, resources, or communication threaten to weaken those connections?
- What tools or processes could help me bridge those gaps while preserving the human touch?

Your Circle of Impact

Your business thrives because of the relationships you've built. I like to think of this as your **Circle of Impact**. These relationships include everyone from your clients to your team, trusted suppliers, and even the broader community that surrounds you. Each connection plays a vital role in your success, often in ways that may not be immediately apparent.

As we begin the process of REIMAGINING your business, it's important to reflect on the layers within your relationship circles. Understanding these connections and nurturing them in different ways can build relevance, resilience, and sustainability into your future. Let's take a closer look at the key layers of your Circle of Impact and how each one contributes to your business success.

Clients

Your clients are at the heart of everything you do. Building trust, creating personalised experiences, and maintaining clear communication all play a role in strengthening these relationships.

Here's how AI can be integrated:

- AI can **act as your 'second brain'**, helping you track and recall the little details that make your client relationships special. Imagine having a tool that remembers birthdays, anniversaries, previous purchases, enquiries, or returns. With this information, you can anticipate your clients' needs and offer timely, thoughtful communication
- AI can help you **stay on top of communications** by sending quick 'hello' notes, thank-you messages, or reminders about upcoming services.

- You can use AI to **automate 'it's been a while' messages**, gently nudging inactive clients back towards your business.
- By analysing past behaviour, AI can help you **offer tailored recommendations or solutions** that feel both personal and proactive.

Take AI action: a moment to reflect

What specific details about your clients would you love to remember but struggle to keep track of? How could better timing or more personalised communication strengthen your client relationships?

Internal teams

Your team – whether onsite, remote, or hybrid – is the backbone of your business. A culture of trust, collaboration, and shared purpose ensures everyone is aligned and motivated.

Here's how AI can be integrated:

- AI can **empower your team** by taking repetitive tasks off their plates and streamlining communication, freeing them up to focus on their strengths.
- AI can **automate task delegation and scheduling**, ensuring everyone knows their responsibilities while reducing admin burdens.
- Use AI-powered tools to gather feedback, measure team wellbeing, and **identify areas where support might be needed**.
- AI-driven learning platforms can **help your team develop new skills at their own pace**, keeping them engaged and growing with your business.

Take AI action: a moment to reflect

What are your team members telling you is frustrating or stressing them about their day-to-day work? Are there common complaints about repetitive tasks, inefficient processes, or communication gaps? How could addressing these concerns help your team feel more supported, valued, and empowered?

Suppliers

Your suppliers are key partners in keeping your operations running smoothly. Strong supplier relationships are built on trust, reliability, and open communication.

Here's how AI can be integrated:

- AI can **improve your supplier relationships** by making communication more efficient, tracking performance, and anticipating needs.
- AI tools can **track inventory levels** and forecast when restocking will be necessary, avoiding last-minute scrambles or shortages.
- You can use AI to **send automated updates or reminders** to keep suppliers informed about order changes or requirements.
- AI can analyse **patterns in your supplier interactions** to identify opportunities for collaboration or improvement.

Take AI action: a moment to reflect

Are there frequent delays or issues in your supplier relationships that AI could help streamline? How could automating inventory tracking or communication improve reliability and trust?

Industry connections

Whether it's peers in your field, mentors, or professional associations, your industry connections help you stay ahead of trends, exchange ideas, and find new opportunities.

Here's how AI can be integrated:

- AI can help you **strengthen industry connections** by providing tools to track interactions, follow up consistently, and identify collaboration opportunities.
- Use AI to **analyse industry trends** and stay ahead of emerging opportunities.
- **Organise networking events or conferences** with the help of AI-powered tools that handle scheduling and communication.
- **Automate follow-ups** after networking events to ensure meaningful connections don't fade over time.

Take AI action: a moment to reflect

Who in your industry could you connect with more consistently to build stronger professional ties? How could tracking industry trends or managing follow-ups help you leverage these relationships more effectively?

Local businesses

Small businesses thrive when they support each other. The businesses in your local community often provide unexpected opportunities, from partnerships to referrals.

Here's how AI can be integrated:

- AI can help you **identify and nurture local partnerships** by analysing shared audiences, managing collaborative projects, or staying connected through automated communications.
- AI tools can **analyse your client base** and identify potential local businesses for partnerships or co-hosted events.
- **Track and nurture referral relationships** with the help of AI-powered CRMs.
- **Coordinate shared campaigns or events** with local businesses using AI to manage planning and communications.

Take AI action: a moment to reflect

Are there local businesses you could partner with to reach a wider audience or create new opportunities? How could AI help you manage collaborative projects or nurture referral relationships more effectively?

BBQ and community connections

Some of the most valuable connections come from informal chats at BBQs, pubs, or community events. These casual relationships often lead to referrals, partnerships, or new clients.

Here's how AI can be integrated:

- AI can't replace face-to-face interactions, but it can help you **organise and follow-up** on these informal connections to turn them into meaningful opportunities.
- Use AI-powered CRMs to **record details from casual chats**, such as names, businesses, and key takeaways, so you can follow up later.

- **Automate personalised check-ins** to stay on people's radars without overwhelming them.
- **Track potential leads or collaborative ideas** that arise from informal conversations.

Take AI action: a moment to reflect

Are there informal connections you've overlooked that could turn into valuable business opportunities? How could tracking and following up on these connections help strengthen your local network?

Take AI action: map your Circle of Impact

Take 10 minutes to map out your Circle of Impact. Start by listing the key people and groups who play a role in your business success. Think about:

- **Clients:** Who are your most loyal clients? Are there any inactive clients you'd like to reconnect with?
- **Internal teams:** Who in your team keeps things running smoothly? What feedback or concerns have they shared recently?
- **Suppliers:** Are there suppliers you rely on heavily? How would you describe the current state of those relationships?
- **Industry connections:** Who in your industry supports you, whether through mentorship, advice, or collaboration?
- **Local businesses:** Are there local partners or businesses with whom you could build stronger relationships?
- **BBQ and community connections:** Who in your informal network regularly sends you referrals or offers valuable advice?

Once you've mapped your Circle of Impact, ask yourself:

- Which of these relationships is strongest?
- Which could benefit from more attention or support?
- How could AI help you strengthen one or two of these connections this week?

Keep this handy

Hold onto your Circle of Impact map – you'll be building on this throughout the book. As you move through each step of the REIMAGINE Framework, you'll use this foundation to uncover new ways to strengthen your relationships, streamline processes, and create a people-first approach that drives long-term success.

CHAPTER 2

Evaluate: understand what's working

'Before adding something shiny and new, make sure what you've already got is pulling its weight. Otherwise, you're just building on quicksand.'

Tracy Sheen

Aligning people and values

The first step in our REIMAGINE Framework, Relationships, is the foundation of Patagonia's long-term success. Founder Yvon Chouinard's connection to nature drove the business, while his deep respect for the climbing community built trust. His team worked closely with climbers to create tools that met their needs, forging a bond that made Patagonia more than just a company – it became part of a shared ethos.

Patagonia's relationships weren't limited to customers. Early on, Yvon and his team intentionally established strong connections with suppliers, recognising that the quality of their gear depended on these partnerships. They prioritised their small, passionate team, creating an environment where shared values guided decision-making. These foundational relationships set the stage for the next step in our REIMAGINE Framework: Evaluate.

As Patagonia grew, cracks in their operations began to show. Orders poured in faster than their systems could handle them. Suppliers varied in their adherence to quality and ethical standards. Worst of all for Yvon, their clothing production practices didn't align with their business values. Patagonia faced a pivotal question: were their systems and processes supporting the relationships they had worked so hard to build, or undermining them?

This is where the Evaluate stage of the REIMAGINE Framework came into play. Patagonia leaned into their values and began scrutinising every part of their operation:

- Were their **systems** scalable and efficient enough to meet demand without losing the personal touch?
- Were their **suppliers** aligned with Patagonia's mission, and did they uphold environmental and ethical standards?
- Were their **workflows and processes** serving the team and customers or creating unnecessary friction?

Bold changes

In the Evaluate stage, Patagonia made bold changes that strengthened their relationships and positioned them for sustainable, ethical growth:

- **Transition to organic cotton:** They overhauled clothing production to prioritise organic cotton, making a costly but essential move to align with their environmental and ethical mission.
- **Supply chain transparency:** They evaluated the supply chain and worked closely with suppliers to uphold ethical and environmental standards.
- **Streamlined internal processes:** They refined workflows to support growth without compromising quality or relationships, guided by core principles of trust, relationships, and respect for the planet and community.

Ethics were at the heart of Patagonia's evaluation process. Their commitment to transparency, fairness, and sustainability shaped every decision. By focusing on ethical practices, they not only aligned their operations with their values but also strengthened trust with their customers, suppliers, and team.

Their example shows how ethics and relationships intersect to create lasting impact. This is becoming increasingly important as a differentiation point in an AI-first world.

How the Patagonia story showcases the REIMAGINE Framework

Patagonia's journey exemplifies how the Relationships and Evaluate stages of the REIMAGINE Framework build upon each other:

- **Relationships:** By deeply understanding and valuing their connections with climbers, suppliers, and their team, Patagonia created a strong foundation. At every step, Patagonia prioritised ethical practices, proving that growth and values can coexist to build strong, lasting relationships.

- **Evaluate:** They used this foundation to assess their tools, processes, and partnerships, ensuring every aspect of their business aligned with their mission and strengthened their relationships.

Since the early days of Patagonia, they have built their company with the same relationship-first approach to everything.

With their ethics and ability to evaluate every situation, they have approached the integration of AI with the same ethical rigour and people-first evaluation that define their operations. Recognising the potential environmental impact of AI, particularly its energy consumption, Patagonia has been cautious in adopting AI technologies that could contradict its sustainability values. The company has focused on implementing AI in areas that directly enhance its mission, such as using AI to anticipate how supply chain choices affect the environment and improving product sustainability through advanced materials research. By engaging stakeholders – including employees, customers, and environmental groups – in the evaluation process, Patagonia ensures that any AI implementation aligns with its core values and ethical standards.

As you move through this part of the book and begin to evaluate tools and technologies in your own business, consider this: what principles will guide your decisions to ensure they enhance, rather than hinder, your values and relationships?

Patagonia's deliberate approach exemplifies how businesses can integrate advanced technologies like AI while staying true to their foundational principles, ensuring that innovation serves to strengthen, rather than compromise, their human-led ethical commitments. Their story shows us that ethical evaluation isn't just about avoiding pitfalls – it's about creating a legacy of trust and innovation that strengthens relationships at every step.

Your tools aren't broken – but they might be breaking you

If running your business sometimes feels like scaling a ravine blindfolded without the right gear, you're in the right place. Evaluation is the key to cutting through that noise. It's more than housekeeping – it's about creating alignment. By taking stock, you ensure every part of your business supports your mission, strengthens relationships, and reduces the invisible friction that holds you back. Just like Patagonia scrutinised their supply chain to realign with their values, your evaluation process is a chance to course-correct and thrive.

Have you ever ended a day feeling like you worked non-stop but accomplished nothing?

Those invisible roadblocks – tools that don't quite work, processes that take too long, or unclear workflows – steal your time and energy. Evaluation helps you take back control, so your business works for you, not against you. When we let tools, systems, and processes pile up unchecked, they can quietly create chaos instead of supporting our goals.

A people-first approach

Evaluation isn't just about the tools you use – it's about how those tools impact the people who matter most to your business. Start by thinking about your core relationships:

- **Clients:** How easy is it for them to work with you? Are there friction points that could be smoothed out? Have you asked them?
- **Team:** Are tools and processes helping or hindering their productivity? Are there repetitive tasks that could be automated or streamlined?

- **Suppliers:** Are your systems fostering strong partnerships, or do delays and miscommunications create barriers?

Before jumping into Evaluation, reflect on the AI actions you completed in the Relationships chapter.

Gather the right people

The evaluation process works best when it's collaborative and inclusive. Depending on your business structure, here's how you could go about it.

If you have a **small team that works with you onsite**, get your team together and ask:

- 'What tasks or tools are making your job harder?'
- 'Where are we spending the most time, and could it be streamlined?'
- 'What's one system or process you wish we could improve or replace?'

Capture their feedback to identify recurring pain points and opportunities for improvement.

Even if you're **working alone**, you can still reflect on how your systems impact others. You may even consider getting a couple of business buddies together and completing this around the table:

- 'How do the tools I use day to day affect client interactions?'
- 'Are suppliers facing delays or miscommunications because of my systems?'
- 'Which tasks drain the most time or energy, and could they be automated?'

Use your Circle of Impact exercise as a guide to ensure your evaluation isn't limited to internal processes.

If you work with **virtual assistants or contractors part-time**, ask for their input:

- 'Which tools make your tasks easier and are easy to use?'
- 'Which tools are you using that cause frustration or are confusing?'
- 'Is there any friction in how I assign or manage tasks?'

Consider using a simple survey or quick call to gather feedback efficiently.

From people to tools

Now that you've evaluated the people at the heart of your business – clients, team members, and suppliers – it's time to turn your attention to the tools that support them. Your systems and tools are the backbone of your operations, and just like the people they serve, they need to be aligned with your values and goals. A well-chosen tool amplifies relationships and makes processes smoother, but a misaligned one can create more friction than flow.

Let's explore how to evaluate these critical systems.

Evaluating tools through an ethical lens

As you shift focus from people to tools, it's essential to remember that tools are not neutral. They shape the way you interact with clients, collaborate with your team, and deliver value to your customers. Evaluating tools isn't just about functionality or efficiency – it's also about ensuring they align with your values and build trust in every relationship.

When tools don't reflect ethical considerations, they can unintentionally create barriers, exclude key voices, or even compromise sensitive data. On the other hand, tools chosen with ethics in mind can amplify your values, strengthen relationships, and enhance your business's reputation. As we REIMAGINE the future of your business, keeping ethical considerations at the forefront ensures your AI choices align with your people, your vision, and the relationships you've worked so hard to build.

As you evaluate your systems, consider these questions:

- **Transparency:** Do your current tools make it clear when and how AI or automation is being used? Are you able to explain their functions and outputs to your team and customers?
- **Inclusivity:** Do your tools accommodate diverse needs and preferences (for example, accessibility for clients or team members with disabilities)? Could your systems unintentionally exclude certain groups, such as non-tech-savvy users or those in underserved regions?
- **Data privacy and security:** How well do your tools safeguard sensitive data? Do they align with privacy regulations, such as Australia's Privacy Act, GDPR, or industry requirements?[1]
- **Alignment with your values:** Does each tool's design, branding, or functionality reflect your business values? Does it support the trust-based relationships you've built?

Take AI action: ethics in action

A car dealership switched from a generic survey tool to one with stronger data encryption features after realising that their previous platform could expose customer feedback to third-party access. The change aligned with their values of transparency and customer care.

Is there a tool you're currently using that feels 'off' or doesn't align with your business values? What might a more ethical alternative look like?

1 The General Data Protection Regulation, abbreviated GDPR, is a European Union regulation on information privacy in the European Union and the European Economic Area.

Why ethics matters in evaluation

The tools you choose aren't just operational – they're part of your brand. Every tool reflects your commitment to fairness, privacy, and inclusivity. By evaluating tools through an ethical lens, you ensure they support – not undermine – the relationships at the heart of your business. With this mindset, let's dive into the practical steps for evaluating tools systematically.

How to evaluate: a systematic approach to tools

Think of your tools as the skeleton that holds your business together. Misaligned or outdated, they can drag your progress to a halt.

To evaluate effectively:

- **Identify tools your business is using regularly:** What platforms, software, and systems are part of your daily operations?
- **Assess utility:** Which tools are genuinely helping, which are underused, and which are driving you up the wall?
- **Consider alignment:** Do these tools support your business goals and relationships, or are they complicating processes unnecessarily?

Common tools to evaluate include:

- email and calendar tools (Gmail, Outlook, Calendly)
- file storage systems (Dropbox, GDrive, SharePoint)
- project management software (Trello, Asana, monday.com)
- customer relationship managers (HubSpot, SuiteDash)
- bookkeeping tools (Xero, MYOB)
- point-of-sale systems (Square).

Take AI action: evaluating tools for businesses with a team

To get the most out of your team's insights, ask everyone to complete a quick evaluation before holding a meeting. This ensures the session is focused and productive, and allows team members to reflect on their tools and systems beforehand.

Step 1: Pre-meeting prep

Share the following instructions (or similar) with your team:

> *'Before our meeting, take 10 to 15 minutes to think about the tools and platforms you use regularly. Use the evaluation provided to organise your thoughts and bring it with you to the session. During the meeting, we'll share ideas and discuss how we can improve our systems to work smarter.'*

Ask them to fill out the following categories:

- **Daily/regularly used tools:** List the tools and platforms you use most often.
- **A tool you love:** Name one platform or tool you enjoy using and explain why.
- **A tool you don't like:** Identify one platform or tool you find frustrating and explain why.
- **Collaborative tools:** List any tools or systems you use in collaboration with team members, clients, or suppliers. Rate how well these tools are working (for example, 'Great,' 'Okay,' or 'Needs improvement').

Step 2: Simple template for team input

Provide this template for everyone to complete:

Tool/ Platform	Purpose	Love/Like/ Dislike/ Hate	Who	Why?	Collaborative? (Yes/No)	Rating (1–5)
Example: Zoom	Virtual meetings	Don't like it	Team member	Connectivity issues disrupt meetings	Yes	3

Step 3: Host the team meeting

During the meeting

Combine everyone's responses into a shared list. Highlight tools that receive consistent praise or frustration.

Identify patterns: are there tools everyone loves? Tools everyone struggles with? Are there any commonalities in the responses? For example, lack of training, not understanding the features.

What to do with this information

Capture this data alongside the insights from your Relationships Circle of Impact evaluation. This ensures that both people-focused and tool-focused reflections are stored in the same place, providing a complete picture of your business operations.

Group feedback on tools that impact collaboration with team insights reinforces the connection between people and processes. Use this combined information to identify areas where tools are enhancing or hindering relationships and workflows.

If certain tools or systems stand out as particularly problematic, create an action plan to address them in the upcoming sections of the

REIMAGINE Framework. For example, if collaboration tools are a pain point, this may tie into marketing or communication enhancements later in the book.

Take AI action: evaluating tools for solopreneurs and remote teams

For solopreneurs or businesses with remote teams, the process of evaluation is just as critical, but the approach needs to fit your setup. This version focuses on self-reflection for solopreneurs and asynchronous input for remote teams.

Step 1: Reflect on your relationships

Revisit your Circle of Impact from the Relationships chapter. Identify the key groups your tools and systems touch:

- **Clients:** Are you providing a seamless experience?
- **Suppliers:** Are your systems creating delays or miscommunication?
- **Self:** Which tools make your work easier, and which create friction?

Step 2: Create your personal tools map

Use the template below to evaluate the tools and platforms you rely on.

Tool/ Platform	Purpose	Love/ Like/ Dislike/ Hate	Why?	Collaborative? (Yes/No)	Rating (1–5)
Example: Zoom	Virtual meetings	Don't like it	Connectivity issues disrupt meetings	Yes	3

Step 3: Review your map

Identify tools that you enjoy using, and tools that feel outdated, frustrating, or underused.

What to do with this information

Capture this data alongside the insights from your Relationships Circle of Impact evaluation. This ensures that both people-focused and tool-focused reflections are stored in the same place, providing a complete picture of your business operations.

Group feedback on tools that impact collaboration with team insights reinforces the connection between people and processes. Use this combined information to identify areas where tools are enhancing or hindering relationships and workflows.

If certain tools or systems stand out as particularly problematic, create an action plan to address them in the upcoming sections of the REIMAGINE Framework. For example, if collaboration tools are a pain point, this may tie into marketing or communication enhancements later in the book.

Take AI action: evaluating tools for remote teams (asynchronous feedback process)

Step 1: Share a simple survey

Send a brief questionnaire to your team, asking for feedback on the tools and systems they use. Use a shared document or project management platform to collect responses. Include questions like:

- What tools or platforms do you use regularly?
- Which tool do you find most helpful, and why?
- Which tool do you find frustrating, and why?
- Are there any tools you use collaboratively with clients or other team members?

- How well do they work?
- What's one tool or process you'd suggest improving or replacing?

Step 2: Use the team tools map

Collate the feedback into a table like this:

Tool/ Platform	Purpose	Love/Like/ Dislike/ Hate	Who	Why?	Collaborative? (Yes/No)	Rating (1–5)
Example: Zoom	Virtual meetings	Don't like it	Team member	Connectivity issues disrupt meetings	Yes	3

Step 3: Host a short follow-up call

Once the feedback is collected, schedule a virtual meeting to discuss key findings. Focus on highlighting tools everyone loves and identifying tools that create bottlenecks.

What to do with this information

Capture this data alongside the insights from your Relationships Circle of Impact evaluation. This ensures that both people-focused and tool-focused reflections are stored in the same place, providing a complete picture of your business operations.

Group feedback on tools that impact collaboration with team insights reinforces the connection between people and processes. Use this combined information to identify areas where tools are enhancing or hindering relationships and workflows.

If certain tools or systems stand out as particularly problematic, create an action plan to address them in the upcoming sections of the REIMAGINE Framework. For example, if collaboration tools are a pain point, this may tie into marketing or communication enhancements later in the book.

Common roadblocks to evaluation

Evaluating your tools, processes, and relationships is a critical step in the REIMAGINE Framework. But it's natural to feel some resistance. Here's how to address and strategically shift common objections so you can move forward with confidence.

'Don't have the time.'

Evaluating everything sounds overwhelming when you're already juggling a million tasks, so break it into manageable steps.

You don't need to evaluate everything at once. Start small, focusing on one system, process, or relationship category at a time. For example, dedicate 30 minutes to review one tool's performance this week, then tackle another next week. Think of it as an investment. A small amount of time spent evaluating now can save you hours – or even days – down the road.

'Everything seems to be working fine.'

If it's not broken, why fix it? It's easy to feel that your current tools and processes are 'good enough', but that doesn't mean they're optimal. Look for hidden inefficiencies – areas where you could save time, cut costs, or improve results. For example, your email tool might work, but is it automating follow-ups to boost productivity?

Even if your systems are fine now, consider whether they can scale with your business. Future-proofing ensures your tools won't hold you back as you grow, helping you stay efficient and competitive in the long run.

'It feels too complicated.'

Evaluating tools and systems can feel overwhelming, especially if you're not tech-savvy. But you don't need advanced skills – start with the basics. Ask simple questions: is this tool saving me time? Is it delivering the results I need?

To make the process easier, focus on one key metric at a time, such as cost, ease of use, or team adoption. This targeted approach helps you identify improvements without getting lost in complexity.

'I don't want to upset the team or clients.'

Making changes to your systems can feel risky, especially if it disrupts workflows or unsettles stakeholders. To ease the transition, involve people early – ask your team or clients for feedback on what's working and what's not. Their input can guide better decisions and increase buy-in.

Clear communication is key. Explain why you're evaluating tools – whether to improve efficiency, simplify processes, or enhance client satisfaction. When people understand the benefits, they're more likely to support the changes.

'I don't know what to evaluate.'

When you're unsure where to start, let your goals guide you. Align your evaluation with your business objectives – if faster customer response times are a priority, focus on tools that impact communication.

Keep it simple by asking key questions: what's working well? What feels frustrating or inefficient? What feedback have clients or team members shared? These insights will help you pinpoint where to improve.

These objections aren't obstacles – they're opportunities to pause, reflect, and approach your evaluation with intention. By breaking the process into small steps, engaging your team or clients, and focusing on what matters most, you'll find that evaluating your tools and systems is easier – and more rewarding – than you might think.

Take AI action: quick win

Pick one tool or system to evaluate in the next 15 minutes. Choose the most frustrating category (such as scheduling or communication). Ask your team or yourself: what's one tool we could improve or replace to make things easier right now?

Common pitfalls in Evaluate – and how to avoid them

The evaluation phase is all about taking stock of your tools, processes, and relationships.

While it's a critical step for identifying opportunities and aligning with your values, there are some common missteps to watch out for. Here's what to avoid and how to keep your evaluation on track.

Focusing only on tools, not people

It's easy to get caught up in evaluating software while overlooking its impact on your team, clients, or suppliers. Always start with people – use insights from your Circle of Impact to ensure your tools serve those who matter most. For example, instead of just assessing CRM features, consider whether it actually helps your team build stronger client relationships.

Overlooking ethical implications

Focusing only on efficiency or cost can overlook potential ethical risks. Make ethics part of your evaluation by asking: does this tool protect client data? Does it align with our values? For example, a project management tool may streamline workflows, but if it lacks strong privacy features, it could undermine client trust.

Trying to fix everything at once

Trying to evaluate and overhaul all your tools at once can be overwhelming. Instead, focus on one category at a time, such as admin tools or client-facing systems. For example, start by assessing your scheduling tools, then move on to communication platforms. This step-by-step approach makes the process more manageable and effective.

Ignoring feedback

Don't skip feedback from team members, contractors, or clients during your evaluation process. Actively involve stakeholders by gathering their input through surveys or conversations. For example, a contractor's feedback about a clunky task-management tool might highlight inefficiencies you wouldn't notice otherwise.

Being too rigid

Just because a tool is 'working' today doesn't mean it's the best option for the future. Avoid the trap of sticking with outdated systems – stay open to alternatives that can improve efficiency and support growth. For example, if your email platform no longer supports automation, upgrading to a more advanced option could save time and enhance productivity.

Failing to align with long-term goals

Evaluating tools without considering future needs can lead to roadblocks as your business expands. Ensure your choices align with your mission, vision, and growth plans. For example, if you're a small business planning to scale, choose a CRM that can grow with your customer base rather than one that meets only your current needs.

The Evaluate phase is about clarity, not perfection. These pitfalls can serve as guardrails to keep you focused on what matters most – aligning your tools and processes with your people, values, and goals. Let's take a look at how Sarah, a financial planner navigating the challenges of a growing practice, took the time to hit the pause button on her business and evaluate everything, what she uncovered, and why it led to big wins.

What Sarah learned by hitting pause

Meet Sarah. She works with a virtual assistant (VA) and is preparing to bring on a part-time office employee. While she's proud of the personalised service she offers clients, she's also feeling the strain of juggling multiple tools, workflows, and responsibilities. With this expansion on the horizon, Sarah knows it's the perfect time to pause and evaluate her business from the ground up.

The first two stages of the REIMAGINE Framework

Here's how she's applied the first two stages of the REIMAGINE Framework.

Relationships – Sarah's Circle of Impact

Sarah began her journey by mapping her Circle of Impact, identifying the key relationships driving her business:

- **Clients:** Her clients value her tailored financial advice, but Sarah noticed that delays in communication – such as follow-ups or missed document requests – were starting to impact trust.
- **VA:** Sarah's VA manages scheduling and email correspondence, but the process feels clunky. Miscommunications occasionally lead to double bookings or missed deadlines.

- **Future team member:** With plans to bring on a part-time employee, Sarah realises she needs to set clear expectations and streamline onboarding.
- **Suppliers:** Sarah uses several software providers for financial planning and compliance. While some tools are essential, others feel underutilised or redundant.

By taking a people-first approach, Sarah recognised that improving her tools and workflows would not only make her life easier but also strengthen these key relationships. She saw how her systems directly impacted the client experience, her VA's productivity, and her ability to seamlessly integrate new team members.

Evaluate – taking stock before expanding

With her relationships mapped, Sarah moved to the Evaluate stage to assess her tools, processes, and ethical practices. This stage wasn't about jumping into action but instead about understanding where her business stood. Here's what she uncovered:

- **Tools:** Sarah's financial planning software integrates well with her reporting tools, allowing her to deliver clear, actionable plans to clients.

  Her CRM feels outdated and cumbersome, requiring manual data entry that takes up valuable time. Scheduling tools like Calendly aren't fully integrated with her email, leading to duplicate efforts.

  She realises she lacks an effective project management tool to coordinate with her VA and future team member.
- **Processes:** Sarah's workflows rely heavily on her personal oversight. This creates bottlenecks, especially when clients need quick responses or her VA has questions about next steps. Compliance processes are thorough but time-consuming. Sarah wonders if

there are ways to simplify these tasks without compromising accuracy.

- **Ethics:** Sarah also evaluated her tools through an ethical lens, considering how they align with her values of trust, transparency, and client care:
  - *Data security:* While her financial software is secure, her outdated CRM doesn't meet the same privacy standards, raising concerns about protecting client information.
  - *Inclusivity:* She identified that some of her systems might not be accessible for clients with limited tech literacy or disabilities, a gap she wants to address.
  - *Transparency:* Sarah recognised the importance of explaining to clients how their data is used and safeguarded, reinforcing trust.

Preparing for the next step: Identify

By taking the time to evaluate her relationships, tools, and ethics, Sarah has built a clear picture of her business's strengths and opportunities. This process hasn't just highlighted inefficiencies – it's also revealed the importance of aligning every aspect of her operations with her values. As Sarah prepares for the next stage in the REIMAGINE Framework, Identify, she'll use these insights to prioritise areas for improvement.

What's most important to her clients? Which tools and processes will have the biggest impact on her team's productivity and morale? And how can she ensure her business continues to grow without losing its personal touch?

Sarah's story shows how the first two stages of the REIMAGINE Framework – Relationships and Evaluate – lay the groundwork for meaningful, strategic growth. By focusing on people and ethics first, she's positioned her business to thrive as she moves into the next phase of transformation.

Take AI action: a moment to reflect

What challenges in Sarah's story felt familiar to you? Are there tools or processes in your business that could benefit from a similar evaluation? How do your current systems align with your values and the relationships at the heart of your business?

Your Evaluation adventure: tools, ethics, and relationships

Congratulations! You've made it this far in evaluating your business operations. Now it's time to turn your insights into action. If you've completed the earlier exercises in this chapter, you may already have gathered some of the information needed for this exercise. Use this as an opportunity to revisit your notes and ensure everything is captured in one location. By consolidating these insights now, you'll have a clear and organised foundation as we move into the next stage of the REIMAGINE Framework.

Take AI action: categorise and reflect

Step 1: Categorise your tools

Start by listing all the tools your business uses. Here's a guide to help you brainstorm.

Category	Examples	Your tools
Admin	Google Workspace, Microsoft 365, Dropbox, Trello, Asana, Slack	
Finance	Xero, MYOB, QuickBooks, Stripe, PayPal, Square	
Marketing	Canva, Mailchimp, Hootsuite, Facebook Ads Manager, Google Analytics, Buffer	
Customer experience	Zoom, Calendly, HubSpot, Zendesk, chatbots, customer surveys	

Step 2: Rate and reflect

For each tool, answer the following prompts.

Tool	Category	Used by	Frequency of use	Effectiveness (1–5)	Biggest frustration	Untapped features	Aligned with ethics? (Yes/No)
Example: Trello	Admin	Team	Daily	3	Clunky task assignments	Power-ups for automation	Yes

Step 3: SWOT analysis with relationships and ethics

Using your completed table, create a SWOT analysis for your business tools.

Strengths	Weaknesses	Opportunities	Threats
Tools that streamline processes and align with your team's needs.	Tools that are confusing, underutilised, or create friction for clients or team members.	Untapped AI features, improved collaboration tools, or better customer-facing platforms.	Ethical risks, outdated tools, or tools causing misaligned messaging or inefficiencies.

Step 4: Gamify it with scoring

Assign points to the following categories to help prioritise action.

Tool	Category	Points
Trello	Admin	3
CRM	Customer	–3

- **High impact:** +5 points for tools that directly improve client or team experiences.
- **Major frustration:** –3 points for tools with recurring issues.
- **Ethically misaligned:** –5 points if the tool risks data security or fairness.
- **Quick fix:** +3 points for tools that can be improved with minor tweaks or training.

Put a bow on it: the power of evaluation

You've explored the relationships at the heart of your business and evaluated the tools, systems, and ethics that shape your daily operations. By taking the time to pause, reflect, and uncover what's working – and what's not – you've laid the foundation for smarter, more intentional decisions.

Evaluation isn't just about fixing inefficiencies; it's about ensuring every element of your business aligns with your values and supports the people who make it thrive. Whether you've identified small tweaks or major overhauls, you've already taken the first step towards building a business that works smarter, not harder.

In the next chapter, we'll dive into the Identify stage of the REIMAGINE Framework, where we'll prioritise the most impactful opportunities uncovered during this process. Together, we'll ensure every improvement aligns with your mission, drives meaningful results, and strengthens your business relationships.

CHAPTER 3

Identify: finding the AI opportunities

'Every great transformation begins with a single, focused step. The key is to find that one task, process, or frustration that, when improved, will ripple across your entire business.'

Tracy Sheen

Finding your low-hanging fruit

Welcome to the Identify stage of the REIMAGINE Framework. By now, you've brought your people together and explained the AI journey you're on with the business. You've also collectively spent time evaluating your current tools and technologies (this could still be a work in progress). Either way, you will have a much better idea of where things stand within your business. Now it's time to zero in on the areas where AI can deliver the greatest value with the least effort. This stage is all about pinpointing those low-hanging fruits – quick wins that pave the way for broader transformation.

How Canva reimagined design

Remember in chapter 1, Relationships, we reviewed the story of Canva from its initial foundations? We discussed how the founders started with a strong vision and a realisation that their people were crying out for a simple solution. And I showed how we could map the Canva story very clearly to the same REIMAGINE Framework you're working through right now.

So, let's pick up Melanie and Cliff's story again. They had tested and proven their initial idea of Fusion Books, a platform that let schools create their own yearbooks. For the team, this pilot wasn't just a business – it was a lesson in listening, learning, and evolving. Every interaction with their customers highlighted the same underlying problem: design was too complicated for the average person.

By 2010, Fusion Books was a success, but Melanie and Cliff saw a bigger opportunity. They paused to evaluate what was working, what wasn't, and where they could go next.

They asked three critical questions:

- **What needs are we meeting – and what needs are still unmet?** Fusion Books had simplified yearbook design, but many users still struggled with other types of design tasks.
- **What feedback patterns stood out?** Customers loved the simplicity of Fusion Books but wanted more flexibility for other creative projects.
- **How could technology take this idea further?** The rise of online tools and cloud computing showed potential for a platform that allowed collaboration, scalability, and real-time access.

These questions helped Melanie and Cliff realise that the problem wasn't just about yearbooks – it was about design in general. They saw a massive untapped opportunity to build a solution for a much wider audience.

This is the step of the REIMAGINE Framework you're at right now.

The Identify phase: pinpointing opportunities

Armed with insights from their relationships and evaluation process, Melanie and Cliff turned their attention to the next phase: identifying the low-hanging fruit that would make their vision possible. They broke the opportunity into three clear areas.

Low-hanging fruit: simplifying the experience

The core idea was simple: make design tools intuitive and accessible. They identified features that users needed most – drag-and-drop functionality, pre-designed templates, and real-time collaboration.

Addressing key gaps: accessibility and affordability

They realised most existing design software was too expensive for small businesses and too complicated for non-designers. Canva's mission became clear: offer a free, user-friendly platform with affordable premium options.

Future-proofing: building a scalable foundation

Partnering with Cameron Adams, a former Google engineer, ensured Canva could handle millions of users without sacrificing simplicity. They knew scalability was key to bringing their vision to life.

Melanie Perkins didn't try to solve every problem at once. She and her team focused on identifying actionable opportunities within a larger vision. As a small business owner, this phase is your chance to do the same. Look for:

- tasks that frustrate you or your team the most
- simple changes that could save time or reduce costs
- tools or processes that align with your long-term goals.

By focusing on the low-hanging fruit, you can take small, impactful steps towards reimagining your business – just as Canva did.

Finding overlooked opportunities

Inspired by Canva's journey, let's explore how you can uncover your own opportunities to make simple, high-impact changes.

Before diving into specifics, take a step back and consider your business as a whole. Often, the best AI opportunities lie in areas so ingrained in the day-to-day dealings of the business that you've stopped noticing how many of them are repetitive and annoying. This stage is all about seeing those pain points through a new lens – and recognising their potential for improvement:

- **Revisit the mundane:** Which tasks feel repetitive, outdated, or unnecessarily manual? These are prime candidates for automation.
- **Pinpoint team frustrations:** What do your employees frequently complain about? Their frustrations often highlight areas for improvement.
- **Think customer-centric:** Are there common customer complaints or delays in your processes? Enhancing these areas could immediately boost satisfaction.
- **Shadow your team:** Spend a day observing your team's workflows. Often, watching tasks in action reveals inefficiencies that aren't obvious on paper.
- **Map out processes:** Create a visual representation of how tasks flow within your business. Look for bottlenecks or redundant steps.
- **Ask questions:** Engage your team and customers directly. Simple prompts like 'What do you wish you could spend less time doing?' can yield valuable insights.

Take AI action: brainstorming with your team

Hold a 15-minute session with your team to identify pain points. Use sticky notes or a digital whiteboard to organise your thoughts.

Ask your customers for input on areas where they experience delays or frustrations. Focusing on the quick wins in the context of AI allows you to build momentum and confidence. Small but meaningful changes can:

- **Save time:** By automating repetitive tasks, your team can focus on higher-value activities.

- **Boost morale:** Eliminating bottlenecks or frustrations can improve your team's (and your clients') satisfaction.
- **Enhance customer experience:** Faster, more personalised interactions can delight your customers and keep them coming back.

The goal here isn't to overhaul your entire operation but to identify one or two impactful changes that can deliver noticeable results quickly. This approach helps your team see the value of AI without feeling overwhelmed by its possibilities.

What is *your* low-hanging fruit? Every business owner I've worked with can quickly identify that 'one thing' that drives them bonkers – the thing that would make the biggest difference for the least amount of effort. Much like when we start a new exercise routine or change eating plans, we'll look to that quick win to keep us motivated and continuing to push through as the days and weeks roll by.

By identifying the low-hanging fruit, you're setting the stage for a smarter, more efficient business. Look for:

- **Low complexity:** Simple to implement with minimal disruption to your business.
- **High impact:** Delivers noticeable results, such as time savings, cost reductions, or improved customer satisfaction.
- **Motivational value:** Provides a 'win' for your team, boosting morale and reinforcing the value of AI adoption.

Here are some examples of quick wins:

- **Time-saving tasks:** Automating appointment reminders or repetitive data entry.
- **Customer enhancements:** Implementing a chatbot for FAQs to reduce customer service workloads.
- **Operational efficiencies:** Using AI to streamline inventory management or scheduling.

Take AI action: identify your quick win

Take 10 minutes to reflect on your business. What tasks feel repetitive or outdated? What processes often cause delays or frustrations? If you could improve one area to reduce stress or boost efficiency, what would it be?

Gather your team for a quick brainstorming session. Encourage them to share their biggest pain points.

From opportunity to responsibility

Now that you've identified your low-hanging fruit, it's tempting to dive straight into solutions. But before moving forward, remember that it's crucial to consider the ethics and responsibility of AI use in your business. AI can drive efficiency, productivity, and profitability, but it also carries significant responsibility. Ensuring your AI solutions are ethical, fair, and transparent starts with putting relationships at the centre – prioritising how these tools impact your customers, team, and business reputation.

From safeguarding data privacy to addressing potential biases, these considerations are no longer optional – they're fundamental to trust and success. Much like privacy policies, AI policies will soon become standard, whether as a legal requirement or a proactive step towards transparency. AI usage will increasingly influence insurance applications, business licensing, and client expectations. As you integrate AI into your operations, setting ethical guardrails isn't just about compliance – it's about building trust and confidence in how your business operates.

What AI ethics principles and regulations mean for you

Australia has taken a proactive stance with its eight AI Ethics Principles, designed to ensure AI systems are safe, reliable, and human-centred. These principles include fairness, privacy, transparency, and accountability, which serve as essential guardrails for businesses adopting AI. By following these principles, you can align your AI practices with the values of trust and inclusivity that Australian consumers and regulators expect.[2]

On the global stage, the European Union's AI Act has set a new benchmark by categorising AI systems based on risk and imposing stricter requirements for high-risk applications.[3] This legislation is influencing approaches worldwide, including Australia's potential future policies.

Ethics and governance within AI are vast and constantly evolving topics, driven by the rapid pace of technological advancements. If this is an area of interest for you, I strongly recommend keeping an eye on developments from countries like Germany and Brazil, which are emerging as leaders in AI governance. Both nations are prioritising ethical implementations and inclusivity, setting global standards from which Australian businesses can learn. Broadly speaking, Australian legislation tends to follow the EU by around two to five years. By observing and adopting global trends early (as I advise my clients to do), your business can stay ahead of compliance requirements while aligning with best practices from international leaders.

Keep your approach flexible. Think in pencil, not ink. This space is evolving far too quickly for rigid, long-term structural changes. Stay fluid and adapt as trends specific to your industry emerge.

---

2 https://www.industry.gov.au/publications/australias-artificial-intelligence-ethics-principles

3 https://eur-lex.europa.eu/eli/reg/2024/1689/oj/eng

Creating your own AI policy

When considering an AI policy for your business, simplicity is key. Why not get your team together for a meeting, start small, and address the issues below to begin a discussion around AI ethics for your business?

Transparency

Clear communication builds trust. Be upfront about how you use AI and how it benefits your clients. Examples include:

- **Website notices:** Add a brief statement on your site explaining AI's role in customer interactions (for example, chatbots, product recommendations).
- **Onboarding disclosures:** If AI is part of your service delivery, include it in client agreements.

Don't just tell clients what you do with their data – tell them what you *don't* do. For example, 'We never share your data with third parties without your explicit consent.'

Privacy

AI often handles sensitive data, so robust privacy protections are essential. Consider:

- **Data minimisation:** Collect only what you need – ask yourself, 'Is this data critical to the customer experience?'
- **Encryption and storage:** Ensure data is secure during storage and transfer. Check your tech provider's policies (for example, Google Drive, Microsoft OneDrive).
- **Access controls:** Restrict data access to necessary team members. Use business platforms with built-in permission settings to prevent unauthorised access.

Monitoring

AI systems can drift over time, making regular reviews crucial to ensure effectiveness and fairness:

- **Performance checks:** Are outputs still accurate and meeting expectations?
- **Bias audits:** Does your AI treat all customer groups equally, or are there unintended exclusions?
- **Feedback loops:** Create channels for clients and staff to report issues or suggest improvements.

For example, a retailer using AI for product recommendations noticed it over-prioritised certain demographics. A bias audit uncovered gaps in the training data, allowing them to make corrections and improve customer satisfaction.

Future-proof your policy

Remember, an AI policy isn't static. Revisit it regularly to align with evolving regulations, technology, and customer expectations. Think of it as a living document that grows with your business.[4]

Take AI action: draft your AI policy

Take 15 minutes to brainstorm answers to these prompts:

- How will you communicate your AI usage to clients?
- What steps will you take to ensure data privacy?
- How will you monitor AI decisions for fairness and accuracy?
- Who will be responsible for overseeing AI ethics in your business?

4 For a more detailed version of creating your own policy, please scan this QR code to be taken to the AI & U Playbook.

Spotting and addressing bias

As you refine your ethical AI practices, one critical area demands attention: bias. AI itself isn't inherently biased – it's just a system of ones and zeros. However, the data and humans behind it inevitably carry biases, whether intentional or not. This isn't about blame; we all have biases shaped by our experiences. The key is recognising how these biases might influence AI systems and ensuring they don't undermine fairness, inclusivity, or business goals.

AI bias occurs when systems produce unfair outcomes due to flawed training data or algorithm design. For example, a hiring algorithm trained on older data might favour male candidates over equally qualified women. Early versions of Alexa struggled with female voices because the system was trained mostly on male data, leading to a poorer user experience for women. A 2019 UN report even found that digital voice assistants with submissive, female voices could reinforce gender stereotypes. These examples highlight why diverse, well-balanced datasets are essential for building fair AI systems.

Bias matters because it can:

- **erode trust**, as clients and customers may lose confidence in your business if they feel excluded or treated unfairly
- **harm inclusivity**, as certain groups may experience poorer outcomes, impacting your business's reputation and effectiveness
- **create legal risks**, as discriminatory outcomes could expose your business to regulatory or reputational damage.

How to identify potential bias

As you explore AI solutions, ask these questions: does this system treat all customer groups equally? Is the data used to train the AI representative of the people it serves? Who benefits the most – and the least – from this AI process?

Take AI action: conduct a bias check

Review the data sources used by your AI tools. Are they inclusive of all demographics?

Test the outputs. Are there patterns that favour one group over another? Collect feedback from employees and customers to spot unintended consequences.

Bias isn't a one-and-done issue – it requires ongoing attention. Regular reviews and updates to your AI systems will help ensure fair and inclusive outcomes as your business evolves. By understanding and addressing bias, you're not just improving your AI tools – you're building a more inclusive and trustworthy business.

Common roadblocks to ethical AI

Identifying opportunities for AI to make a difference in your business might feel straightforward, but it's common to encounter hesitations or mental blocks. Here's how to tackle the most frequent objections and move forward with clarity and confidence.

'I don't have any obvious opportunities.'

Even if your business runs smoothly, small inefficiencies might still exist.

Start with small irritations. Look for tasks that feel repetitive or outdated. Even minor frustrations can reveal big opportunities. For example, automating appointment reminders can save time.

Employees often notice inefficiencies you might miss. Ask what tasks they'd like to spend less time on.

'I'm not sure how AI can help.'

AI can seem complex, but the key is to focus on solving real problems. Focus on the problem, not the tool: identify challenges first, then explore AI solutions. For example, AI chatbots can handle customer queries 24/7.

Start small. You don't need advanced AI – simple tools like scheduling assistants or data-entry automation are great starting points.

'What if I pick the wrong opportunity?'

Fear of making the wrong choice can lead to inaction, but every step is a learning opportunity.

Think of it as a test. Small, low-risk experiments provide valuable insights. For example, automating one task can reveal broader opportunities without major commitment.

Use a prioritisation map (discussed later in this chapter). Focus on tasks that offer quick wins and high impact.

'I'm worried about overwhelming my team.'

Change can feel like extra work, but the right improvements reduce workload.

Focus on tasks that reduce workload. Choose solutions that ease pressure on your team, such as automating data entry, which saves hours for more valuable work.

Communicate the benefits. Frame changes as ways to make work easier, not just business optimisations.

'I don't know where to start.'

When everything seems like a priority, narrowing your focus is key.

Prioritise based on impact. Ask which tasks cause the most frustration or waste the most time. For example, start with manual inventory updates if they take too long but add little value.

Follow the REIMAGINE Framework. Use what you've already assessed – like tools and impact mapping – to guide your next steps.

These objections aren't roadblocks – they're opportunities to pause, reflect, and think strategically. By starting small, prioritising wisely, and involving your team, you'll uncover impactful opportunities and build the momentum needed for broader AI integration.

Common pitfalls in Identify – and how to avoid them

The Identify phase is where opportunities for quick wins and meaningful improvements come into focus. But like any critical step in your business journey, it's easy to stumble if you're not prepared. Here are the most common pitfalls to watch out for – and how to navigate them with confidence.

Focusing on the wrong opportunities

It's easy to become caught up in tasks that feel urgent but don't create real value. Instead of spending time optimising minor back-office processes, focus on changes that drive meaningful results, like improving customer response times to boost satisfaction and loyalty.

Use your prioritisation map (explained later in this chapter) to assess each opportunity based on its impact and ease of implementation. This ensures you're directing resources towards what truly moves the needle, rather than just checking off tasks that have little effect on your business success.

Overthinking your first step

Waiting for the 'perfect' opportunity can lead to inaction. Instead, start small with an area where you can make a quick improvement and treat it as an experiment rather than a final decision.

Choose a low-risk, high-reward change, like automating appointment reminders or adding an AI chatbot for FAQs. Small wins build momentum and provide valuable insights for bigger improvements down the line.

Ignoring team input

Overlooking the people who work closest to a process can lead to missed insights. Engage your team early by asking about pain points and inefficiencies – they often see gaps that others miss. For example, a customer service rep might point out that automating common inquiries could save hours each week. Involving your team ensures that improvements are practical, effective, and widely supported.

Trying to do too much at once

Trying to tackle too many improvements at once can lead to burnout and inefficiency. Instead, focus on one to three high-impact opportunities that align with your business goals and deliver measurable results. For example, start by automating data entry before moving on to more complex changes like workflow redesigns. This step-by-step approach keeps progress manageable and sustainable.

Failing to align opportunities with business goals

Choosing improvements that don't fit your broader goals can waste time and resources. Use your business objectives as a filter – ask: does this directly support my mission, vision, or bottom line? For example, if customer retention is a priority, focus on enhancing client communication rather than optimising an internal admin task.

Keeping your efforts aligned ensures meaningful, long-term impact.

Assuming opportunities are 'one and done'

Treating opportunities as one-time fixes can limit their potential. Instead, view each change as part of a continuous improvement cycle – implement, evaluate, and refine. For example, using AI for customer inquiries may work well at first, but ongoing adjustments based on client feedback can make it even more effective over time.

Overestimating resources

Selecting improvements without assessing time, budget, or skills can lead to frustration and stalled progress. Before committing, ask: do we have the capacity to implement this effectively right now? For example, automating a simple process might be manageable, but developing a custom AI solution could overwhelm your team. Aligning opportunities with available resources ensures sustainable success.

Disregarding short-term wins

Focusing only on big, long-term changes can slow progress. Instead, identify at least one low-effort, high-impact opportunity to see immediate results and build momentum. For example, automating invoice reminders can save time and improve cashflow while you work on larger projects. Small wins keep motivation high and demonstrate early success.

Choosing tools before identifying needs

Adopting technology without a clear purpose can lead to wasted time and resources. Always identify the pain point first before choosing a solution. For example, instead of using AI just because it's trendy, focus on solving specific issues like reducing time spent on manual tasks. Let the problem guide your technology choices, not the other way around.

Ignoring competitor insights

Ignoring industry trends can mean missing valuable opportunities. Observe what competitors are doing and how their innovations might apply to your business. For example, if they're using AI for personalised customer outreach, explore how you can implement similar strategies tailored to your unique audience. Learning from others can help you stay competitive and inspire new solutions.

The Identify stage isn't about perfection – it's about discovering what's possible. By avoiding these pitfalls and focusing on opportunities that align with your goals, resources, and values, you'll set your business up for meaningful progress and momentum.

The price of doing nothing

Choosing not to act or adopt AI is, of course, a decision in itself. In today's fast-moving landscape, ignoring AI's potential will come at a significant cost to your business.

Sometimes we're better off adopting a 'wait and see' approach, while other times it's imperative that we remain agile and adapt as we recognise a trend. So, what is the 'real' cost to your business if you choose to wait and see where AI is headed?

- **Missed efficiencies:** Competitors who automate mundane tasks will free up time for innovation while you remain bogged down.

- **Employee frustration:** Teams stuck with tedious, repetitive tasks may feel undervalued and disengaged.
- **Lost customers:** Slower, less personalised service can drive your customers straight to competitors.

Imagine this: a competitor automates their customer service, reducing response times from hours to minutes. Not only are they providing faster answers, but their customers also enjoy a seamless, satisfying experience. How would your business compete against that?

The low-hanging fruit you identified earlier represents the first step towards avoiding these opportunity costs. Acting on these smaller, impactful changes will help you build momentum for more transformative shifts.

The sunk cost dilemma

Opportunity cost often goes hand-in-hand with another common trap: sunk costs. Businesses hesitate to pivot or invest in new solutions because they've already spent significant time, money, or effort on existing processes or systems. But clinging to outdated methods can be even more costly in the long run. Consider this: if you've invested in a manual customer database, you may feel reluctant to move to an AI-powered customer relationship manager because of the time and money already spent setting up your current system.

However, by sticking with outdated tools, you might miss out on opportunities to automate customer insights, improve marketing effectiveness, or streamline operations.

Let's consider a small café competing with a nearby franchise. The franchise uses AI to predict peak times, optimise staffing, and personalise marketing offers. As a result, they have shorter wait times, targeted promotions, and happier customers. The local café, still relying on manual processes, struggles to keep up, losing customers to the franchise. The opportunity cost here isn't just the lost revenue – it's the long-term impact on customer loyalty and brand reputation.

Take AI action: mapping your low-hanging fruit

Having spent the time to identify your low-hanging fruit and considered ethical and strategic foundations, it's time to organise your insights. A prioritisation map helps structure your opportunities, ensuring you start with the most impactful and feasible tasks. Remember, our goal here isn't to tackle everything at once but to focus on the opportunities that offer the biggest return with the least complexity.

The prioritisation map

This simple tool will help you organise your ideas and identify the best place to start. Think of it as plotting your opportunities against three key criteria:

- **Biggest pet peeves:** The tasks or processes that drain your energy, frustrate your team, or consistently cause problems. Examples are manual invoicing that takes hours each week, and customer service delays causing complaints.
- **Most rewarding changes:** Areas or tasks where even small improvements could make a noticeable difference to your bottom line or customer satisfaction. Examples are having a scheduling tool to allow customers to book an appointment without needing to speak to you, and reducing errors in data entry to improve accuracy.
- **Easiest wins:** Opportunities where implementation requires minimal effort but delivers immediate results. Examples are automating appointment reminders, and using an AI tool to streamline inventory tracking.

Write down key tasks or processes that need improvement. For example: 'Responding to repetitive customer questions takes too much time.' Then, evaluate each opportunity based on its impact and feasibility.

Consider these dimensions: biggest annoyances (tasks that drain energy), most rewarding changes (improvements that boost customer satisfaction, revenue, or efficiency), and easiest wins (quick solutions requiring minimal resources). This helps prioritise where to start.

Here is an example prioritisation map.

Opportunity	Biggest annoyance	Most rewarding change	Easiest win
Automating appointment reminders	High	Moderate	High
Streamlining inventory tracking	Moderate	High	Moderate
Personalising customer communications	Moderate	High	High

CHAPTER 4

Mapping: charting your path to AI success

'Mapping your AI journey turns your ideas into achievable steps. Success is never an accident; it's a well-charted course.'

Tracy Sheen

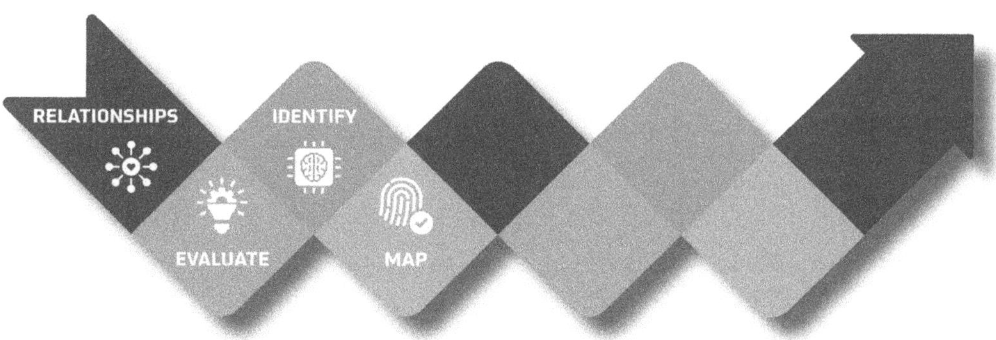

I'm a fan of the US band OK Go. Their music videos are legendary for their intricate planning, creating stunning results when put into action. You may remember their treadmill choreography for *Here It Goes Again*. But when I think about mapping or planning anything, my mind always goes to the video they did for *The One Moment*.

The entire music video took just 4.2 seconds to film. That's it – 4.2 seconds!

The planning and mapping that went into it? Months of meticulous effort. Every single element, from paint explosions to balloons popping, had to occur at the perfect moment in precise sequence.

Take AI action: breaking glass and exploding guitars

Take 10 minutes to watch these two videos with your team. Just scan this QR code. I dare you to find a better example of the importance of mapping the outcomes you're looking for.

Start with the behind-the-scenes making of the clip, then watch the final edited version.

Now, imagine trying to execute that level of precision without planning. It would have been chaos.

The difference? A well-thought-out map ensures your efforts lead to exponential impact – not confusion.

That's exactly where we are now in the REIMAGINE Framework: Mapping.

Mapping a strategic evolution

Let's take another trip back in time. It's the early 2010s, and the world of work is undergoing a seismic shift. For the first time, we're really starting to hear about the 'gig economy'. Platforms like Upwork and Fiverr are springing up, offering small business owners access to specialised skills on demand. Hot-desking and communal workspaces are making headlines, giving freelancers and startups places to collaborate without committing to long-term leases. The rules of business are changing. Teams no longer need to be in the same room – or even the same country – to deliver results. Agile methodologies, once confined to software developers, are becoming mainstream.

Businesses are scrambling for tools to keep up with the pace of change. At the centre of this evolving landscape is Mike Cannon-Brookes, an unassuming Sydney entrepreneur with a big vision. Back in 2002, Mike and his university mate Scott Farquhar co-founded Atlassian out of a student apartment, using a $10,000 credit-card debt. They wanted to solve a simple problem: help teams work better together. Their flagship tool, Jira, became a game-changer for developers, enabling technical teams to track bugs and manage workflows. Confluence followed, helping businesses centralise and share knowledge.

By the early 2010s, Atlassian had already achieved global success, but Mike and Scott weren't content to rest on their laurels. They knew the world of work was evolving fast – and they wanted Atlassian to evolve with it.

Enter Trello: the evolution continues

Mike Cannon-Brookes and Scott Farquhar saw an opportunity. While Jira and Confluence had become staples for technical teams, they realised the growing demand for a tool that appealed to non-technical teams as well. These were marketers juggling campaigns, operations managers coordinating across departments, and startups wearing every hat at once. Enter Trello. Created by Fog Creek Software, Trello was gaining traction as a simple, intuitive tool for organising work. Its Kanban-style boards, cards, and lists provided clarity for teams navigating the chaos of tasks, deadlines, and priorities. It wasn't just a tool – it was a way of thinking about work that resonated with users.

Atlassian recognised Trello's potential as the missing piece in their ecosystem. Rather than reinvent the wheel or compete head to head, they decided to acquire Trello in 2017 for $425 million. It was a bold move that instantly expanded Atlassian's reach, giving them access to millions of Trello users while reinforcing their reputation as leaders in team collaboration.

But this wasn't just a business acquisition – it was a carefully planned evolution. Atlassian didn't simply bolt Trello onto its product lineup. They integrated it thoughtfully, ensuring it complemented rather than competed with their existing tools. Trello retained its simplicity, charm, and loyal user base, while benefiting from Atlassian's resources and expertise. This wasn't about doing more for the sake of it. It was about aligning with Atlassian's mission of empowering teams to work better together. By evolving intentionally, Atlassian expanded its influence without losing focus on what it did best.

As the business landscape continues to evolve, Atlassian hasn't stopped there. By integrating AI into their tools – with the introduction of Atlassian Intelligence in 2023 – they've shown how emerging technologies can amplify collaboration and streamline processes, all while staying true to their core mission.

This highlights an essential principle of evolution: leveraging innovation to enhance what already works, rather than chasing change for its own sake.

How Atlassian REIMAGINED evolution

Atlassian's journey with Trello isn't just a story of smart business decisions – it's a masterclass in intentional evolution. Every step they took, from recognising a gap to integrating Trello into their ecosystem, aligns with the principles of the REIMAGINE Framework. This wasn't luck or guesswork; it was a deliberate process of evaluating opportunities, building relationships, and evolving in ways that strengthened their mission.

Let's take a closer look at how Atlassian's decisions mapped to the first few steps of the REIMAGINE Framework and what it can teach us about evolving with clarity and purpose.

Relationships

Atlassian's evolution started with a strong foundation of customer relationships. By listening to their users – both technical and non-technical – they understood the challenges faced by different teams. They recognised that non-technical teams were underserved and needed simpler, more intuitive tools.

Evaluate

The Atlassian team assessed their existing ecosystem – Jira and Confluence – and identified a gap. While their tools excelled for structured workflows and technical teams, they lacked a solution that worked for creative, marketing, and other non-technical teams.

Identify

Rather than building a new tool from scratch, Atlassian identified Trello as the ideal solution. Its simplicity and growing popularity made it a perfect complement to their existing offerings.

Map

Atlassian developed a clear plan for integrating Trello into their ecosystem. They ensured that Trello retained its identity while enhancing its value through alignment with Atlassian's other tools.

Setting up your dominos

Your roadmap is a blueprint based on the insights gathered from your relationships, evaluations, and identified opportunities. Think of it as setting up dominos – each step triggering the next in sequence. Instead of jumping into action, this stage is about organising your findings to define goals, prioritise quick wins, and set milestones. Starting small and celebrating early wins will keep progress on track while ensuring sustainable success.

So far, you've laid a strong foundation with three key steps: Relationships, Evaluate, and Identify. In Relationships, you engaged your team, clients, and community to align on a shared vision. In Evaluate, you assessed current systems, uncovering inefficiencies and opportunities for smarter operations. In Identify, you turned those insights into actionable goals, pinpointing where AI can create the biggest impact. These steps weren't just about gathering data – they built the clarity and confidence needed to move forward effectively.

Mapping is where it all starts to come together. But without the groundwork you've already done, creating a roadmap would feel overwhelming or disconnected. Thanks to the work you've put in, you have clarity on where your business needs AI the most. You have alignment within your team, so everyone is rowing in the same direction. You have focus, knowing which goals to prioritise and how to measure success. Now, it's time to pull it all together.

Take AI action: framing your roadmap

To help you create a clear and actionable roadmap, we'll use my five-step FRAME process:

- **F: Focus on goals** – Define specific, actionable objectives to guide your efforts.
- **R: Roadmap milestones** – Break down your goals into clear, manageable steps.
- **A: Assess success metrics** – Identify how you'll measure progress and results.
- **M: Maximise quick wins** – Prioritise high-impact actions to build momentum.
- **E: Empower responsibility** – Assign ownership to ensure accountability and execution.

Each step in FRAME builds on the work you've already done in the earlier stages of the REIMAGINE Framework – Relationships, Evaluate, and Identify. With your frame in place, you'll have a clear picture of where you're headed and how to get there.

Step 1: Focus on goals

Clear, specific goals give you direction. Without them, you risk wandering aimlessly, implementing tools that don't solve real problems or align with your priorities. By setting precise objectives, you:

- provide your team with a shared vision
- make it easier to measure success and track progress
- ensure every action contributes directly to meaningful outcomes.

How to define goals using the FRAME process

From the Evaluate step: what processes or areas did you identify as needing improvement?

From the Identify step: what are the priorities you set and the quick wins you spotted?

Include the input of team members to ensure goals are realistic and aligned with daily operations.

Make them SMART goals:

Specific: Define exactly what you want to achieve.

Measurable: Include benchmarks or numbers.

Achievable: Set targets your team can realistically meet.

Relevant: Align with your business's core goals.

Time-bound: Set deadlines to ensure it happens.

Here are some example goals:

- Automate appointment scheduling to save four hours per week.
- Generate two new qualified leads per week using an AI tool.
- Improve inventory forecasting accuracy by 30% within six months.

With your goals clearly defined, you're ready to start building the rest of your FRAME.

Step 2: Roadmap milestones

Once you've set your goals, the next step is to break them into smaller, actionable pieces. Think of milestones as the stepping stones that lead you to your destination. Without them, you can easily get overwhelmed or lost. Milestones help you:

- create a clear path to follow
- make progress manageable by focusing on one step at a time
- build momentum with small wins that keep your team motivated.

Look at your goal and ask: what are the major steps required to achieve this? For example, if your goal is to reduce appointment booking time by 50%, your milestones might include:

- researching AI scheduling tools
- selecting and testing the best tool
- training your team on how to use it
- implementing the tool fully in daily operations.

Each milestone should build on the previous one. Think of them like dominos – when one falls, it sets the next in motion.

Example roadmap milestones

Goal: Automate appointment scheduling to save four hours weekly.

Milestone 1: Research and shortlist AI scheduling tools (week 1).

Milestone 2: Select the best tool and test it with five customers (weeks 2–3).

Milestone 3: Train team members on the tool (week 4).

Milestone 4: Launch the tool fully for all appointments (weeks 5–6).

With your milestones in place, you've created a step-by-step plan to achieve your goal. Next, let's talk about how to measure success.

Step 3: Create success metrics

Setting success metrics is how you ensure your roadmap is delivering the results you want. Without clear metrics, it's impossible to know if your AI integration is working. Metrics help you:

- measure progress objectively
- celebrate wins with your team
- identify when adjustments are needed to stay on track.

Metrics provide clarity and accountability. They show your team what success looks like and keep everyone focused on achieving it.

Step 4: Maximise quick wins

Quick wins are the lifeblood of momentum. They're the small, manageable actions that deliver immediate value, helping your team see the benefits of AI integration early in the process. Quick wins keep everyone motivated, build confidence in your roadmap, and create the energy needed to tackle bigger challenges.

Look at the inefficiencies and opportunities you highlighted earlier.

Which tasks or processes can AI improve quickly and easily? Choose tasks that are easy to automate or enhance with minimal investment or training. Pick quick wins that will free up significant time or deliver visible results.

Ask team members to suggest tasks they find repetitive or time-consuming. Their input ensures the quick wins you choose will be meaningful to their roles. For example, what's one thing you do every week that feels like a time sink? Could we automate that?

Even quick wins need a measurable outcome. Define how you'll know the win is successful.

Step 5: Empower responsibility

A great roadmap is only as strong as the team behind it (that's why we begin our REIMAGINE roadmap with relationships). Assigning clear responsibilities ensures that each step of your plan is executed effectively. When everyone knows their role and what's expected of them, your roadmap moves from a plan to a reality. Without accountability, even the best plans can stall.

Empowering your team with clear responsibilities transforms your roadmap into a collaborative, actionable plan. It ensures everyone knows their role and feels invested in the success of your AI journey.

Now that you've seen how the FRAME process comes together, it's time to create your own roadmap! Gather your team, bring your insights from earlier steps, and work through the above process together.[5]

5 If you'd like a hand pulling it all together, the AI & U Playbook includes ready-to-use templates and worksheets to guide your team step by step. Simply scan the QR code to check it out.

Common pitfalls in Mapping – and how to avoid them

The Mapping phase translates your ideas into actionable steps, but it's easy to trip up if you're not prepared. Here are the most common pitfalls to watch for and how to sidestep them.

Overcomplicating the roadmap

Trying to map out every detail at once can lead to overwhelm. Start simple. Focus on one goal and build out milestones step by step. For example, map out how to automate appointment scheduling before adding other processes.

Neglecting success metrics

Without clear metrics, you won't know if your roadmap is working. Tie every goal to a measurable outcome. For example, track time saved weekly after implementing a scheduling tool.

Failing to adjust the plan

Sticking rigidly to your roadmap, even when it's not working, leads to wasted effort. Treat your roadmap as a living document. Review and adjust regularly. For example, if a tool isn't delivering expected results, explore alternatives.

Lacking team accountability

Assigning tasks without follow-up can stall progress. Assign clear ownership for each milestone and track progress through regular check-ins.

Forgetting the 'why'

Don't focus too much on tasks and lose sight of your broader goals. Start every roadmap milestone with a clear objective tied to your mission or vision. For example, frame tasks like 'implement AI scheduling' as part of a larger goal, such as 'reduce admin workload by 20%'.

Gaining clarity, momentum, and flexibility

Phew! You made it. Congratulations – you've tackled one of the most critical steps in the REIMAGINE Framework! The purpose of mapping is gaining clarity, momentum, and flexibility. By addressing objections and avoiding these common pitfalls, you'll create a roadmap that not only delivers results but also keeps you aligned with your values and goals.

Mapping is the backbone of your AI journey. By working through the FRAME process, you've:

- focused on clear goals to guide your efforts
- created milestones to break down your goals into actionable steps
- established success metrics to measure progress and outcomes
- identified quick wins to build momentum
- empowered responsibility by assigning clear roles.

This is no small feat. The Mapping stage often feels like heavy lifting, but the effort you've put in now will save you time, money, and frustration in the long run. You've built a roadmap that ensures every action you take moves your business closer to success.

Remember, success is never an accident – it's the result of careful planning and purposeful execution. By investing in this process, you've done what many skip: laying a solid foundation for long-term growth. Every client of mine who's seen real transformation with AI has started where you are now – with a detailed roadmap that turns possibilities into a clear path forward. If it feels like you're wading through custard, take a breath and celebrate how far you've already come.

What's next? Activate.

CHAPTER 5

Activate: testing AI solutions in the real world

'AI isn't about waiting for the perfect moment – it's about starting where you are, with what you have. Activation is how you build momentum one small step at a time.'

Tracy Sheen

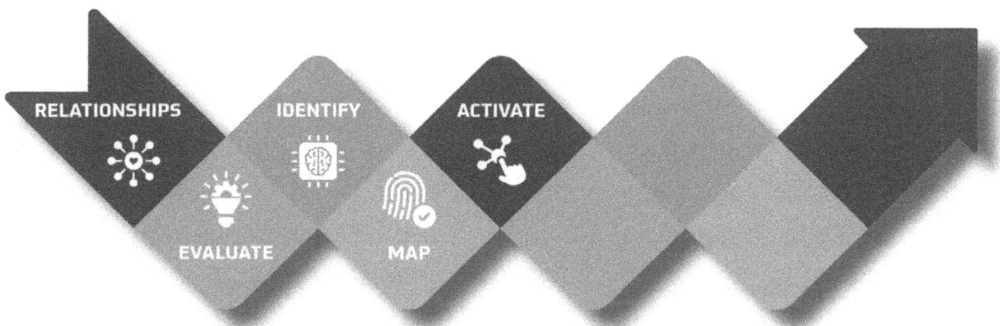

Lighting the spark of change

In the 1980s, everything felt big. Big hair, big music, and big cultural moments. Blue Light Discos were the highlight of my social calendar, and I'd spend hours perfecting my 'Moon Patrol' skills on the two-player Atari game I'd talked my parents into putting in our general store.

It was a time when everything seemed to be about daring moves and bold statements. It wasn't just individuals vying for the spotlight – brands were too. The Cola Wars were raging, with Pepsi and Coca-Cola locked in fierce competition. Pepsi was gaining ground, using campaigns like the Pepsi Challenge to position itself as the choice of a younger, trendier audience. (Anyone else remember Michael Jackson's famous – and fiery – commercial?)

Coca-Cola, the undisputed titan of the beverage world, found itself losing market share and knew it had to act. In 1985, Coca-Cola made a daring move – they activated their plan to launch a completely new formula: 'New Coke'. This wasn't just a minor adjustment; it was a full-scale reinvention of one of the world's most iconic brands.

Their decision was driven by relationships. Extensive taste tests showed that younger consumers preferred a sweeter flavour, and Coca-Cola mapped out a bold strategy to align with these changing preferences. But even the best-laid plans can go sideways. What Coca-Cola underestimated was the depth of emotional loyalty their existing customers felt for the original formula. The activation was bold and strategic, but it revealed a critical gap in their planning. When backlash came, it was swift and loud. (What happened next is a story we'll revisit later.)

For now, let's focus on what it takes to activate with purpose. Coca-Cola's story is a powerful example of how activation relies on preparation, relationships, and ethics. It shows us the importance of timing and ensuring your actions align with your values and audience needs.

How Coke learned the hard way

The New Coke story reminds us that even bold steps can lead to invaluable lessons when guided by the right framework. That's where the REIMAGINE process comes in. Each step you've taken so far – Relationships, Evaluate, Identify, Mapping – feeds into activation, providing a foundation for success while helping you navigate potential challenges.

Here's how the story of 'New Coke' maps onto these steps, and how you can apply these lessons to activate your AI journey with confidence and purpose.

Relationships: the foundation of activation

The New Coke story reminds us that no activation happens in isolation. Coca-Cola's decision to launch was based on relationships – they studied their audience, leaned into their insights, and took a bold step forward.

For your business, activating AI isn't just about pressing 'go' on a tool. It's about understanding how your customers, team, and community will experience the change and ensuring those relationships remain at the heart of every decision.

Evaluate: timing activation to values and capacity

Coca-Cola's misstep also underscores the importance of evaluating timing. Is your team ready for this change? Does this activation align with your values and the expectations of your customers? Activation must be more than a reaction to trends – it's a deliberate step that considers your capacity to handle what comes next.

Take AI action: assess readiness

Before you activate, ask yourself: how does this change strengthen your relationships? Who needs to be involved in making this successful?

Assess readiness before you activate, ensuring the timing aligns with your team and customer expectations.

Identify: focus on the right opportunity

Activating AI isn't about doing everything at once. Much like Coca-Cola's attempt to solve one specific problem – appealing to younger consumers – you need to focus your activation on the opportunities with the biggest potential impact. Whether it's automating a repetitive task or improving customer engagement, start small and build confidence.

Map: charting New Coke

For Coca-Cola, mapping their strategy for New Coke was all about turning insights into action. They used taste-test data to identify their goal – appealing to younger consumers – and built a roadmap to achieve it. The plan was detailed: reformulate the product, launch an innovative marketing campaign, and roll it out nationwide.

Coke's map was thorough but lacked a holistic view of relationships and long-term goals. A good map not only outlines steps but also considers roles, responsibilities, and how each decision aligns with your values.

The ethics of activation

Activation also demands a commitment to ethics. When Coca-Cola faced a backlash, their response was rooted in transparency, humility, and action. They didn't hide behind marketing spin – they addressed customer concerns head-on and made changes. For your business, ethical activation means ensuring your AI solutions align with your values, are transparent to your customers, and improve rather than disrupt the trust you've built.

Take AI action: before you activate

Before activation, ask:

- Does this align with our core mission and values?
- How will we communicate this change to customers and team members?
- What systems are in place to handle feedback or ethical concerns?

Lighting the spark

Activation is the moment when planning transforms into progress. Like Coca-Cola's bold activation of New Coke, your business is now at a tipping point. Planning has brought you to this moment, but it's the act of moving forward – taking deliberate, courageous steps – that will turn your vision into reality.

Before you take the first step into activation, let's pause and revisit everything you've achieved so far. Each step of the REIMAGINE Framework has prepared you for this moment, giving you the tools, clarity, and confidence to move forward. By pulling together the resources you've created, you can refine your plans and ensure everything is ready for a successful launch. Think of this as your final pre-launch check – a moment to ensure alignment, confirm readiness, and reconnect with the people and purpose driving your AI journey.

Measure twice, cut once

I'm married to an engineer. If you know any engineers, you'll understand exactly where I'm going with this. Pete is the most practical and methodical person I've ever met. Before he makes a decision, he spends months researching every possible angle and scenario. He's the epitome of the saying 'measure twice, cut once'.

When it comes to REIMAGINING your business, we're talking about something so transformative that your operations will never look the same again. You're stepping into uncharted territory while still keeping the day-to-day running smoothly. That's why taking this final moment to reflect is critical. Imagine activating a pilot programme only to discover it disrupts a connected system, inconveniences your clients, or frustrates your team. These are the kinds of risks you can avoid by reconnecting with the work you've done so far. Taking this time to measure twice ensures that when you make the final cut, it's precise, deliberate, and impactful.

This check-in is about more than reviewing documents or plans. It's about strengthening your confidence, refining your approach, and ensuring the people who will make your activation successful are informed and aligned. By taking this step, you're not just preparing – you're setting the stage for success. When you're ready, read on and step into your activation journey with confidence.

What activation looks like

Activation doesn't have to start with sweeping changes. Small, focused steps can build the momentum you need for long-term success. Here are some ways you can get some quick wins:

- **Run a pilot programme:** Trial a new AI tool in one department and gather feedback.
- **Automate processes:** Automate a repetitive task, like sending reminders or collecting data.
- **Boost customer engagement:** Use AI to better understand your clients' needs and improve interactions.

Every action – no matter how small – is a spark that ignites something bigger. The time you save, the confidence you build, and the trust you strengthen with your team and clients all add up to a business that feels lighter, faster, and more focused on what truly matters.

Take AI action: create your action plan

Now that you've reflected on your progress, it's time to put your plans into action. Use this exercise to consolidate everything you've worked on so far and ensure you're ready to activate with confidence. This is your final pre-launch step: a hands-on exercise to organise your thoughts, confirm your plans, and ensure you're fully prepared for activation. Whether you're a soloprepreneur, working with a virtual assistant, or leading a team, this step will help you tailor your activation to your specific needs.

How long will this take?

Solo entrepreneurs: 30 to 60 minutes for focused reflection and planning.

With a VA: 1 to 2 hours to collaborate and confirm roles.

Small teams (2 to 10 members): 2 to 3 hours, likely involving a short meeting.

Larger teams (10+ members): Half a day to a full day for stakeholder alignment.

What will you need?

Templates and resources from the REIMAGINE Framework that you have prepared so far:

- Circle of Impact and relationship mapping
- SWOT analysis
- quick win worksheet
- prioritisation map
- AI policy draft
- bias check
- FRAME roadmap.

Workspace and tools

Notebook, whiteboard, or digital workspace (for example, Google Docs, Notion, or Trello). Communication tools (for example, Zoom, Slack) if collaborating with others.

Who should you involve?

Solo entrepreneurs: Work independently, but consider consulting a mentor or peer for feedback.

If you have a VA or remote team: Brief your VA and collaborate on task allocation and preparation.

If you have a team: Involve your team or key stakeholders to review, refine, and align on the plan.

Step 1: Define your activation plan

Begin by clarifying the specifics of your activation project.

Use the template below as a guide for what to include.

Step	Notes (example)
Project	*What specific project or initiative are you activating?*
Goal	*What measurable result are you aiming to achieve? (e.g. reduce response time by 20%)*
Low-hanging fruit	*What quick-win opportunities will this project address?*
Responsibilities	*Who is responsible for overseeing this project? What are their specific tasks?*
Metrics	*What will you track to measure success? (e.g. inquiries resolved, customer satisfaction, revenue)*
Timeline	*What is the timeline for this activation? Include key milestones (pilot, evaluation, expansion).*
Communication plan	*How will you inform your team or customers about this activation?*
Risks or challenges	*What risks have you identified, and how will you address them?*
Feedback plan	*How will you gather feedback during and after activation?*

Step 2: Review for readiness

Use the launch checklist below to ensure you've covered all your bases.

Revisit your map:

- Have I reviewed the project goals, metrics, and responsibilities?
- Does the roadmap reflect our priorities and available resources?

Prepare for launch:

- Is the tool or system fully configured and tested?
- Have I uploaded or created all required content (scripts, workflows, data)?
- Has the team been briefed on their roles and expectations?

Pull the trigger:

- Have I communicated the launch details to internal and external stakeholders?
- Am I starting small to test and refine before full-scale activation?
- Is a feedback process in place to evaluate early results and make adjustments?

Step 3: Align your team

Activation isn't just about tools; it's about people:

- **For solo entrepreneurs:** Hold yourself accountable with clear deadlines.
- **If you have a VA or remote team:** Delegate specific tasks and ensure your VA has access to all necessary tools and resources.
- **If you have a team:** Clarify everyone's role in the activation process. Set up check-ins to ensure alignment and address concerns.

Step 4: Create a launch timeline

Set a clear timeline with realistic milestones. For example:

Week 1: Pilot the project with limited scope.

Week 2: Gather feedback and make adjustments.

Week 3: Expand the activation to full-scale implementation.

Step 5: Take action

Activation is where your plans become progress. By starting small, aligning your team, and staying flexible, you'll not only gain confidence but also build momentum for the rest of your AI journey.

From the Mapping stage, you already know what to do and who's responsible. Activation is simply about following through. By taking this step, you're moving closer to REIMAGINING your business and building momentum for the rest of your AI journey.

Common roadblocks in the Activate stage

At this stage of the REIMAGINE Framework, it's common to feel a sense of hesitation – or as I like to call it, 'the wobbles'. You've done the groundwork and made your plans, and now you're on the verge of putting them into action. That's when the enormity of REIMAGINING everything you've ever done starts to sink in.

It's normal.

In fact, it's more than normal – it's a *good thing*. Feeling a little uneasy means you're thinking deeply about the changes ahead. You're considering your team, your clients, and the long-term impact of your decisions. You might wonder:

- How will my team adjust?
- Will my clients cope with the changes?
- Am I really ready to take this leap?
- Things are okay now – do I need to do this?

Let me reassure you: hesitation is part of the process. It's a sign you're taking this seriously. It means you're thinking everything through and evaluating every angle. But as natural as this hesitation is, it's important to address it head-on so it doesn't hold you back. By reviewing your own roadblocks now, you gain the clarity and confidence to move forward, knowing you've done the hard work to prepare.

'What if it doesn't work?'

It's natural to worry that an AI tool might not deliver the results you're hoping for. But that's exactly why we start with a pilot – an experiment, not a long-term commitment. Even if it doesn't work perfectly at first, you're still making progress. Set realistic expectations and focus on testing, not perfection. Start with a small, manageable task where even modest improvements feel like a win.

'Will my team resist change?'

Change can be challenging, especially if your team is comfortable doing things a certain way. That's why early buy-in is crucial. If resistance arises, take a step back and address their concerns. Involve your team from the start, ask for their input, and show them how the tool solves their pain points. Celebrating small wins along the way can help shift mindsets and build momentum.

'I'm already overwhelmed.'

If you're a solo operator or managing a small team, the thought of adding something new to your workload might feel overwhelming. But AI is meant to lighten your load, not add to it. The key is to start small. Choose just one repetitive task – like sending appointment reminders – and automate it. Even dedicating 30 minutes to setting it up can make a noticeable difference.

'How do I engage my remote or part-time team?'

Managing a dispersed team comes with its own challenges, but success lies in clarity and communication. Remote and part-time teams thrive when they have a clear roadmap and ongoing involvement. Use shared tools like Trello or Slack to assign roles, track progress, and set clear milestones. Keeping tasks visible and checking in regularly ensures everyone stays aligned and engaged.

'I can't afford this.'

Budget concerns are valid, but AI adoption doesn't have to be expensive. Many tools offer free or low-cost versions that allow you to test their value before making a bigger investment. Start by exploring existing tools that might already have useful features. Focus on cost-saving opportunities, like automating repetitive admin tasks, and seek advice from experts who can guide you towards low-cost implementation options.

'Will this disrupt my business?'

The fear of AI disrupting operations or confusing customers is understandable. But that's why you're starting small – testing one thing in one area rather than making sweeping changes. Begin with an internal task that won't directly affect customers. Clear communication with your team or clients about what to expect can ease any concerns, and keeping the pilot contained and manageable will help you assess its impact without unnecessary risk.

Key ethical questions to ask

Before you flip the switch, take a moment to reflect on these critical questions to ensure your activation is both ethical and people-first:

- **Relationships:** How does this activation strengthen or maintain trust with your clients and team? Have you consulted your team and key stakeholders about how this change will impact them?
- **Transparency:** Have you communicated to clients and stakeholders how your activation will affect them? Are you clear about what's being automated and why?
- **Collaboration:** Have you involved your team in planning the activation? Have you sought input from clients or stakeholders to understand their concerns or expectations?
- **Bias:** Is the tool or system you're using trained on diverse, unbiased data? How are you monitoring for unintended biases that could negatively affect clients or outcomes?
- **Accountability:** Who is responsible for overseeing the activation and ensuring it meets expectations? How will you handle issues or feedback during the pilot phase?
- **Alignment with values:** Does this activation reflect your business's mission and core values? How does it enhance the relationships and trust you've worked hard to build?

- **Long-term impact:** How will this activation impact your clients and team in the long run? What systems will you put in place to review and improve the tool over time?

Wrapping up activation: looking ahead

Congratulations – you've reached a major milestone in your AI journey! Activation isn't just about taking action; it's about lighting the spark for meaningful change in your business. By following the steps of the REIMAGINE Framework and keeping ethics at the heart of your decisions, you've set the stage for success.

But activation is only the beginning. Every obstacle you overcome and every small win you celebrate is part of the process. The next step, Gather, is where you'll start to uncover the insights that will guide your journey forward. This isn't about perfection – it's about learning. Think of Gather as the feedback loop that refines your process and builds momentum. You'll use this phase to:

- discover what worked really well and why
- identify areas for improvement
- uncover unexpected opportunities that your activation has revealed.

If you're feeling stuck or overwhelmed, use the Troubleshooting Checklist opposite to identify one small step forward. Remember, progress – not perfection – is the goal.

Take AI action: troubleshooting checklist

When things don't go as planned, don't panic – here's a checklist to help you stay on track and keep moving forward.

The tool feels overwhelming

- **Break it into smaller steps:** Focus on setting up one feature at a time.
- **Check for tutorials or help guides:** Most tools offer quick-start resources to simplify the process.
- **Ask for help:** Reach out to the tool's support team or online forums for guidance.

Your team isn't on board

- **Revisit the 'why':** Remind your team how the tool benefits them directly.
- **Show quick wins:** Share early results or time savings to build enthusiasm.
- **Offer extra support:** Provide additional training or resources to boost confidence.

It's not working as expected

- **Check the setup:** Review your configurations and ensure the tool aligns with your goals.
- **Test in smaller increments:** Start with a single task or workflow to identify issues.
- **Reassess the fit:** If the tool isn't right, revisit the Identify phase to choose another option.

You're feeling stuck or overwhelmed

- **Pause and refocus:** Step back and revisit your Mapping notes for clarity.

- **Simplify:** Choose one small action to move forward – progress over perfection.
- **Reach out:** Connect with peers, mentors, or communities to gain perspective and support.
- **Reflect:** What's one roadblock you've encountered so far, and what's one small action you can take to address it today?

Take AI action: celebrate your first step

Before diving into the next phase, take a moment to pause, reflect, and celebrate this milestone. Activation isn't just about launching a pilot – it's about building momentum and confidence in your AI journey.

Just the beginning

Activation isn't just about using AI – it's about proving to yourself that you're ready to lead your business into the future. The spark you've lit today is just the beginning of what's possible. If you're running this journey solo, remember that even small progress is monumental. You're not just reimagining your business – you're proving that you have the courage and vision to shape your future.

In the next step, you'll uncover the insights that will take your results to the next level.

CHAPTER 6

Gather: fitting the pieces together

'Gathering insights isn't just about data – it's about uncovering the stories behind the numbers. Every insight is a stepping stone, guiding you to smarter decisions and a clearer path forward.'

Tracy Sheen

The Gather stage in our REIMAGINE Framework is where the pieces of your AI journey start to fit together. It's not about drowning in spreadsheets or getting lost in dashboards – it's about uncovering the story behind the numbers.

Every piece of data you collect has a purpose: to validate your decisions, reveal what's working, highlight areas for improvement, and uncover hidden opportunities. Think of this stage as detective work. The insights you gather will act as a compass, guiding you towards smarter, more focused decisions that align with your goals. It's about taking the lessons from your pilot activation and transforming them into a clear roadmap for the next phase.

But not all data is created equal. The key is to focus on the metrics that matter most – those that directly align with your goals and tell you whether your pilot is heading in the right direction. By narrowing your focus, you'll avoid the overwhelm of endless reports and zero in on actionable insights. The Gather phase is more than just a task; it's how you learn, adapt, and build momentum for the future. With the right insights, you'll move closer to creating a smarter, more agile business that's ready to evolve.

To see what this looks like in action, let's revisit Patagonia – a company that has mastered the art of gathering insights to refine its processes and make values-driven decisions.

Patagonia: gathering insights for purposeful action

Patagonia's journey highlights how gathering data can drive transformation. In the Evaluate stage, its commitment to values led to bold decisions, such as shifting to organic cotton – a move that reinforced the power of reflection and adaptation. Today, Patagonia extends this approach to AI, using data to align its operations with its mission. By forecasting the environmental impact of materials, analysing customer sentiment, and optimising internal efficiency, AI helps Patagonia make more informed, sustainable choices. Rather than replacing values, AI amplifies them, allowing the company to stay true to its purpose while driving innovation.

While Patagonia operates at scale, its principles apply to any business. Data – whether from AI tools or traditional methods – provides clarity and direction. Whether tracking customer feedback, measuring team efficiency, or assessing a pilot activation, the process remains the same: focus on meaningful insights and let them guide your next steps. Just as Patagonia aligns data with its mission, you can use the Gather stage to ensure your actions reflect your values, goals, and customer needs.

Not all data is created equal

Whatever pilot you choose to Activate, you've likely realised that most AI platforms and solutions offer an overwhelming amount of data, from graphs to detailed reports. But here's the secret: you don't need it all. The key is to concentrate on the data that aligns directly with your goals and tells you what you need to know to move forward. Trying to analyse *everything* can lead to what's known as 'analysis paralysis', where too much information prevents meaningful action. Instead, by focusing on key metrics that align with your business goals, you'll ensure the data you collect drives progress and informs smart decisions.

Take AI action: reflect on your pilot's data needs

Before you get caught up in the flood of information available, take a moment to focus.

How long should this take?

Solo business owners: Spend 20 to 30 minutes reflecting on questions, with an optional 15-minute follow-up after reviewing data.

Small teams (2 to 10 people): Allocate 30 to 60 minutes for a collaborative discussion, gathering input from all relevant team members.

Remote or larger teams: Plan a 1- to 1.5-hour structured session, using pre-prepared materials to guide discussion and ensure stakeholder participation.

Who needs to be involved?

Solo business owners: Complete the exercise solo but seek feedback from trusted advisers, mentors, or close collaborators.

Small teams: Involve key team members affected by the AI pilot, such as customer service reps for client tools or operations staff for internal processes. Ensure everyone can provide input on meaningful data.

Remote or larger teams: Engage stakeholders across departments, including managers overseeing the pilot, employees using the AI system, and IT or analytics specialists familiar with data tools.

Ask the following key questions and jot down the responses:

- What was the problem I was trying to solve for the business?
- What is the metric that will show me if my pilot is moving towards success?
- What information do my people or clients need?
- What feedback or metrics would build my team's confidence in the changes?
- What results would reinforce trust and show my clients the benefits of the AI solution?

- What ethical considerations should I keep in mind?
- What insights do I need to make better-informed decisions about how the pilot is tracking?

What data should you gather?

To get started, use the questions above to pinpoint the data that directly supports your goals. The type of data you gather depends on your pilot project's goals. Use this list to focus on metrics that matter:

- **Customer interactions:** Track total inquiries, response times, and customer satisfaction (for example, ratings or surveys).
- **Efficiency metrics:** Measure time saved per task and error reduction compared to manual processes.
- **Engagement data:** Monitor open rates, click-through rates, campaign conversions, and customer feedback on recommendations.
- **Operational insights:** Assess workflow improvements, team efficiency, and problem areas resolved.

Take AI action: your data collection action plan

This step-by-step guide will help you collect, organise, and act on the data that matters most to your AI pilot. It's designed to keep you focused, ethical, and impactful as you refine your strategy.

How long will this take?

Solo business owners: Allocate 1 to 2 hours total for setting up and reviewing data collection.

Small teams (2 to 10 people): Plan a 1-hour collaborative session to review and align.

Larger teams or remote setups: Use a structured 1- to 1.5-hour meeting, with pre-distributed materials, to ensure alignment across stakeholders.

Step 1: Define your metrics

Identify two to three key metrics tied to your goals (for example, response times, customer satisfaction scores, time savings).

Ask yourself: what problem am I solving? Which data will clearly show progress towards my goal?

Step 2: Set a review cadence

Decide how often to check your data:

Short-term pilots: Review weekly for immediate feedback.

Longer pilots: Review monthly to identify trends. Block time in your calendar for reviews (for example, 30 to 60 minutes per session).

Step 3: Choose tools for collection

Use tools that fit your needs and simplify tracking: AI dashboards, CRM reports, or spreadsheets. Involve your IT or analytics team (if available) to ensure efficient data setup.

Step 4: Involve your people

Team input

Engage your team to gather on-the-ground insights and qualitative feedback.

Customer feedback

Use surveys or interviews to gauge how the pilot is impacting their experience.

Step 5: Consider ethics

Ask yourself

Are we protecting customer privacy and data security? Have we ensured that the data we collect doesn't create biases or exclusions? Are we transparent about how and why we're using this data?

Step 6: Organise for clarity

Use a simple format to summarise your findings, such as a table showing key metrics, trends, and action points or a dashboard that highlights progress at a glance. Keep it concise – focus on actionable insights, not every detail.

Step 7: Spot trends and act

Look for patterns, anomalies, or opportunities in your data. Are you meeting your goals? What's working well, and what needs tweaking? Use these insights to refine your pilot with small, incremental adjustments.

Step 8: Celebrate wins

Share early successes with your team and customers to build momentum and motivation and reinforce trust in the process.

What to do with the results

Share key insights with your team and stakeholders in a simple report or presentation. Make small adjustments based on what the data tells you. Use your insights to inform your next steps in the Iterate phase.

Paul's pilot success

Paul, an accountant based in Port Macquarie, has built strong long-term relationships with his clients, many of whom have worked with him for over a decade. However, as governance requirements in his industry grew, he found it harder to maintain the same level of engagement. To address this, Paul explored AI-driven solutions and decided to pilot an AI email assistant to streamline communication. Concerned about maintaining trust, he was transparent with clients about the change, reassuring them that AI would complement, not replace, his personal touch. While some clients, particularly older ones, were initially sceptical, Paul kept communication flexible, continuing to offer phone and Zoom consultations where needed.

To measure success, Paul analysed his existing client communication, noting low email engagement rates and limited responses. He structured a three-week pilot, selecting 50 clients and setting clear goals. By categorising clients based on their communication preferences, he automated emails for tech-savvy clients while preserving personal interaction for others. The results were immediate – open rates rose by 25%, response rates rose by 15%, and clients appreciated the increased frequency of useful updates. However, some older clients found the volume overwhelming, prompting Paul to adjust email frequency based on feedback.

The pilot revealed valuable insights, showing that AI-enhanced emails worked best for certain clients, while others still preferred personal touchpoints. Paul refined his approach, improving email templates, scheduling quarterly Zoom calls for clients who preferred direct interaction, and allowing clients to choose their communication preferences. Throughout the process, he maintained ethical transparency, ensuring clients understood how their data was being used to enhance services. By leveraging AI while staying true to his values, Paul successfully balanced efficiency with client trust, improving engagement without compromising relationships.

Common roadblocks in gathering

Life has a way of throwing curveballs, especially when you're tackling something as transformative as REIMAGINING your entire business! Here are some of the most common challenges my clients face around this stage, along with ways to reframe and address them to ensure you maintain momentum and success.

The data doesn't match your expectations

You've set clear goals for your pilot, but the numbers just aren't adding up. Maybe your open rates are lower than you hoped, or the results don't seem to align with your efforts. It's natural to feel frustrated, but this isn't the end of the road – it's a valuable learning moment.

Were your goals realistic for this pilot project? Adjust your expectations to reflect what's achievable at this early stage.

Consider what might be happening outside your business. For example, are seasonal trends or market shifts influencing customer behaviour?

Refocus on what's working. Even if the overall picture isn't ideal, look for small wins or positive trends to build on. For example, did a specific customer segment respond better than others?

Unexpected data isn't failure – it's feedback. Use what you've learned to refine your goals and focus on incremental improvements that align with your business.

The feedback is conflicting

You're hearing mixed opinions from customers, your team, or other stakeholders. Some love the changes, others are sceptical, and a few might even push back. This can feel overwhelming, but conflicting feedback is often where the best insights live.

Identify recurring themes across the feedback to guide your next steps. Beware the 'survey of one'! If you hear it once, park it. If you hear it multiple times, take action.

Focus on the feedback that matters most to your goals. For example, pay attention to customers who represent your target market and team members closest to the process.

Quantitative feedback (like open rates) is critical, but qualitative insights provide the 'why' behind the numbers.

Conflicting feedback isn't a problem – it's a roadmap. By prioritising patterns and stakeholder needs, you'll gain clarity and create meaningful progress.

You (or your team) feel overwhelmed

AI pilots, data collection, and feedback loops can feel like a lot. When everything is new, it's easy to feel like you're in over your head. But overwhelm is just a sign to simplify and focus.

Start small. Choose one or two key metrics to track. Focus on the essentials before expanding your scope. Then, tackle the process in smaller steps. Instead of analysing all the data at once, prioritise by time period or category.

Engage your team. Assign specific tasks or data points to individuals to lighten the load and build ownership.

By scaling back to what matters most, you'll make the process more manageable – and more impactful.

Ethical or people concerns arise

Building team buy-in is crucial for successful AI adoption. Instead of viewing AI as a replacement for human roles, position it as a tool that enhances productivity and decision-making.

Share successes and insights to keep your team engaged. Ethical concerns are a chance to lead with integrity. By addressing them openly, businesses can foster trust, strengthen relationships, and establish themselves as forward-thinking, values-driven organisations.

Common pitfalls in Gathering – and how to avoid them

As you address objections and begin putting your data collection into action, it's important to be aware of potential stumbling blocks. The Gather phase is where real insights start to emerge, but it's also where some common missteps occur. Think of this as your guide to avoiding the most frequent mistakes I've seen businesses make during this stage. By keeping these pitfalls in mind, you'll stay focused, ethical, and purposeful.

Gathering too much data

Trying to track every metric leads to overwhelm. Avoid this by focusing on one or two key metrics that align with your goals. For example, if client engagement is your priority, track open rates and customer feedback instead of 20 data points. 'Less is more': quality insights drive better decisions.

Ignoring feedback trends

Ignoring feedback because it seems conflicting or unclear can be a mistake. To avoid this, look for patterns and recurring themes rather than reacting to individual comments. For example, if several clients mention difficulty understanding a new feature, focus on simplifying communication instead of changing course based on one opinion.

Misinterpreting data

Jumping to conclusions without context can lead to misguided decisions. Avoid this by combining quantitative data, like open rates, with qualitative insights, such as customer feedback, for a fuller picture. For example, a drop in email responses might seem negative, but feedback could reveal that clients prefer a different communication method.

Overlooking team involvement

Handling data collection alone can lead to missed insights. Avoid this by involving your team in gathering, reviewing, and interpreting data. Assign specific metrics or feedback areas to team members to make the process more collaborative and effective.

Focusing only on short-term gains

Focusing on quick wins without considering long-term goals can limit growth. Avoid this by balancing short-term improvements with strategies that align with your broader vision. For example, an AI tool might streamline client follow-ups now, but also think about how it can scale to enhance long-term customer relationships.

Overreliance on AI insights

Relying on AI data as absolute truth can overlook valuable human intuition and experience. Avoid this by using AI insights as a starting point, not the final decision-maker. For example, if AI recommends optimising a service for one customer segment, balance it with team input to ensure alignment with broader business goals.

Overloading clients with changes

Making too many changes at once can overwhelm both customers and your team. Avoid this by rolling out adjustments gradually, testing each one for effectiveness before adding more. For example, if clients prefer personalised emails, start with one campaign instead of overhauling your entire communication strategy.

Take AI action: questions for reflection

For solopreneurs

What's one task or challenge that feels lighter since activating your pilot? What new opportunities has the pilot created for your business? How has this step boosted your confidence to keep going?

For teams or larger businesses

What feedback from your team has been the most surprising or impactful? How has the pilot improved workflows or boosted morale? Which customer reactions or feedback have stood out the most?

For everyone

What's the most exciting insight you've uncovered? How has AI already made things easier for you or your business? What's one action you can take based on what you've learned so far?

Ethics and people: guiding principles for data collection

Gathering data isn't just about numbers – it's about respecting the trust your customers and team place in you. By prioritising ethics and transparency, you create a foundation of respect and fairness that strengthens both your business and relationships. In Australia, the Australian Privacy Principles (APPs) provide a clear framework for ethical data collection, emphasising transparency, accountability, and privacy. Aligning with these principles ensures your approach not only builds trust but also meets legal standards.

A strong ethical approach to data collection includes three key principles:

- **Transparency** fosters trust – clearly communicate why you're collecting data, how it will be used, and how it benefits customers and employees.
- **Respect** means honouring individual preferences, offering opt-outs, and ensuring data use aligns with expectations.
- **Fairness** ensures data practices are unbiased and inclusive, avoiding favouritism or unintended exclusions.

By embedding these values into your AI and data strategies, you can drive innovation while maintaining integrity.

Take AI action: ethics and people check-in

Take a moment to reflect on your approach and write down your thoughts on the following:

- Am I being transparent?
- How am I explaining my data collection practices to stakeholders?
- Have I communicated how this data will benefit them?
- Am I respecting preferences?
- Have I asked customers and team members about their communication preferences?
- Do I have clear opt-out options in place?
- Am I ensuring fairness?
- Have I reviewed my data and practices for potential biases?
- Does my process reflect the diversity of my clients and team?

Write one action step for each principle to strengthen your ethics-driven approach.

Where creativity meets strategy

The data you've gathered isn't just a reflection of your pilot's performance – it's the raw material for something extraordinary. This is where creativity meets strategy. Iteration allows you to test, tweak, and transform, turning small adjustments into significant breakthroughs. It's not about starting over – it's about starting smarter.

Take AI action: putting it all together

As you wrap up the Gather phase, it's time to consolidate everything you've learned and set the stage for what's next. This practical exercise will help you organise your insights, prioritise actions, and prepare for the Iterate phase.

Step 1: Reflect on your data insights

Take a moment to revisit the key insights you've gathered. Ask yourself:

- Which metrics have shown the most progress? (For example, increased open rates, reduced response times.)
- What feedback from customers or team members stands out most? (For example, recurring themes, surprising trends.)

What's one small win you can celebrate right now? (For example, new efficiencies, improved relationships.)

Step 2: Revisit your foundations

Go back to the exercises you completed in earlier chapters and assess your current progress towards your original goals:

- **Circle of Impact:** Are there any new stakeholders or relationships to prioritise based on your data?
- **Customer journey:** Does your data suggest new touchpoints or gaps in your customer experience?

- **AI policy and bias check:** Are your practices still aligned with your values and ethical standards? Reflect on how these earlier exercises connect to your data insights.

Ask yourself:

- Have my priorities shifted based on what I've learned?
- Are there areas I overlooked that need attention now?

Step 3: Time-saving tips for data review

As a small business owner, your time is precious. Use these tips to make your data review process manageable and efficient:

- Dedicate just 30 minutes per week to reviewing your data insights.
- Focus on one key metric or trend each session to avoid overwhelm.
- Automate repetitive tasks like data collection or reporting with tools like Google Forms, Airtable, or Trello.
- For larger teams, assign specific data responsibilities to team leads.

Step 4: Action plan for iteration

Finally, turn your insights into an action plan for the next stage:

- Choose one key area to improve; for example, refine email campaigns, adjust communication frequency.
- Set a small, achievable goal for iteration; for example, test a new email subject line, or personalise outreach to a specific client group.
- Schedule your next review. Block time in your calendar to reflect on progress during the Iterate phase.

By completing this exercise, you'll enter the Iterate phase with a clear focus on what's working, what needs refining, and how to prioritise your efforts. The insights you've gathered are more than just numbers – they're a roadmap for what's next. Every small adjustment you make builds on the progress you've already achieved, bringing you closer to REIMAGINING your business.

CHAPTER 7

Iterate: continuously improving your AI strategy

'Iteration isn't about starting over – it's about starting smarter. Each tweak brings you closer to the solution your business truly needs.'

Tracy Sheen

Just as Coke did in the '80s, it's our role as business owners to be on a constant journey of iteration, always looking for the next process that can be tweaked. How can we refine? How can we serve our clients better? Where can we increase efficiencies? Whatever it is, iteration is not about failure – it's feedback in action.

For small businesses, the lesson is clear: no tool, platform, or strategy will be perfect from the start. Success comes from testing, learning, and refining until it fits your business and your customers perfectly. This chapter is all about mastering the art of iteration.

Whether you're adjusting your AI tools, reworking workflows, or rethinking how you use customer data, iteration is the key to staying agile and getting the most from your efforts.

The journey so far

You've been on a journey to bring AI into your business, following the REIMAGINE Framework. As you review the steps you've already taken, you may notice that you have actually been iterating and refining the process at every step. Those tweaks, the recognition of a platform the business is already using that could be used 'better'. The team discussions around which task to prioritise and activate first. Each of those micro-decisions are actually iterations designed to refine and improve the process along the way:

- **Relationships:** You started by mapping your ecosystem – your customers, staff, and partners – to understand who stands to benefit from AI and how. As you dived into these conversations, you 'iterated' on your beliefs and refined the things that really mattered.
- **Evaluate:** You then explored your current processes and tools; you went through iterations of what tools are working, which ones

could be improved, and which, perhaps, needed to be completely overhauled.

- **Identify:** From there, you pinpointed the specific tasks, processes, or opportunities that, with the assistance of AI, could improve your overall business operations … iteration in action.
- **Map:** With clear goals in mind, you created a roadmap to integrate AI effectively, balancing priorities and resources. You negotiated with your team to prioritise what would happen first, and you assigned roles and responsibilities. These negotiations and mapping processes are all examples of the everyday iteration process we use without thinking.
- **Activate:** You took the first step, implementing AI in a focused way, and began seeing the initial results. Results that may have fallen short helped you to recognise where they needed to be tweaked (iterated).
- **Gather:** Finally, you collected feedback and data, capturing what's working, what's not, and what needs to undergo an iteration process.

Now, it's time to take that feedback you've gathered so far and iterate some more. This step is where the real magic happens. It's the phase where you refine, adjust, and optimise your AI integration so that it truly serves your business.

Why iteration is key

In business, as in life, our first attempt, sadly, is rarely the best. Whether it's crafting the perfect marketing message, writing a book, training a new employee, or learning how to use a tool like AI, improvement comes from action, reflection, and adjustment. That's iteration in action. It's tempting to think of AI as a 'set-and-forget' solution, but that mindset often leads to frustration and wasted opportunities. AI works best when you treat it as a living, breathing part of your business – one that grows and evolves as your needs and the needs of your business change.

There are three reasons iteration is essential:

- **Your business is dynamic:** Your business today is not the same as it was five years ago – or even last year. And I guarantee it will not look even remotely similar in the next five years. Customer needs, market conditions, and technology are constantly evolving. Iteration ensures that your AI solutions keep up with these changes, adapting to serve your business as it grows and shifts.
- **AI is a tool, not a crystal ball:** Even the smartest AI (or human) doesn't know everything about your business on day one. It learns and improves as it's used, but only if you guide it. By iterating – adjusting settings, refining inputs, and rethinking applications – you unlock its full potential. Just like training a new human team member!
- **Mistakes are inevitable:** Every business makes mistakes when adopting new technology. Maybe your CRM tool is too rigid, or your chatbot isn't delivering the right responses. That's not failure – it's feedback. Iteration turns those missteps into stepping stones, helping you fine-tune your tools until they work seamlessly.

Iteration vs perfection

One of the most common traps in business is the quest for perfection – waiting until everything is 'just right' before launching. The truth is, perfection is a moving target. Iteration shifts the focus to progress: small, meaningful improvements that add up over time.

Have a think about your mobile phone or your computer. When was the last time you did a software update? Pretty regularly, right?

The apps and tools we use daily are constantly updated with new features, bug fixes, and refinements. Those updates aren't signs of failure – they're signs of a team committed to making their product better for the user. If you think about AI adoption for your business in the same way, you'll save yourself a mountain of frustration and headaches.

Iteration in action: how do you know what to fix?

Iteration isn't about changing everything, or, as my Mum used to say, 'throwing the baby out with the bathwater'. It's about focusing your efforts where they'll make the biggest impact.

But how do you know what needs tweaking, what's working, and what's not? The answer lies in the feedback and data collected in our Gather stage. Whether it's numbers, customer reviews, or your gut instinct about a clunky process, these clues tell you where to start.

Let's break down how to pinpoint these opportunities and turn them into meaningful improvements for your business.

Not every process or tool in your business needs constant attention, and that's a good thing – you've got a lot on your plate already. The key to iteration is knowing where to focus your time and energy. It starts with identifying the gaps, inefficiencies, or opportunities in your current AI setup.

Here are some signs it's time to iterate:

- **Results aren't matching expectations:** You rolled out an AI tool with specific goals – maybe faster response times or better customer engagement. If the results you're seeing fall short of what you envisioned, it's time to figure out why.

- **Customer or team feedback highlights gaps:** Comments like 'this feels clunky' or 'it takes too long' are goldmines for identifying what needs improvement. Whether it's your chatbot giving incorrect answers or a process that's confusing for your team, feedback shows you exactly where to dig deeper.
- **You're doing too much manually:** AI is supposed to save you time and energy, not add to your workload. If you're still doing tasks by hand that should be automated, it's a sign a tool isn't set up correctly or isn't the right fit.
- **Your business priorities have shifted:** Maybe you started with AI to streamline admin tasks, but now you're focused on improving customer retention. Goals evolve, and your AI tools need to evolve with them.
- **The market or your industry is changing:** External forces, like new competitors, new products or shifting customer preferences, might demand a new approach. If your AI isn't keeping pace, it's time to tweak or rethink your setup.

Take AI action: the iteration opportunity finder

Use this exercise to evaluate your AI tools and processes based on the feedback and data gathered during your pilot programme activation. Follow these steps to uncover the areas that will benefit most from iteration.

Step 1: Assess your AI tools with these questions

Time efficiency

Are your AI tools saving you time or creating more work?

Goal alignment

Are the outputs (for example, insights, automations, responses) aligned with your business goals?

Feedback quality

Is the feedback from customers or your team generally positive, neutral, or negative?

Relevance to current needs

Have your business needs or market conditions changed since implementation?

Measurable results

Are there clear, measurable improvements since you started using the tool?

Ease of use

Is the tool easy for you and your team to use, or does it require too much technical know-how?

Cost vs benefit

Are the results justifying the time and money you're investing in the tool?

Scalability

Can the tool grow with your business, or will it need replacing as your needs evolve?

Integration

Does the tool integrate well with your existing systems, or is it causing compatibility issues?

User feedback trends

Are certain types of users (for example, staff, customers) struggling more than others with the tool?

For any question where your response is 'no' or 'not sure', flag that as an opportunity for iteration. These flagged areas will form the foundation for your next steps.

Step 2: Rank your priorities

Once you've flagged areas that need attention, the next step is deciding where to focus your efforts. Not all problems are created equal, and tackling the right ones first can save you time, money, and frustration.

How to rank opportunities

Use these categories to prioritise your flagged areas:

- **High impact:** These changes will significantly improve customer experience, team productivity, or profitability; for example, fixing a chatbot that's confusing customers, leading to lost sales or increased complaints.
- **Moderate impact:** These changes will add noticeable value but aren't urgent; for example, enhancing AI-generated reports for greater clarity or usability.
- **Low impact:** These changes are nice-to-haves but won't make a big difference right now; for example, adjusting the tone of automated email responses for a slightly friendlier feel.

Using the information from your pilot programme, create a simple table like the one below to prioritise your flagged areas.

Flagged	Impact level	Why this matters
Chatbot responses	High	Losing customers due to inaccurate replies
CRM workflow automation	Moderate	Saves team time but not customer-facing
Dashboard visualisation	Low	Nice-to-have but non-essential right now

Step 3: Dive into the data

Your flagged areas and priorities are a great starting point, but to make informed changes, you'll need to dig into the details you collected during your Gather stage. This step is all about turning raw information into actionable insights.

Quantitative data (the numbers)

- How much time are AI tools saving you or your team?
- Are customers receiving faster replies?
- Have sales or sign-ups increased since implementing the tool?

Qualitative feedback (the stories)

Dive into comments from customers, staff, or stakeholders. Ask yourself:

- What are they frustrated with?
- What do they find helpful?
- Are there recurring themes or common complaints?

Behavioural trends (the patterns)

Analyse how people are interacting with your AI tools:

- Are customers dropping off at a certain step in the process?
- Are staff consistently bypassing or avoiding certain features?

Use these tools and techniques to make sense of your data:

- Create follow-up surveys for customers or staff to clarify vague feedback.
- Use analytics dashboards to track trends over time. (These are often built into the platforms or software you are using.)
- Review error logs or system reports for recurring issues.

As you analyse the data, look for the following:

- Where are delays or inefficiencies occurring?
- Are AI outputs matching your expectations and goals?
- Are features or tools being ignored?

For each flagged issue, write down:

- What's not working, and how is it affecting your business?
- What does the data suggest is causing the problem?
- How could resolving this improve your results?

Step 4: Plan your iteration

Iteration isn't just about making changes – it's about making the *right* changes in a deliberate, measurable way. This step focuses on crafting a plan that maximises the impact of your adjustments while minimising disruption to your business.

Define the problem

Start by clearly outlining the issue you're addressing. What isn't working? Be specific – vague goals lead to vague results. How does it impact your business? Tie the issue to measurable outcomes, such as customer satisfaction, efficiency, or revenue.

For example, if customer drop-off rates during online checkout are too high, you'll have reduced sales and frustrated customers.

Identify the change

Decide on the specific adjustment you'll make to address the problem. Is it a small tweak or a major overhaul? Start small when possible to reduce risk. What resources are required? Consider time, tools, and team involvement.

For example, you could reduce page load times by optimising the AI-powered recommendation tool.

Set a measurable goal

Define what success looks like for your iteration. What's the outcome you want to see? How will you measure it? Use metrics like response time, conversion rate, or team satisfaction scores.

For example, you could decrease checkout drop-off rates by 15% within two weeks of implementing changes.

Create an action plan

Map out the steps required to make the change. Who will implement them? What tools or resources are needed? When will they be completed?

Use a simple format like this:

Action	Who	Deadline
Review customer feedback	You	10 June
Adjust chatbot settings	Admin/Vendor	15 June
Test the updated checkout	Admin/Team	30 June

Step 5: Test and measure

Iteration isn't complete without testing your changes to ensure they're delivering the results you need. This step is about making sure your efforts are paying off and gathering insights for future iterations.

Set a testing timeframe

Decide how long you'll observe the impact of your changes. A few days to a month is usually sufficient, depending on the scope of the iteration. For example, if you've adjusted chatbot responses, test them for two weeks during peak customer service hours.

Choose key metrics

Measure success using the same metrics you used to identify the problem in the first place. Examples include:

- conversion rates (for example, how many customers complete a purchase)
- customer satisfaction scores (for example, survey feedback)
- efficiency gains (for example, time saved by staff).

Run controlled tests

For small changes, introduce them fully and observe the results. For larger changes, consider testing with a small segment of your audience or team first to limit disruption. For example, if you're testing new chatbot responses, roll them out to 20% of your website visitors before a full-scale launch.

Collect and compare data

Use your tools to gather fresh feedback, survey results, and metrics. Compare the results to your baseline data from before the iteration to see if your changes had the desired impact.

Adjust based on results

If the iteration worked, scale the change across your business. If it didn't work as planned, analyse why and make further tweaks based on what you've learned.

Practical testing checklist

By testing and measuring your changes, you close the loop on iteration. Every adjustment brings you closer to a system that truly works for your business. Remember: iteration isn't a one-time event – it's an ongoing process that helps your business stay agile and competitive.

Use a checklist like the below to keep track of your iteration process.

Step	Action	Completed?
Set testing timeframe	Decide how long to monitor changes	
Choose success metrics	Define how you'll measure success	
Test in a controlled way	Roll out changes to a small audience first	
Collect feedback	Use surveys, analytics, and team insights	
Compare data	Review results against your baseline	
Make adjustments	Refine changes based on what you've learned	

Tailoring the iteration process to your unique setup

No two businesses look the same, and how you approach iteration will depend on the size and structure of your team. Whether you're working solo, leading a small team, or managing a remote workforce, here's how to tailor the iteration process to your unique setup.

For solo operators: making iteration manageable

When you're running the show solo, time and energy are everything. Stay efficient by focusing on one or two high-impact changes at a time to avoid overload, using automation tools like Trello or Asana to handle repetitive tasks, and treating iteration steps like client projects – schedule them with clear deadlines to keep yourself accountable.

For small teams: collaborate and prioritise

With a small team, collaboration is a strength – but coordination is essential. Clearly delegate roles so each team member owns a part of the iteration process, such as one person gathering customer feedback while another tests adjustments. Regular check-ins keep everyone aligned, allowing the team to address challenges and track progress efficiently.

Encouraging team buy-in is key – explaining the value of iteration helps boost engagement and reduce resistance to change. Using shared tools like Slack, Monday.com, or Google Workspace streamlines collaboration, making it easier to track tasks and ensure smooth execution.

For remote teams: iteration across distances

When your team works remotely, maintaining alignment and productivity requires extra planning. Choose the right tools, such as Notion or ClickUp, to manage tasks, share insights, and track iterations across time zones. Create asynchronous workflows so team members can contribute on their own schedules without bottlenecks – for example, one person gathers feedback during the day while another analyses it overnight.

Overcommunicate to keep everyone on the same page. Use video calls for key planning sessions and keep detailed notes to ensure clarity on next steps. Leverage time zones by staggering tasks, allowing global team members to keep the iteration process moving 24/7.

Quick tips for all teams

No matter your structure, these principles will help ensure your iteration process is smooth and effective:

- **Start small:** Focus on high-impact changes before tackling larger, more complex problems.
- **Measure results:** Use feedback and data to track whether your iterations are working.
- **Iterate regularly:** Treat iteration as an ongoing habit, not a one-time task.

Focus on the big wins first

With your priorities ranked and your plan in place, it can be tempting to tackle everything at once. But when resources are limited – and they always are for small businesses – it's critical to focus your efforts where they'll have the greatest impact.

Quick wins build momentum, keeping your team motivated and reinforcing that you're on the right track. Maximising ROI ensures that time and money are invested in changes that deliver the greatest impact. Avoiding burnout is just as important – tackling too much at once can overwhelm your team and stall progress entirely.

How to identify a big win

A big win usually checks these boxes:

- It solves a problem that's **causing major pain** for your customers or team; for example, fixing an AI-powered recommendation tool that's frustrating users and causing drop-offs.
- It aligns directly with **your business goals**; for example, streamlining your CRM workflows to reduce admin time and improve client follow-ups.
- It delivers **measurable, noticeable results**; for example, a 20% boost in customer satisfaction scores after improving chatbot responses.

Pick one or two high-impact areas to address first. Once you've seen results, use the momentum to tackle moderate-impact changes.

Use the 80/20 rule

The 80/20 Rule (also known as the Pareto Principle) states that 80% of your results often come from 20% of your efforts. Focus on the 20% – the changes that will deliver the biggest impact for your business.

It's not me, it's you – when to ditch a platform and find something new

Iteration is a powerful process – it can refine workflows, improve tools, and uncover opportunities for growth. But as you focus on the big wins, you may find that some problems refuse to budge. No matter how much effort or creativity you invest, the results just don't improve.

When that happens, it's time to ask the hard question: is the problem with the process, or is it with the platform itself? This distinction is critical. If the tool is fundamentally misaligned with your business needs – lacking the features, flexibility, or scalability you require – no amount of iteration will fix it. Continuing to tweak something that isn't designed to work for you will lead to frustration, wasted time, and lost resources. Sometimes, the smartest move isn't another round of iteration – it's making the decision to start fresh with a better fit.

Knowing when to stop iterating and move on can save you time, money, and frustration. Here are some signs it's time to move on:

- **The tool can't keep up with your business:** Your business has grown or changed, but the platform hasn't. It may lack the features, flexibility, or scalability you now need; for example, a basic scheduling tool might have worked when you had five clients, but as your client base grows, it struggles to handle more complex scheduling needs.
- **The costs outweigh the benefits:** If you're pouring money and time into a platform but seeing little return on investment, it's time to reassess; for example, a CRM that requires constant troubleshooting and external consultants might not be worth the ongoing expense.
- **You're compromising too much:** If the platform forces you to change your workflows in ways that feel unnatural or inefficient, it's not serving you; for example, a rigid AI tool that can't integrate with your current software, requiring manual workarounds that eat up time.

- **Feedback isn't improving:** If customers or team members continue to express frustration despite multiple iterations, it's a sign the tool might be the problem, not the process; for example, a chatbot that customers consistently avoid or complain about because it doesn't deliver useful responses.
- **The platform is stagnant:** Technology evolves quickly. If the platform provider isn't releasing updates, addressing bugs, or keeping up with trends, it may no longer be competitive; for example, a social media automation tool that doesn't support new platforms or features that your competitors are already leveraging.

How to transition smartly

If you've decided it's time to move on, here's how to approach the transition:

- **Identify what went wrong:** Reflect on why the current platform didn't work to avoid making the same mistakes with the next one.
- **Define your must-haves:** Create a list of features, integrations, and scalability requirements that your new tool must deliver.
- **Research alternatives:** Ask peers, read reviews, and take advantage of free trials. Take your time to find the best fit.
- **Plan the transition:** Avoid disruption by migrating data and training your team in phases.
- **Evaluate early:** Assess the new tool's performance quickly to confirm it's the right choice. Don't wait months to act if something feels off.

Additional considerations include:

- **Hidden costs of switching:** While switching to a new platform may seem like the best solution, it's crucial to consider the hidden costs. Data migration can be time-consuming and expensive, requiring effort to transfer information seamlessly. Training time is another factor – learning a new system could lead to downtime and reduced productivity. Additionally, customer impact should be assessed, as the transition might temporarily disrupt service or user experience.

- **Long-term vendor stability:** There's a reason Google and Microsoft are the two most dominant players in the cloud-based business operating space. They've been around a long time, they have huge databases, and a seemingly bottomless pit of finances behind them. That means you can be sure (well, as sure as anyone can be about anything) that they will be around in years to come, and they will keep iterating and evolving their own business.

  When it comes to considering changing platforms or suppliers, it is equally important to weigh up the long-term viability of the company you are switching to.

Common pitfalls in Iteration – and how to avoid them

You've done the hard work of activating your AI pilot, and now you're ready to refine it. But if you're like many of the business owners I work with, you're probably thinking, 'I don't have time for this!' or, 'What if I mess it up?'

The truth is, every business faces these doubts. And it shows that you're thinking things through from every angle. The difference between those businesses that thrive when it comes to AI adoption and those that stall is how they respond to these challenges. Let's take a look at the most common objections to iteration and turn them into opportunities for growth.

'I don't have time for this!'

Time is the one thing every small business owner wishes they had more of. Adding iteration to your to-do list might feel impossible. It is true that initially adopting AI into your business may add a little to your workload … but only for a very short time. After that, the statistics typically show you'll gain between two and eight hours back each week. I reckon it's worth pushing through for that kind of reward:

- **For solopreneurs:** Focus on one high-impact change at a time. Dedicate just 30 minutes a week to reviewing feedback or testing a tweak. Using automation tools will minimise those repetitive tasks in the long run.
- **For small teams:** Delegate tasks based on team strengths and hold short weekly check-ins to stay on track.
- **For remote teams:** Use collaboration tools like Trello or Slack to streamline communication and keep iteration manageable across time zones.

'I've already chosen the perfect platform!'

It's tempting to think of your platform as a 'done deal'. But even the best tools need ongoing fine-tuning to perform at their best. Remember, even our laptops and phones go through regular updates – and we think they're already working pretty well! Here are some solutions for all business types:

- **Treat your tools like apps on your phone:** Regular updates and tweaks are what keep them effective.
- **Reassess regularly:** Periodically review your tools against your evolving business goals to ensure they're still the right fit.

'I'm overwhelmed with feedback!'

It's easy to feel buried under an avalanche of suggestions, metrics, and customer input. Often at this point, the loudest voice can win out, so we need to 'beware the survey of one' and learn to separate emotion from facts. If I get feedback from one person, I'll thank them and keep moving forward. If I hear the same thing a few times, that's when I pay attention and decide what action to take next.

Here are some solutions:

- **For solopreneurs:** Break feedback into categories: quick fixes, moderate tweaks, and big-picture changes. Start with quick fixes for immediate wins.
- **For small teams:** Assign one person to collect and sort feedback so others can focus on solutions.
- **For remote teams:** Use shared dashboards or project management tools to track and organise feedback collaboratively.

'What if I make it worse?'

Fear of making a mistake can stall progress and cause us to second-guess our decisions. What if your iteration doesn't work or creates new issues? What if the team or clients hate it? What if … What if … What if …? If this is where things are at for you, take yourself for a walk and get some fresh air. It's time to remove the emotion from the data and take a good hard look at what it is you really want for your business, your clients, and your team. What if you could make things so much better?

Here are some solutions for all business types:

- **Start with controlled tests on a small audience or team:** If something doesn't work, most tools allow you to roll back changes.
- **Learn from missteps:** Frame mistakes as valuable feedback to guide the next round of iteration.

'This feels like a never-ending process!'

I think Michael Jordan sums this one up best: 'I've missed more than 9000 shots in my career. I've lost almost 300 games. Twenty-six times, I've been trusted to take the game-winning shot and missed. I've failed over and over and over again in my life. And that is why I succeed.'

Here are some solutions:

- **For solopreneurs:** Focus on the areas that deliver the most visible results – this will build momentum.
- **For teams:** Celebrate milestones, no matter how small, to keep morale high.
- **For all business types:** Balance iteration with stability. If something is working well, don't feel pressured to change it unnecessarily.

'I don't understand AI well enough to iterate it.'

A lack of technical knowledge can feel like a major barrier, especially for small business owners just starting with AI. That's why you've done all the hard yards working through my REIMAGINE Framework. It takes the guesswork out of what area(s) in your business you want to improve, why you want to improve them, and how to get yourself the best bang for your buck.

Here are some solutions:

- **For solopreneurs:** Focus on the basics – what's working and what isn't. Let your instincts and feedback guide you.
- **For teams:** Assign a tech-savvy team member to explore platform options or reach out to support teams.
- **For all business types:** Leverage free tutorials or customer support to get the guidance you need to make informed adjustments.

'I'm afraid my team will resist changes.'

Employees may push back on constant adjustments, especially if changes disrupt their workflow or feel unnecessary. If you put the time in with them during the Relationships section of the framework, though, they will be on board with the programme and cheering on everything the business is doing.

Here are some solutions:

- **For small teams:** Involve your team early in the iteration process (go back and visit RELATIONSHIPS) to gain their input and buy-in.
- **For remote teams:** Communicate changes clearly and share the 'why' behind them to get buy-in.
- **For all business types:** Show results. Use quick wins to demonstrate the benefits of iteration and build trust.

'I don't want to upset my customers.'

None of us do; without them, we don't have a business. But our customers are looking to engage with businesses that can work with them in personalised ways. Upsetting or frustrating your clients will only occur if the change has not been communicated properly in the Identify part of the framework. Involve your clients in the journey every step of the way. Seek their feedback and listen to their concerns and suggestions.

Here are some solutions for all business types:

- **Communicate proactively:** Let customers know about updates and why they're being made.
- **Start small:** Test changes quietly before rolling them out broadly.
- **Listen closely:** Act on customer feedback quickly if adjustments aren't landing well.

Remember, iteration isn't about perfection – it's about progress. By addressing objections head-on, you can create a process that feels doable, not daunting. Every step you take makes your AI adoption and your business stronger, more efficient, and better aligned with your goals.

Lego: the never-ending process of building and improving

If you've been following me on social media, been to any of my workshops or keynotes, or basically have any awareness of who I am outside of my day-to-day work life, you'll know I'm an AFOL (Adult Fan of Lego). When work and life are stressing me out, I turn to those little bricks and zone out for hours.

Apart from being my happy place, they are also a fascinating story in business iteration. It's a story of persistence, customer engagement, and trend-watching – knowing when to refine what's working while still innovating for the future.

The birth of the brick: iteration in action

Okay, here's a super-quick Lego history lesson so this all makes sense.

Lego started in the 1930s as a small Danish company making wooden toys. It wasn't until 1949 that Lego introduced its first plastic brick, but even then, the design wasn't perfect. The early bricks lacked the interlocking system that makes today's Lego so iconic. They were loose and didn't hold together well, frustrating builders. For nearly a decade, they tested new designs and manufacturing techniques. In 1958, they landed on the interlocking brick system we know today, with its clever tube-and-stud design that made creations sturdy and versatile. It was a game-changer – a design so timeless that bricks from the 1950s still fit perfectly with today's models.

When you think you're done, you're not

By the 1990s, Lego was riding high – but cracks began to show. The company started expanding into too many areas – clothing, video games, theme parks – and their iconic brick was getting lost in the chaos. Sales began dropping dramatically in the early 2000s, and Lego faced bankruptcy.

What did they do? They went back to their roots. Lego iterated again – not on the brick itself, which was already perfect, but on their business model. They focused on what they did best: inspiring creativity through play. By introducing new themed sets, collaborating with franchises like Star Wars, and launching crowd-sourced designs through Lego Ideas, they rebuilt their brand brick by brick. And guaranteed that kids and AFOLs like me would remain hooked for years to come.

The balance of iteration and consistency

Lego's story proves that iteration is never truly done – but it's also about knowing when to stop refining what works. Lego stopped iterating on the core design of the brick in 1958 because it was already perfect. They knew further tweaks wouldn't add value.

On the other hand, Lego has never stopped iterating on how they use the brick – whether it's through new product lines, digital games, or experiences like Lego Masters on TV. Everything they do and everything they iterate feeds clients (like me) back to the brick itself. This dual approach – refining what's not working while preserving what is – has kept Lego relevant and beloved for over 90 years. Genius!

But what do tiny plastic bricks mean for your business?

Like Lego, you don't need to iterate endlessly on everything. Some things, once refined, can be left to shine on their own. Remember the story of the Tim Tam from the beginning of the book? That biscuit recipe has stayed the same since Arnott's perfected it, but the business keeps evolving with new flavours, seasonal editions, and playful marketing like the Tim Tam Slam. And then there's Nike. The Air Force 1 sneaker's classic design hasn't changed in decades – it doesn't need to. But inside the business, Nike is constantly pushing boundaries in performance gear, digital experiences, and sustainability initiatives like their Move to Zero campaign.

The lesson? Iteration is about more than just tweaking endlessly – it's about knowing what works and letting it shine, while focusing your efforts on evolving the parts of your business that can grow, adapt, and stay relevant. In other words, iteration is never really done – but when done well, it creates a foundation that can support your next big leap.

How a Perth business coach iterated her way to success

Emma is a business coach based in Perth who works with small businesses across Australia.

Her setup is lean – she manages the day-to-day operations herself but relies on two part-time virtual assistants (VAs) located in different countries. Emma recently adopted a new AI-driven CRM tool to streamline client onboarding and manage communications. At first, the CRM seemed like the perfect solution.

But within a few weeks, Emma started noticing problems:

- Some automated emails were confusing clients.
- The VAs were bypassing the CRM entirely because they found it clunky.
- Emma was spending more time fixing issues than reaping the promised efficiency benefits.

It was clear something had to change. Emma used the REIMAGINE Framework to iterate and refine her CRM processes:

- **Relationships:** Emma identified key stakeholders and their needs – clients wanted clearer, more supportive communication, while VAs needed simpler processes to embrace the CRM. Gathering input from both groups highlighted key friction points.
- **Evaluate:** Reviewing data and feedback, Emma found that clients were confused by poorly timed, overly formal emails; VAs found the CRM unintuitive and reverted to spreadsheets; and she herself felt overwhelmed by the learning curve.
- **Identify:** Rather than tackling everything at once, Emma prioritised fixing email templates to match her coaching style, creating a short tutorial for VAs, and streamlining the onboarding workflow.
- **Mapping:** Emma created a clear plan with deadlines – rewriting email sequences, recording a VA tutorial, and testing a simplified onboarding process with a new client.
- **Activate:** Over two weeks, Emma implemented the updates, making email templates more conversational and creating a 10-minute video highlighting key CRM features for her VAs.
- **Gather:** After the rollout, feedback showed positive results – clients appreciated the more personal emails, VAs felt more confident using the CRM, and Emma saved 30 minutes per client with a simpler onboarding process.
- **Iterate:** Encouraged by the results, Emma made further refinements, tweaking email timing and turning the VAs' onboarding process into a checklist to reduce errors.

The results

By following the REIMAGINE Framework, Emma:

- reduced onboarding time by 30%
- increased client satisfaction scores by 20%
- empowered her VAs to fully embrace the CRM, freeing her to focus on growth.

Emma's journey highlights that iteration isn't just about fixing problems – it's about refining processes to create a stronger foundation for the future.

Take AI action: your quick guide to refining success

Every small tweak builds a stronger foundation for growth. This quick guide will help you undertake the iteration process in five steps:

Identify

Choose one product, process, or strategy to refine. What's not working as well as it should?

Gather

Collect data and feedback from metrics, customers, and team members. What does the data or feedback reveal about this issue?

Prioritise

Rank changes by impact and urgency, focusing on high-priority areas first. Which change will have the biggest impact right now?

Map

Outline actions, assign responsibilities, and set deadlines. What's my next small, actionable step?

Test and reflect

Roll out changes on a small scale and review results. What worked, and what can I improve next?

Common pitfalls to avoid

Common pitfalls to avoid include the following:

- **Fixing everything at once:** Start small and focus on one or two high-priority areas.
- **Ignoring feedback:** Don't rely solely on gut instincts – listen to your customers and team ... but also beware the survey of one!
- **Skipping the testing phase:** Always test changes before rolling them out widely.

Iteration is the heartbeat of progress

It's about refining what you've built, learning from the results, and making thoughtful adjustments that move your business closer to its goals. Whether it's perfecting a product, streamlining a process, or enhancing a strategy, iteration creates the foundation for growth.

The key isn't doing it all at once – it's starting small, focusing on what matters most, and building momentum with each success. If you use the tools and strategies in this chapter, you will have everything you need to make iteration an integral, manageable part of your business.

Once you've fine-tuned the elements that matter most, it's time to Narrow your focus. The next step of the REIMAGINE Framework will show you how to zero in on what truly drives results, helping you cut through the noise and prioritise the areas that will take your business to the next level.

CHAPTER 8

Narrow: boost what works – cut what doesn't

'Success doesn't come from doing more – it comes from doing the right things. Narrowing your focus isn't about cutting back; it's about creating clarity so you can grow.'

Tracy Sheen

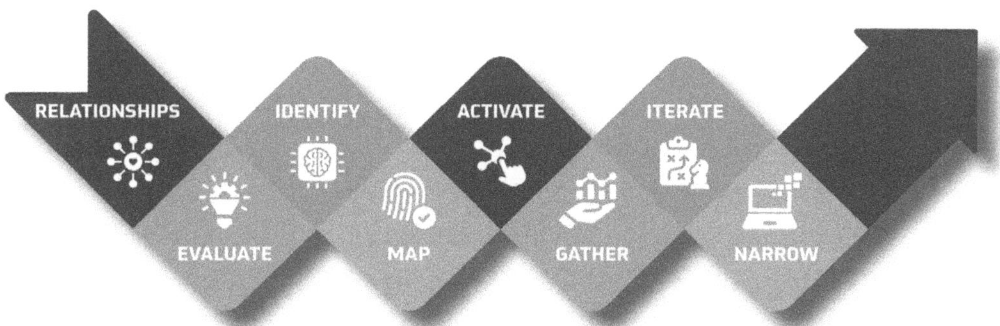

Janine Allis didn't set out to create an empire – she just wanted to solve a problem. In the late 1990s, while on a trip to the United States, she noticed something curious: smoothie bars were popping up everywhere. People were lining up for drinks that were fresh, healthy, and fast.

Back home in Australia, nothing like this existed. Janine saw an opportunity and decided to take a chance. She didn't have a business degree or a hospitality background, but what she had was vision: a smoothie bar that would deliver healthy, delicious drinks in a vibrant, fun atmosphere.

From the start, Janine's decisions followed the principles of the REIMAGINE Framework. Her focus on understanding her customers, refining her offerings, and doubling down on what worked created a strong foundation for Boost Juice to grow.

Focusing on what mattered

From the beginning, Janine understood that success wouldn't come from trying to do it all.

While other cafés and fast-food outlets packed their menus with everything from burgers to frappuccinos, she stuck to one thing: smoothies. That decision wasn't just strategic – it was revolutionary. By narrowing her focus, Janine could pour all her energy into making Boost Juice the best in its category. She invested in perfecting her recipes, creating a distinctive brand voice, and delivering an in-store experience that matched the health-conscious energy of her drinks.

Using a narrow focus to scale

As Boost Juice grew, Janine resisted the temptation to expand into too many categories too quickly. While competitors experimented with larger menus or complex offerings, she kept her focus tight. Instead of diluting the brand, she refined what worked:

- **Customer experience:** Janine focused on delivering quick, friendly service that made customers feel good about their choices.
- **Brand identity:** From the vibrant green branding to the energetic atmosphere, every detail reinforced Boost Juice's fun, fresh image.
- **Menu evolution:** When Boost added items, they enhanced the core offering – smoothies with added benefits like protein or superfoods – and were not distractions.

This relentless focus allowed Boost Juice to grow strategically. By the time competitors tried to copy her model, Janine's brand had become synonymous with smoothies in Australia.

How Boost Juice REIMAGINED smoothies

If we dissect Janine's brand story, we can see how it directly maps across to the REIMAGINE Framework you've been working on throughout the book.

Relationships: understanding what Australians wanted

Janine didn't jump straight into action. She started by observing her audience. Australians were ready for a healthy, fast alternative to typical café offerings. She understood that customers wanted more than a drink – they wanted to feel good about their choices. By focusing on these needs, she built a brand that resonated emotionally and practically, creating loyal customers who kept coming back for more.

Evaluate and Identify: pinpointing the opportunity

Janine evaluated the market and saw a clear gap: simplicity. Where other cafés overloaded their menus, she focused on one thing: smoothies. She identified her key priorities:

- perfect the recipes for taste and health
- create a vibrant in-store experience
- make ordering fast and easy for time-poor customers.

This clarity guided her decisions and helped her avoid distractions that could have diluted the brand.

Mapping and Activate: setting the plan in motion

Janine didn't dive in blindly. She mapped out a clear plan for launching Boost Juice:

- Focus on high-traffic locations, like shopping centres, to reach her target customers.
- Design stores to be bright and energetic, reflecting the brand's fun and fresh vibe.
- Train her team to deliver fast, friendly service that matched the health-conscious energy of the drinks.

By activating this plan, she brought her vision to life and made Boost Juice a destination, not just a drink stop.

Gather and Iterate: refining the formula

Early feedback showed that customers loved the smoothies but wanted more personalisation. Instead of rigid recipes, Janine allowed customers to customise their drinks, adding protein powders or superfoods to suit their tastes. She also refined store operations, improving workflows to reduce wait times and keep customers happy during busy periods. Every tweak was guided by customer feedback, helping Boost Juice maintain its edge.

Narrow: boosting what works, cutting what doesn't

As Boost Juice grew, Janine faced a critical choice: expand into other categories, like full-service cafés, or double down on what was already working. She chose to stay focused. Janine narrowed Boost Juice's efforts to three key priorities:

- **Customer experience:** Delivering quick, friendly service that makes customers feel good.
- **Core offerings:** Keeping the menu simple, with smoothies at the heart of the brand.
- **Scalable systems:** Streamlining operations by incorporating technology to ensure every store runs efficiently.

This narrow focus allowed Boost Juice to scale without losing its identity. Even as competitors tried to replicate her model, Janine's brand remained synonymous with smoothies in Australia.

What you can learn from Boost Juice

Janine's success wasn't about doing everything – it was about doing the right thing exceptionally well. By narrowing her focus, she was able to:

- build a strong foundation that resonated with her audience
- simplify her operations, making it easier to scale
- double down on what worked, instead of chasing distractions.

Like Janine, narrowing your focus lets you amplify what's working while eliminating distractions. It's about embedding success into your business and freeing up resources to invest where it matters most.

The success of Boost Juice shows the transformative power of narrowing focus. By concentrating her efforts on perfecting one thing – smoothies – Janine built a brand that scaled strategically and became synonymous with its niche. Just as Boost Juice refined its offerings and amplified what worked, you can use AI to streamline your business and create clarity for growth.

Let's explore what narrowing means for you.

What narrowing means in the Framework

In the context of REIMAGINING your business through AI adoption, narrowing means intentionally simplifying and refining how AI integrates into your business. It's not about scaling back – it's about doubling down on what works and creating clarity to grow strategically.

Here's how this ties into some of the steps you've already taken:

- **Activate:** You launched a pilot AI programme to explore its potential.
- **Gather:** You collected data to see what's working, what's not, and where the opportunities lie.
- **Iterate:** You refined your systems based on early insights, improving performance.

Now, in the Narrow phase, you ask: what AI initiatives should we embed? Which ones should we cut?

Here's how narrowing AI works in practice:

- **Embed what works** by fully integrating AI tools that have delivered measurable results. For example, if AI-driven email marketing increased open rates by 20%, make it a core part of your strategy.
- **Cut what doesn't** by identifying underperforming AI tools or processes and letting them go. If a chatbot failed to improve customer satisfaction, remove it and focus on more effective solutions.

- **Streamline for simplicity** by consolidating overlapping tools and efforts to reduce complexity. For example, replace two similar analytics platforms with one comprehensive solution.

By narrowing your focus, you create the foundation for scaling AI in your business.

The insights you embed now will drive long-term growth while preventing overwhelm. By maintaining clarity and focus, you stay aligned with your business goals. Optimising resources frees up time and investment for high-ROI areas, while simplifying AI efforts ensures sustainable, strategic scaling.

Take AI action: cut the noise, amplify success

Here's how to cut the noise and amplify success:

- **Set aside time:** Dedicate 10 to 20 minutes for this exercise. If you have a team, consider bringing them together to work through these prompts as a group. For solo or remote workers, you can complete this reflection independently or use a virtual brainstorming tool to collaborate with others.
- **Review your AI efforts:** Take stock of all the AI tools or processes you've piloted or integrated. If you're working with a team, share observations from different areas of the business to ensure a comprehensive view.
- **Work through the prompts:** Answer the questions on page 176 to assess what's working, what's not, and where you can simplify. For teams, facilitate an open discussion and capture collective insights. Solo workers can reflect on their own or bounce ideas off a trusted peer.
- **Create an action plan:** Whether you're working alone or with a group, identify one or two immediate actions to embed, cut, or streamline. Assign clear next steps to ensure follow-through.

Prompts to guide your reflection

By reflecting on these prompts, you're naturally applying key steps like Gather, Identify, and Evaluate – ensuring your decisions are grounded in the framework's principles:

- **Embed what works** by integrating AI initiatives that have delivered the most measurable impact into your operations.
- **Cut what doesn't** by identifying AI tools or processes that consume resources without clear results and phasing them out.
- **Streamline for simplicity** by eliminating overlaps and inefficiencies, consolidating tools, and optimising workflows for scalability.

When you've completed this exercise, review your action plan. Prioritise your next steps and schedule a time to implement them. Narrowing your focus today will pave the way for streamlined growth tomorrow.

The hidden costs of doing too much

At this stage, you've activated your AI pilot programme, gathered valuable data, and iterated on your processes. But if we stop at iteration, all of the hard work you've achieved could easily stall. Narrowing your focus gives you the time to embed what's working into your daily operations. It helps maximise your achievements and eliminate the noise that's holding you back. Narrowing provides the space for you to see the new gaps and opportunities facing the business so you can prioritise the next low-hanging fruit to focus on.

Now that you're aware of the potential pitfalls, let's dive into the practical steps you can take to avoid them by embedding what works, cutting distractions, and streamlining your efforts.

The law of diminishing returns

When it comes to AI (or any business strategy), doing too much can lead to diminishing returns. Without narrowing your focus, you risk creating inefficiencies that can hold your business back instead of propelling it forward. Here's what can happen if you don't narrow your AI strategy:

- **Scattered efforts lead to mediocre results** when time, money, and energy are spread too thin across multiple AI tools or projects; for example, implementing five AI tools at once without optimising any of them limits their potential.
- **Wasted time and resources** occur when ineffective AI initiatives drain budgets and overwhelm teams; for example, troubleshooting an underperforming chatbot instead of refining a successful email campaign.
- **Team burnout** arises when small teams juggle too many systems, leading to frustration and disengagement, while solopreneurs face constant overwhelm and decision fatigue.
- **Missed opportunities for growth** happen when businesses fail to double down on successful AI strategies, losing the chance to scale and maximise ROI; for example, neglecting a high-performing AI sales tool because resources are tied up elsewhere.

Why narrowing matters now

In today's fast-moving AI landscape, trying to 'do it all' isn't just inefficient – it's unsustainable. Narrowing your focus is about working smarter, not harder. It allows you to:

- free up resources to refine and scale
- highlight the wins your business has already achieved through AI implementation
- build confidence in your AI tools and processes

- stay aligned with your long-term business goals
- provide space to focus on future opportunities within the business.

When you narrow your focus, you're not just optimising for today – you're reimagining the future of your entire business.

Take AI action: spot the hidden costs

This reflection ties directly into the REIMAGINE Framework. As you evaluate your AI efforts, you're naturally applying steps like Gather, Identify, and Evaluate. Use this exercise to prepare for the Narrow phase and beyond.

Take 10 to 15 minutes to reflect on your AI strategy so far:

- **Are your efforts too scattered?** Assess how many AI tools you're managing and whether any overlap or add complexity. Ask your team if the pilot has created extra work or confusion.
- **What's draining resources?** Identify AI tools consuming time, money, or energy without delivering results. If you had to drop one today, which would it be and why? Gather feedback from your team, clients, or suppliers.
- **Are you missing opportunities to double down?** Focus on the AI initiative showing the most promise. Have you optimised or scaled it? Check with clients or suppliers to see which tools they find most valuable.
- **How does this impact you or your team?** Small teams may feel overwhelmed managing multiple systems, while solopreneurs might be spending too much time on tools instead of high-value activities. Identify where the strain is highest.

If you work with a team, bring them into the conversation. For solopreneurs, consider checking in with clients or trusted peers to gather fresh perspectives.

Turning insights into impact

Once you've worked through these prompts, take time to reflect on the bigger picture. Here's how to turn your insights into actionable steps:

- **Spot the patterns** by identifying recurring themes in your answers. Look for tools or processes repeatedly flagged as ineffective and initiatives that consistently stand out as successes.
- **Prioritise action** by choosing one immediate step to simplify, cut, or double down. Start small – progress builds momentum.
- **Collaborate and share** by reviewing results with your team and agreeing on top priorities. Solopreneurs can share insights with a mentor, peer, or trusted client to validate decisions and uncover blind spots.
- **Prepare for the next phase** by organising your insights and setting a clear direction. This will guide you into how to narrow effectively (see below), where you'll learn strategies to embed, cut, and streamline your AI efforts.

How to narrow effectively

It's natural to hesitate when letting go of certain tools or processes, but narrowing isn't about cutting – it's about focusing on what works best. We'll explore this more shortly in a section around common roadblocks during the Narrow stage. For now, though, you've identified what's working and what's not, so it's time to take action. Narrowing effectively means embedding successful practices, cutting distractions, and streamlining your AI processes to focus on what truly matters.

Embedding what works

Embedding successful AI tools means fully integrating them into your operations. These are the tools that deliver measurable results and align with your business goals. However, before committing to an AI tool or workflow, it's crucial to revisit your ethical foundations. Ask yourself whether the tool:

- respects customer data privacy
- avoids reinforcing biases
- aligns with your business's core values.

For example, a local café using AI analytics to predict top-selling items ensures the tool complies with data privacy laws and only collects necessary information before embedding it further. By reinforcing ethical practices alongside AI adoption, you build long-term trust and scalability in your business strategy.

This isn't a step; it's a mindset

It's around this step in the process that many of my clients begin to realise the REIMAGINE Framework steps actually come into play at every stage along the journey to AI integration. This isn't just a process you go through once – it's a way of thinking that becomes part of every action in your business.

As you narrow your focus, you'll see how naturally each phase flows into the next:

- **Relationships:** It's always about the people – your team, your customers, and your community.
- **Evaluate:** Every narrowing decision involves reviewing what's working and what isn't.
- **Identify:** You're constantly pinpointing what to amplify or let go of.

- **Mapping:** Narrowing focus is about creating a clear plan for what to embed, cut, or simplify.
- **Activate:** Once you've mapped it out, you take action – embedding what works and letting go of distractions.
- **Gather:** Narrowing requires collecting and reflecting on data to guide your choices.
- **Iterate:** As you refine your focus, you continue to test, tweak, and adapt.
- **Narrow:** And here you are – narrowing isn't the end of the framework; it's another way to reinforce and embed this cycle into your business thinking.

By narrowing your focus, you're not just improving today's outcomes – you're embedding this framework-style thinking into the DNA of your business. Narrowing isn't just a framework step – it's your opportunity to create clarity, focus, and momentum. Start today by applying one principle from this section, and watch your business transform.

Cut what doesn't work

Narrowing your focus requires letting go of what's not delivering results. While it can feel counterintuitive, removing the clutter isn't just about cutting back – it's about creating the space to fully appreciate and amplify what's already working. If there's too much noise, it's hard to see the forest for the trees. Think back to the Boost Juice story: Janine Allis could have easily been tempted to expand into coffee, pastries, or salads. But she knew that cluttering her menu with distractions would only dilute her brand and overwhelm her customers. By keeping the focus on smoothies, she gave Boost the clarity it needed to thrive and grow. In your business, cutting what doesn't work gives you the same opportunity: clarity. It frees up time, resources, and energy to double down on the strategies and tools that are already delivering value.

What it looks like in practice

This step aligns with the Evaluate phase of the REIMAGINE Framework, where you review performance data and decide what to prioritise:

- **Identify low performers** by reviewing data and feedback to find AI tools that aren't meeting expectations. For example, a boutique owner phases out a chatbot that hasn't improved customer satisfaction and reallocates resources to email marketing automation.
- **Evaluate alignment** by assessing whether a tool supports your business goals. If it doesn't, reconsider its place in your strategy. For example, an e-commerce store pauses an AI recommendation tool that suggests irrelevant items and seeks a better solution.
- **Make space for what works** by cutting underperforming tools to free up resources for successful strategies to grow and thrive.

Clarity isn't just about knowing what works; it's about having the courage to let go of what doesn't. Narrow your focus, and watch your business grow.

Streamline for simplicity

Just as Boost Juice chose to focus on smoothies, you can simplify your AI processes to reduce noise and amplify what's working. Simplicity is your ally for successful AI implementation.

Streamlining doesn't mean stripping back to the bare minimum – it's about reducing complexity to maximise efficiency and focus. The REIMAGINE Framework helps make this an ongoing practice: the Map phase charts a clear, simple path forward, while the Iterate phase ensures you can refine and adapt as needed.

Simplifying your workflows connects directly to the Map phase, where you chart a clear and scalable path forward:

- **Consolidate redundant tools** by identifying overlap and combining where possible. For example, a solopreneur using two similar analytics platforms switches to one, saving time and subscription costs.
- **Automate repetitive tasks** to eliminate manual work and free up valuable time. For example, a retail team automates weekly sales reporting, allowing them to focus more on strategy.
- **Simplify workflows** by removing unnecessary steps to improve efficiency. For example, a café integrates an AI system to track stock levels and automate reordering, reducing time spent on inventory management.

Simplification isn't just about efficiency today – it's about creating systems that are easy to adapt as your business evolves, guided by the continuous cycle of Mapping and Iterate. As you narrow your focus, the practical steps of embedding, cutting, and streamlining can cause doubt to creep in. What if you're making the wrong decision? Or letting go of something with untapped potential? These are natural hesitations, and addressing them is part of building a stronger, more confident strategy.

Common pitfalls in Narrow – and how to avoid them

It's natural to worry about letting go of something that could improve later. Remember: narrowing isn't permanent. It isn't about eliminating possibilities; it's about focusing on what works best to free up capacity for growth.

'What if I let go of something that could improve later?'

Cutting isn't permanent – it's strategic. The Iterate phase allows you to revisit and refine choices over time, ensuring you focus on what truly delivers value.

'I've already invested so much – shouldn't I give it more time?'

Sunk costs can be misleading. Holding onto an underperforming tool drains resources that could be better spent elsewhere. Ask yourself: 'If I were starting fresh with what I know now, would I choose this again?'

'Won't cutting back limit my options?'

Narrowing focus doesn't reduce possibilities – it amplifies what works. By removing distractions, you create space for more effective solutions and fresh opportunities.

'What if my team or clients push back?'

Transparency is key. Share data-driven insights and involve stakeholders in the decision-making process. Emphasise how these changes will improve efficiency and overall results.

'What if I upset existing clients by cutting a tool or service they use?'

Not all tools are equally valued. Gather feedback to determine if the tool is essential or if a more efficient alternative can meet their needs without disruption.

'How do I know if I'm cutting too much?'

Narrowing is about focus, not scarcity. Start with small, nonessential cuts and monitor the impact. You're not stripping away what makes your business thrive – you're strengthening it.

Every decision in the narrowing process is about prioritising clarity and growth. Trust the framework, and don't be afraid to revisit or adapt as you move forward.

Take AI action: your narrowing tools

Narrowing your focus is easier when you have the right tools. These exercises will help you evaluate your strategies, clarify your priorities, and confidently decide what to embed, ditch, or simplify.

The Embed or Ditch? decision framework

The Embed or Ditch? decision framework helps you evaluate your current strategies, tools, and processes. The goal is to identify what's working and should be amplified (embed) versus what's not delivering value and should be stopped or replaced (ditch).

Take 10 minutes to complete the table overleaf. List your AI tools, strategies, or tasks and evaluate them using the Embed or Ditch framework.

Here's how it works:

- In the first column, list your current strategies, tools, or tasks.
- In the second column, decide whether to embed or ditch based on their value to your business.

Strategy/Task	Decision: embed or ditch?
Automating customer emails	Embed
Manual invoicing	Ditch
Outdated analytics tool	Ditch
High-performing chatbot	Embed

Value vs Effort matrix

Once you've worked through the Embed or Ditch? decision framework, you'll have a clear sense of which tools, tasks, or strategies are worth keeping and which ones need to go. But narrowing your focus doesn't stop there. The next step is to prioritise your efforts by mapping these decisions onto the Value vs Effort matrix. This process ensures that you're not just making decisions about what to embed or ditch – you're also determining where to focus your energy for maximum impact. The Value vs Effort matrix is a prioritisation tool that helps you focus on tasks delivering the greatest impact with minimal effort.

Here's how the matrix works:

- **High value, low effort:** tasks to prioritise immediately.
- **High value, high effort:** tasks worth pursuing but that may need additional planning.
- **Low value, low effort:** tasks to push down the list.
- **Low value, high effort:** tasks to ditch.

Take 15 minutes to map your strategies, tools, or tasks onto the matrix. Use the quadrants below to organise them.

	High effort	Low effort
High value	High-performing chatbot	Automating customer emails
Low value	Outdated analytics tool	Manual invoicing

Here are the results from the example on the previous page:

- **High value, low effort:** Automating customer emails delivers strong results with minimal upkeep, making it a priority to embed.
- **High value, high effort:** A high-performing chatbot is worth keeping but requires maintenance, so it's not an immediate priority.
- **Low value, low effort:** Manual invoicing offers little benefit despite requiring minimal effort, making it a good candidate to eliminate.
- **Low value, high effort:** An outdated analytics tool drains resources without delivering results and should be removed.

From overwhelmed to optimised – a Gold Coast architect's journey

Meet Ling, a Gold Coast architect juggling multiple tools, processes, and services. Like many small business owners, Ling initially believed that offering a wide range of services and using every available tool would set her apart. But instead, it left her overwhelmed, with her team stretched thin and clients receiving inconsistent results.

When Ling decided to narrow her focus, everything changed. Here's how she applied the principles of narrowing to streamline her business and scale sustainably:

- **Embed what works:** Ling kept her project management CRM, which improved collaboration and communication. She fully integrated it into her workflow, ensuring team members and clients stayed aligned from concept to delivery.
- **Cut what doesn't work:** She eliminated a 3D rendering tool that clients found too technical and replaced manual invoicing with automation. These changes freed up hours of administrative time each week.

- **Streamline for simplicity:** Ling consolidated time tracking and budgeting into her CRM and created a shared template for design reviews. This reduced redundancy, allowing her team to focus more on delivering exceptional designs.

The outcome

By narrowing her focus, Ling:

- improved team efficiency and client satisfaction
- increased her capacity to take on larger, higher-value projects
- built a business foundation that was easier to scale without adding unnecessary complexity.

What we can learn from Ling's story

Ling's story shows that narrowing isn't about doing less – it's about doing what works best. By embedding successful tools, cutting distractions, and simplifying her processes, she transformed her business into one that runs smoothly and delivers consistent value to her clients.

What tools or processes in your business could you embed, cut, or streamline to create the same clarity and efficiency?

Take AI action: are you on the right path?

Use this list to ensure your strategy is aligned with your goals:

- Have you identified the tools, tasks, or strategies delivering the most value?
- Have you let go of distractions or efforts that don't align with your priorities?
- Have you simplified workflows to reduce complexity and increase efficiency?

- Are your decisions guided by ethical principles and customer needs?
- Are you using the REIMAGINE Framework to guide and refine your focus?

Before we move on

By now I hope you can see that narrowing isn't about scaling back – it's about making smart, focused decisions that clear the way for growth. By embedding what works, cutting what doesn't, and streamlining your processes, you create a business that's not just efficient but built for long-term success.

Before we move on, you should:

- **Reflect on what matters:** Revisit your Embed or Ditch? decision framework and Value vs Effort matrix. Identify one thing you can embed, cut, or simplify today.
- **Bring others along:** Involve your team or clients in these decisions. Collaboration creates alignment and can uncover valuable insights you might have missed.
- **Embrace iteration:** Narrowing is an ongoing process. As your business evolves, revisit and refine your choices to stay agile and effective.
- **Prepare to evolve:** This foundation sets the stage for innovation. In the next step, you'll build on this clarity to adapt, future-proof, and grow your business.

Every decision you've made here is setting the stage for what's to come. By narrowing the noise, you give yourself and your business the gift of focus. This isn't just about optimising for today – it's about creating a strategy that thrives as your goals and the world around you evolve. Clarity isn't the endgame; it's the starting point for something bigger.

CHAPTER 9

Evolve: shaping your future business

'Evolution is not about staying ahead of the game – it's about creating the game you want to play.'

Tracy Sheen

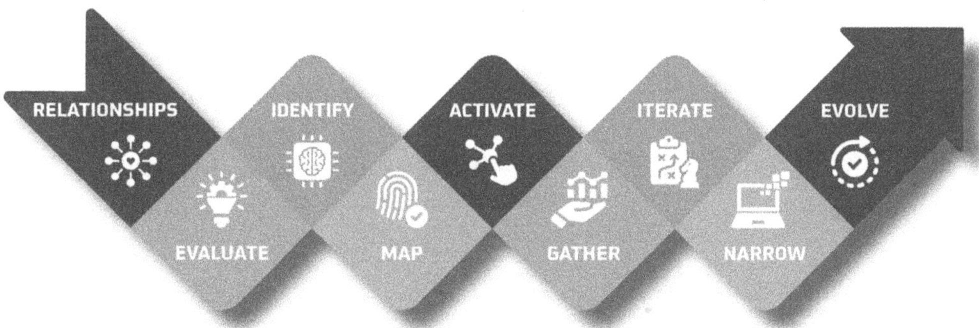

Adapting with intention

Way back in our section on **Mapping** (feels like a lifetime ago, doesn't it?), we explored the story of Atlassian – how Mike Cannon-Brookes and his university mate Scott Farquhar took a $10,000 gamble on a big idea with nothing but a credit card and ambition.

Fortunately for them (and the rest of us), that gamble paid off – big time. But their journey didn't stop there. Let's revisit their story and explore how the remainder of the REIMAGINE Framework fits seamlessly into their continued evolution.

But first, let's set the scene. Jump in our time machine and dial it back to 2010. The penultimate *Harry Potter* film was breaking box office records (I'm still not over Dobby, by the way), Adele was belting out 'Rolling in the Deep', and *Breaking Bad* had us all glued to our screens. Startups were popping up in coffee shops, remote work was gaining traction, and the 'gig economy' was rewriting the rules of business.

For small business owners, the landscape was full of promise – but also full of challenges. How do you adapt to so much change without losing sight of your goals? Let's check back in with Mike and Scott, whose journey with Atlassian is a perfect example of what it means to evolve with intention.

Evolving from strength

By 2010, Atlassian's tools – Jira and Confluence – had revolutionised collaboration for technical teams. But co-founders Mike Cannon-Brookes and Scott Farquhar weren't content to stick with the status quo. They saw the business world changing around them and knew Atlassian needed to evolve to stay relevant. Their mission? Empower *all* teams – not just developers – to work better together. This wasn't just about adding new tools or chasing trends. It was about listening, learning, and making deliberate choices that aligned with their core values.

From gaps to growth

Atlassian's first step was recognising a gap: while Jira and Confluence were powerful for structured workflows, they weren't solving the challenges faced by non-technical teams.

This gap wasn't a weakness – it was an opportunity to grow. By stepping back and assessing their ecosystem, Atlassian saw a way to expand their reach without losing focus on what they did best.

In 2017, Atlassian made a bold move to acquire Trello, a Kanban-style tool that was rapidly gaining popularity. For many companies, acquisitions are a risky proposition.

What made this evolution successful? It wasn't just the acquisition itself; it was how Atlassian thoughtfully integrated Trello into their ecosystem. They didn't try to make Trello fit into Jira's mould or strip away what made it unique. Instead, they enhanced its strengths while aligning it with their broader vision.

Evolution in action

Atlassian's journey highlights an important truth: evolution isn't about doing everything; it's about doing the right things. By following deliberate steps, they turned challenges into opportunities. Here's how their approach maps to the REIMAGINE Framework.

Relationships: listening and learning

Atlassian's evolution began with deep relationships. They actively engaged with their customers – both technical and non-technical – to understand their challenges and aspirations. These insights guided every decision. Great evolution starts with listening. Your relationships hold the key to understanding what's next.

Evaluate: assessing strengths and gaps

Rather than rushing to innovate for the sake of it, Atlassian paused to evaluate. They looked at what was working (Jira and Confluence) and what wasn't (support for non-technical teams). This clarity allowed them to make informed decisions.

Identify: finding the right fit

When Atlassian identified Trello as the missing piece, they didn't see it as competition. They saw it as a complement to their ecosystem – a tool that filled the gap they couldn't ignore. The best opportunities aren't always the ones you create. Sometimes, they're the ones you recognise.

Mapping: planning for impact

Atlassian's roadmap for Trello wasn't about immediate wins; it was about long-term alignment. They retained Trello's simplicity while integrating it into their ecosystem, ensuring a seamless experience for users. Intentional evolution requires a clear roadmap. Success comes from balancing vision with practicality.

Activate: targeted campaigns

Following the acquisition in 2017, Atlassian rolled out Trello to a broader audience. They launched targeted campaigns that highlighted Trello's simplicity and versatility, reaching both existing and new users.

Gather: the feedback loop

Atlassian collected user feedback from Trello and its other tools to refine how they worked together. This ongoing feedback loop ensured the integration enhanced the experience for all users. Evolution is powered by feedback. Listen to your users and refine your strategy to ensure your changes deliver real value.

Iterate: evolution isn't one-and-done

Based on feedback, Atlassian introduced new features to Trello, like templates and integrations, that aligned with user needs. These updates made Trello more robust without compromising its simplicity. Evolution isn't a one-and-done process. Small, iterative improvements ensure you stay aligned with user needs.

Narrow: amplify what works

Atlassian focused on Trello's core strengths, resisting the temptation to overcomplicate it. By keeping Trello simple and intuitive, they ensured it complemented their ecosystem without diluting its purpose. Staying focused is critical. Amplify what works, and don't let complexity dilute your impact.

Evolve: an intentional process

Through this intentional process, Atlassian successfully evolved their business. The acquisition of Trello allowed them to expand their audience, strengthen their product offerings, and reinforce their mission to empower teams everywhere.

Atlassian's ongoing evolution

Atlassian's acquisition of Trello marked a pivotal moment in their journey, but their evolution didn't stop there. Today, Atlassian continues to adapt and innovate, showing us what it means to embrace evolution as an ongoing mindset. From AI-powered tools to strategic acquisitions, Atlassian demonstrates that staying ahead in a fast-changing world requires both bold moves and consistent refinements.

Adopting AI to enhance productivity

In 2023, Atlassian introduced Atlassian Intelligence, integrating OpenAI's technology to streamline workflows and empower teams. From automating repetitive tasks to providing actionable suggestions, this AI enhancement is a testament to Atlassian's commitment to amplifying productivity.

A year later, they launched Rovo, an AI-powered 'teammate' that brings intelligent insights and automation to team collaboration. Atlassian's approach to AI shows that evolution isn't about replacing effort – it's about making better use of time and resources. Evolving with AI doesn't mean adopting every tool; it's about choosing innovations that align with your vision and values.

Strategic acquisitions to meet modern needs

Atlassian's growth strategy also includes smart acquisitions. In late 2023, they acquired Loom, recognising the need for asynchronous video communication in remote and hybrid workplaces. Just a year later, they acquired Rewatch, an AI-powered meeting recorder, further embedding video into their ecosystem.

These acquisitions demonstrate how Atlassian aligns its growth with evolving team behaviours, ensuring every move strengthens its core mission of empowering collaboration.

Focusing on user-centric enhancements

Atlassian continues to refine its tools to serve users better. In early 2025, they plan to roll out a modern navigation system across Jira, Confluence, and other products, improving consistency and efficiency. Updated data security policies offer admins greater control over content, reflecting their commitment to usability and trust. Refining the user experience can be as impactful as adding new features.

Championing flexible work

While other tech giants roll back remote work policies, Atlassian remains a staunch advocate for flexible work models. By prioritising remote and hybrid work options, they demonstrate adaptability to cultural and workforce shifts. Adaptability isn't just about technology – it's about evolving your culture to meet the needs of your team and clients.

The essence of evolution: progress, not perfection

Atlassian's ongoing evolution highlights the importance of intentional growth. They haven't succeeded by chasing trends or adopting every new tool – they've succeeded by aligning their decisions with a clear mission and following a framework.

Strong relationships should always be at the heart of every decision – consider how each change impacts your team and clients. Stay open to new opportunities, but ensure they align with your goals. Growth isn't about doing more; it's about focusing on what strengthens your core.

Evolution happens through small, intentional steps rather than one big leap. By refining and aligning your strategies, you create sustainable progress. How will you take inspiration from Atlassian to shape your own business's evolution?

By now, you've probably figured out that I'm not about chasing every shiny new trend or overhauling everything in your business all at once. Sure, that might feel exciting for a moment – but it's also the fastest way to burn out, waste resources, and lose focus.

As 'boring' as it might sound, a methodical, framework-driven approach is far more likely to help you build sustainability into your evolution. Just like we've seen throughout the REIMAGINE Framework, each step builds on the last, creating a clear, sustainable path to evolution. Evolution isn't about doing it all – it's about doing what matters most. It's about progress – intentional, strategic, and aligned with your goals.

In the context of AI and reimagining your business, this means expanding capabilities, staying agile, and leveraging the clarity you've already built to grow strategically. Let's explore how to expand your capabilities, stay agile, and leverage clarity to grow strategically – ensuring your evolution feels achievable and aligned with your vision.

Expanding capabilities while staying aligned with goals

Evolution offers the opportunity to expand what your business can do, but that growth only works when it aligns with your goals and values. This is where the REIMAGINE Framework becomes your guide:

- **Evaluate and Identify:** Before expanding, you've already evaluated what's working and identified gaps. Evolution builds on this foundation, ensuring any new capability strengthens your business rather than distracting from your mission.
- **Mapping and Activate:** Expanding capabilities is about aligning new tools or strategies with your broader plan. By mapping where these changes fit and activating them thoughtfully, you ensure they serve your goals without adding unnecessary complexity.

Integrate AI tools to streamline workflows or enhance client experiences, but only in ways that fit your mission and strategy. For example, a retailer uses AI to optimise inventory management and predict customer demand, enabling them to grow without losing the personal touch that defines their brand.

Anticipating change and staying agile

The pace of change in technology and customer expectations is accelerating; your evolution is about staying ahead by remaining adaptable. The REIMAGINE Framework gives you the tools to anticipate and respond to change effectively:

- **Relationships and Gather:** Staying connected to your customers, team, and industry allows you to spot emerging trends and gather valuable insights early.
- **Iterate and Narrow:** Agility comes from making small adjustments as you go, refining what works and letting go of what doesn't.

Keep an eye on industry trends, listen to customer feedback, and make small adjustments before they become urgent. For example, a graphic designer spots a rise in demand for animated content and partners with a freelance animator, staying ahead of client needs while expanding their capabilities.

Leveraging clarity to embrace strategic growth

Narrowing your focus earlier in the REIMAGINE Framework gave you clarity about what works, what doesn't, and where to focus your resources. Now, evolution allows you to build on this foundation and grow strategically rather than reactively:

- **Narrow and Mapping:** By narrowing your priorities, you've eliminated distractions and created space for what matters most. Strategic growth means using that focus to map out logical next steps that align with your goals.

- **Activate and Iterate:** Strategic growth doesn't happen all at once. It's about activating small, high-impact changes and iterating based on feedback and results, ensuring each step moves you closer to your vision.

Use the insights from your streamlined operations to identify the next logical step for growth, whether it's new offerings, partnerships, or markets. For example, a consulting firm that narrowed its services to AI strategy now uses that expertise to target larger clients, leveraging its niche to scale effectively.

Progress over perfection

Perfection is an impossible goal, but progress is always achievable. Evolution isn't about getting everything right the first time – it's about taking small, intentional steps that align with your vision, adapting as you go. The REIMAGINE Framework is designed to support this mindset. By continuously iterating, narrowing, and evolving, you're building a business that thrives on progress, not perfection. Each step you take is informed by clarity and purpose, turning challenges into opportunities and change into growth.

Take AI action: a moment to reflect

What does evolution look like for your business? How can you expand, adapt, or grow in ways that align with your goals and vision?

The human factor in evolution

Evolution isn't just about tools, processes, or strategies – it's about people. Whether you're working with a team, managing remote collaborators, or steering the ship as a solopreneur, the success of your evolution depends on how well the people around you adapt, align, and thrive.

It's no coincidence that we started our REIMAGINE journey with Relationships. A human-centred approach isn't just the first step – it's the foundation for everything that follows. Evolution succeeds when it empowers people, respects their needs, and encourages inclusion. By aligning your team and collaborators, you're not just evolving effectively – you're evolving ethically. Building trust and respecting the needs of your people ensures your evolution strengthens relationships rather than strains them. But evolving with people isn't a one-size-fits-all process. The way you approach it will depend on the structure of your business.

For solopreneurs: balancing growth and focus

For solopreneurs, evolution can feel overwhelming, but the key is to focus on incremental growth:

- **Leverage support where needed:** Don't try to do it all yourself. Consider hiring a VA or freelance specialist to handle specific tasks, freeing you to focus on what you do best.
- **Automate where it makes sense:** Use AI tools to streamline repetitive tasks like scheduling or email marketing. This creates space for you to focus on creative or high-value work.

If you have a team: empower and align

For business owners managing a team, evolution means creating alignment and empowering your individuals to grow:

- **Engage your team in the process:** Involve your team early. Explain why changes are happening and how they align with the business's goals.
- **Foster ownership:** Create opportunities for employees to contribute ideas or lead initiatives, helping them feel invested in the evolution.
- **Invest in training and resources:** Equip your team with the tools and knowledge they need to adapt to new processes or technologies confidently.

Just as we saw in the Relationships step of the REIMAGINE Framework, bringing people along for the journey ensures they feel supported and aligned, making your evolution smoother and more effective.

Studies show that 70% of change initiatives fail due to lack of employee buy-in. Bringing your team into the process early dramatically increases the likelihood of success.[6]

For remote and VA collaborators: building alignment across distance

If you rely on remote contractors or virtual assistants, evolving together means creating clear expectations and fostering alignment:

- **Set up simple systems:** Use tools like Trello or Asana to create shared workflows that keep everyone aligned and accountable.

6 https://www.mckinsey.com/featured-insights/leadership/changing-change-management

- **Prioritise secure access:** Ensure remote workers can access your systems and client data securely, with clear guidelines on handling sensitive information.
- **Communicate regularly:** Regular check-ins, even brief ones, help contractors feel connected to your vision.
- **Ethical evolution:** When working with remote collaborators, evolving ethically means ensuring everyone has access to the tools and training they need while protecting client and business data. Clear communication and secure systems build trust and accountability.

Evolving with your clients

While evolving your business, it's easy to focus on internal changes – your team, tools, and processes. But your clients are just as crucial to your success. After all, their needs and expectations often spark the evolution itself. Including them in your process not only ensures you're aligned but can also build stronger, longer-lasting relationships.

Here's how to involve your clients in the evolution process:

- **Listen and adapt:** Gather regular feedback through surveys, conversations, or analytics to track shifting client needs. For example, an accounting firm introduces a secure client portal after learning clients want easier digital access to financial reports.
- **Keep communication open:** Be transparent about changes and how they benefit clients to build trust. For example, a boutique marketing agency briefs clients on how AI tools will improve campaign performance and streamline communication.
- **Involve clients early:** Invite key clients to test new processes before a full rollout to refine and strengthen adoption. For example, an

e-commerce store pilots an AI-driven personalisation feature with trusted clients, adjusting it based on their feedback.
- **Make changes seamless:** Ensure new tools and processes are intuitive, accessible, and aligned with client preferences. For example, a graphic designer simplifies project approvals with an AI-powered feedback tool that clients can use without a steep learning curve.

Ethical evolution with clients

When evolving with clients, consider the ethical implications of your changes:

- **Data security:** If your evolution involves new tools or processes, ensure client data remains secure and protected.
- **Fairness and transparency:** Be upfront about how changes impact their experience and avoid overpromising results.
- **Respect their workflows:** Don't disrupt established client workflows without a clear benefit to them.
- **Understand industry requirements:** In some industries, clients may have specific security or regulatory standards that dictate which systems or processes you must use. Aligning your evolution with these requirements ensures compliance and builds trust. For example, a consultant working with government agencies uses secure, approved platforms for data sharing to meet compliance standards, even if it means adapting their internal workflows.

Remember, evolving with clients isn't just about meeting their needs today – it's about building trust for tomorrow.

Take AI action: a moment to reflect

What changes in your business could directly enhance your clients' experience, and how can you involve them in your evolution?

From resistance to buy-in

Evolving with people means navigating different personalities, preferences and – sometimes – resistance. Whether it's a hesitant team member, a sceptical client, or your own overwhelm as a solopreneur, challenges are natural. The key is recognising where the resistance is coming from and addressing it accordingly.

Team resistance: hesitation and uncertainty

Change can feel unsettling for teams, especially when they don't fully understand why it's happening or how it will impact their roles. Common concerns include fear of disruption, worries that AI might replace jobs, uncertainty about added workload, or a lack of clarity on the benefits. Addressing these fears early helps smooth the transition and fosters team buy-in.

To overcome resistance, communicate the why behind the evolution and how it benefits both the team and the business. Involve employees in the process by seeking their input on implementation, helping them feel ownership over the changes. Highlight success stories from similar transitions, using case studies or internal wins to illustrate positive outcomes.

Most importantly, reframe AI as a tool that enhances roles rather than replacing them – automating repetitive tasks so employees can focus on creative or strategic work. For example, when a small marketing agency introduces an AI project management tool, they hold a brainstorming session to discuss integration ideas, easing concerns and building enthusiasm.

Client resistance: adapting to new changes

Clients may resist unfamiliar changes, particularly if they disrupt existing workflows. Their hesitation often stems from fear of added complexity or scepticism about how the changes will benefit them.

Without clear communication, they may view new tools or processes as unnecessary hurdles rather than valuable improvements.

To ease client concerns, position changes as direct enhancements to their experience – such as faster communication, greater efficiency, or more personalised service. Offer training, walkthroughs, or tutorials to make adoption seamless. Creating a feedback loop ensures clients feel heard and have input on adjustments. For example, a consultant transitioning to a secure client portal provides a live demo and written guide, addressing usability concerns while emphasising improved data security.

Solopreneur overwhelm: the weight of doing it all

As a solopreneur, balancing business evolution with daily operations can feel overwhelming. Limited resources, fear of taking on too much, and uncertainty about prioritisation often make it difficult to move forward. Without a clear plan, the pressure of managing everything alone can lead to burnout and stalled progress.

To stay on track, start small: focus on evolving one area at a time rather than overhauling everything at once. Delegate or outsource time-consuming tasks using freelance platforms or a virtual assistant. Automate repetitive processes with AI, freeing up energy for strategic growth. For example, a graphic designer hires a VA to handle invoicing and scheduling, allowing them to focus on onboarding new clients while evolving their business.

Take AI action: a moment to reflect

What resistance might you encounter from your team, collaborators, or clients as you evolve your business? How can you address their concerns – whether it's fear of disruption, AI adoption, or adapting to new workflows – while building trust and alignment?

Progress with purpose: evolving responsibly

In the context of AI adoption, evolution isn't just about staying competitive – it's about growing in ways that align with your values and build trust. For many of you, the idea of introducing advanced technologies like AI might still feel a little intimidating or even alien, especially if it seems like a world apart from traditional ways of operating. But ethical AI evolution isn't about abandoning what you know; it's about thoughtfully integrating new tools to enhance, not replace, your core practices. It's a chance to build deeper trust with your employees, customers, and community by showing that innovation has a natural place alongside integrity and care.

As we navigate this evolution, it's essential to recognise that AI adoption is not just a technological upgrade – it represents a shift in how we think about business, decision-making, and the role of technology in our lives. Embracing AI ethically requires moving beyond questions of capability ('What *can* AI do?') to a deeper focus on responsibility ('What *should* AI do?'). This shift also means reimagining success. It's no longer just about efficiency and profitability but about building trust, ensuring fairness, and fostering a workplace where technology complements rather than competes with human talent.

For many, this change in mindset will require stepping outside of traditional comfort zones, questioning long-standing practices, and being willing to experiment with new ways of working. It's important here to pause and explore some of these paradigm shifts in more detail to understand how they create opportunities for growth, resilience, and meaningful change.

As AI becomes an integral part of business operations and ubiquitous across society at large, it is asking us to fundamentally rethink long-held assumptions.

Here are the key paradigm shifts that can help businesses evolve responsibly while harnessing AI's potential.

From 'Can AI do this?' to 'Should AI do this?'

Historically, technological advances have been driven by the question, 'What's possible?' With AI, however, the stakes are higher, and I believe our focus needs to shift to, 'What's responsible?'

Not every technological solution aligns with your business values or serves your customers' best interests. By framing decisions through this lens, businesses can avoid unintended consequences, maintain ethics, and build on the trust and relationships their brands have developed over time.

Beyond efficiency to trust and fairness

AI often promises speed and cost-saving, but our customers and employees are looking for more than just faster and cheaper. They want to know our business values fairness, transparency, and ethical practices – and not just values but actively works to implement and maintain these ethics. Within this operating landscape, trust isn't just a competitive advantage in a reimagined environment – it's a business necessity.

For example, you have the opportunity to incorporate AI for hiring a new team member. While automating résumé screening will save time, you recognise it could inadvertently amplify biases if the algorithm favours certain demographics based on historical data. In addressing this challenge by auditing algorithms, involving diverse teams and remaining transparent during the hiring process, your business not only builds trust but also ensures fairer outcomes.

AI as a team member, not a competitor

According to a McKinsey report, by 2030, activities accounting for up to 30% of hours currently worked across the US economy could be automated.[7] While this statistic might seem disconcerting, we need to recognise that AI's role in the workplace is more about collaboration rather than elimination. By automating the mundane and routine tasks, AI frees up team members to focus on creative and strategic aspects of their roles, fostering innovation and job satisfaction.

From data collection to data responsibility

Many small businesses are beginning to realise the value of their data, but with that comes the responsibility to manage it ethically and securely. Customers are increasingly aware of how their data is being used and expect transparency and respect for privacy.

For example, a small e-commerce store collecting customer preferences for personalised recommendations must ensure this data is stored securely and used only for its intended purpose. Breaches or misuse can quickly erode trust, particularly in smaller, community-driven businesses.

From immediate ROI to long-term sustainability

Due to tighter budgets, we often focus on immediate ROI opportunities. But as we evolve with AI, the benefits will often unfold over a longer time. Investments in areas like customer service, inventory management, or marketing automation may take months to show results but can lead to sustained growth and market relevance in the face of market changes.

---

7 https://www.mckinsey.com/mgi/our-research/generative-ai-and-the-future-of-work-in-america

For example, a café might use AI to predict demand for specific items based on seasons or events. While the initial setup may seem costly, over the longer term the system significantly reduces waste and optimises inventory, leading to better margins.

From DIY to leveraging partnerships

Small business owners are a resourceful bunch; we've had to be. But AI adoption is one area where going it alone can be counter-productive. Just as we seek out business coaches, accountants and others to assist us with our business, consider looking for an AI guide – someone who can ease the learning curve, assist your team with streamlining, and reduce the time and energy required to get (and stay) up to speed.

Take AI action: reflecting on the shifts

Take a moment to reflect on these paradigm shifts and how they apply to your business. Consider the challenges you currently face, the opportunities AI presents, and the areas where you might need to adjust your approach to align with these new ways of thinking. This reflection will help you identify the shifts most relevant to your goals and create a foundation for the ethical and strategic integration of AI into your operations.

From 'Can AI do this?' to 'Should AI do this?'

- Are there areas where AI could improve your processes but might create ethical concerns?
- How do you ensure your AI decisions align with your values and customer expectations?

Develop a decision-making framework that evaluates the ethical, social, and long-term implications of adopting specific AI tools. For example, use a checklist that considers privacy, inclusivity, and fairness before implementing new AI systems.

Beyond efficiency to trust and fairness

- How do you currently measure success in your business?
- Could focusing on trust and fairness improve customer loyalty or team morale?

Incorporate regular reviews of AI practices to ensure they remain aligned with your core values and meet the expectations of your community.

AI as a team member, not a competitor

- What tasks or roles in your business could AI complement rather than replace?
- How can AI free up your team to focus on creative and meaningful work?
- What training programmes are available to enable team members to effectively leverage AI tools?

Encourage your team to brainstorm how AI could be built into their job descriptions, allowing them to engage in more meaningful and impactful work. Cultivate a culture that embraces change and views AI as an opportunity for collaboration and growth rather than a threat.

From data collection to data responsibility

- Are you transparent with your customers about how you collect and use their data?
- Do you have processes in place to ensure data security and privacy?
- What are your policies around data collection, storage, and usage?

From immediate ROI to long-term resilience

- Are there AI tools or strategies you've considered but dismissed due to upfront costs?

- How could a long-term perspective shift your approach to AI investments?

From DIY to leveraging partnerships

- Are you trying to manage AI integration entirely on your own?

Explore partnerships and resources, such as grants for digital transformation and AI guidance, shared AI tools, or training programmes.

Action steps

- **Identify:** Which of these shifts resonates most with your business?
- **Assess:** Are there areas where your mindset or practices need to evolve?
- **Plan:** Jot down one or two actionable steps you could take to start embracing these shifts.

By working through these questions and action steps, you'll not only clarify your next moves but also set the stage for evolving ethically with your team, your customers, and your broader community.

Evolving with your people

As you consider the shifts your business needs to make to reimagine and adapt in an AI-driven world, one of the most critical areas to focus on is your people – your employees, customers, and the community your business serves.

Evolving ethically and responsibly with AI means keeping them at the heart of your journey, ensuring that technology supports and strengthens the relationships that underpin everything you do. Change management plays a pivotal role in this evolution. A recent survey found that 77% of workers feel AI tools have reduced their productivity and increased their workloads, underscoring the need for thoughtful and inclusive implementation.[8]

Teams: involve and empower

Open communication is essential to making your team feel included and valued during business changes. Share the why behind AI adoption, showing how it aligns with your mission and values. Involve team members early by seeking their input, addressing concerns, and clarifying how AI will support – not replace – their roles. Emphasise benefits such as freeing them from repetitive tasks so they can focus on more creative, impactful work.

To ensure a smooth transition, communicate the vision, encourage feedback, and provide upskilling opportunities. Foster a culture of curiosity by allowing team members to experiment with AI tools and recognise early successes to build confidence. However, avoid overwhelming them with sudden or excessive changes. Frame AI as an enhancement, not a replacement, and provide extra support where needed to ensure all team members – regardless of skill level or experience – can adapt successfully.

Remote workers and contractors: align with clear protocols

For remote teams and contractors, maintaining security and alignment is crucial. Establish clear protocols for handling sensitive data, limiting access to AI tools based on roles and responsibilities. Provide training that ensures they can use AI effectively while maintaining compliance with your business's security and workflow standards. Regular check-ins help remote workers stay aligned with company goals and give them the support they need to succeed.

---

8 https://www.businessinsider.com/ai-workers-productivity-survey-2024-8

Investing in the right collaboration tools and secure communication platforms ensures consistency across distributed teams. Setting clear expectations for how AI tools should be used in workflows prevents misunderstandings and security risks. However, don't assume remote workers will adapt without training, and don't neglect their sense of inclusion – fostering engagement and alignment is just as important as enforcing security measures.

Clients: build trust through transparency

When introducing AI-driven changes that impact clients, transparency is key. Clearly explain how AI will enhance their experience – whether through faster service, more personalised interactions, or streamlined processes. Address any concerns about privacy or disruptions to their workflows, encourage feedback, and ensure that AI solutions simplify, rather than complicate, their journey.

Maintain trust by openly communicating AI's benefits, aligning changes with existing workflows, and providing clients with options to customise or opt-in to AI-driven interactions. Use case studies or real-world examples to illustrate the improvements. Avoid over-complicating explanations, making disruptive changes without input, or overpromising AI capabilities – setting clear, realistic expectations builds stronger, long-term client relationships.

Connecting ethics to industry requirements

Along with your commitment to bring your people along on the journey to REIMAGINE your business, it's equally critical to ensure your AI adoption aligns with the broader standards of your industry. Maintaining compliance not only protects your business from potential risks but also strengthens trust with your team, customers, and stakeholders. Many of the steps you take to foster transparency and accountability will naturally align with industry regulations. By staying ahead of these requirements, you'll not only ensure your business remains compliant but also position yourself as a leader in ethical, forward-thinking practices.

Industries are constantly evolving, with new regulations and standards shaping the way businesses integrate and adopt AI usage. While staying informed about these changes can feel overwhelming, it is critical for your future success and compliance that you focus on the essentials and build a proactive approach that will keep your business compliant and trustworthy.

Monitor changes proactively

Keeping up with changes in data privacy laws, security standards, and ethical guidelines is essential to maintaining compliance. Use trusted sources such as industry publications, webinars, and government resources to stay updated. Setting aside regular time – monthly or quarterly – for a review of emerging regulations will help you avoid surprises.

Adapt processes to stay compliant

Compliance is an ongoing process, not a one-time fix. Regularly evaluate your current practices to ensure they meet evolving standards. For example, if new data protection laws are introduced, update your policies, train your team, and audit your systems to reflect these changes. Remember, AI is such an evolving space that you need to consider writing everything in pencil, not ink. That way, you always have one eye on the future and how best to incorporate changes as you see them coming.

Leverage industry relationships

Build relationships with advisers, industry groups, or local business associations to stay informed without feeling overwhelmed. These connections can provide insights, updates, and resources that make navigating compliance more manageable.

Why compliance matters beyond regulations

Meeting industry requirements isn't just about avoiding penalties – it's an opportunity to build your reputation as a business that values trust, safety, and responsibility. Customers, employees, and partners are more likely to remain loyal to businesses they see as responsible and proactive. It is an opportunity for your business to set itself apart from the pack as one that values ethics and transparency above all else. As the AI landscape evolves, these are increasingly attractive traits to clients, suppliers, and industry contacts.

Let's explore a practical framework to guide these critical decisions.

Take AI action: a framework for ethical decision-making in AI adoption

As your business integrates AI, you can use this framework to ensure your decisions align with your values, maintain trust, and drive positive outcomes for everyone involved. Take a few moments now to jot down some thoughts on the following questions:

- **Who benefits?** How does this AI implementation create value for your team, clients, and the business? Are there any groups – employees, customers, or partners – who might feel left behind or negatively impacted?

- **Are there risks?** Could this implementation introduce risks, such as data breaches, biased algorithms, or overcomplication? What proactive steps can you take to identify and mitigate these risks before they become issues?
- **Have you communicated?** Have you explained to employees, clients, and others how this AI change will benefit them? Have you sought feedback and addressed concerns or misconceptions to build understanding and trust?

Common pitfalls in Evolution – and how to avoid them

As your business evolves through AI implementation, frameworks and guiding questions can help you make thoughtful, ethical decisions. But even with the best intentions, gaps can form – between plans and execution, people and technology, or trust and transparency. These gaps can lead to missteps that undermine progress, erode trust, or even stall your AI journey altogether.

Recognising these potential pitfalls ahead of time is crucial to navigating AI evolution successfully. This section highlights the most common Evolve mistakes I've seen and the proactive steps you can take to avoid them. To ensure your AI journey is smooth, sustainable, and impactful, I've grouped these pitfalls into four key areas:

- people and relationship challenges
- operational challenges
- strategic challenges
- ethical and compliance challenges.

Let's explore how to address these challenges and set your business up for success.

People and relationship challenges

AI is meant to support your people – employees, clients, and the community. However, poorly managed transitions can lead to disengagement, resistance, or even lost trust. Let's examine common people and relationship pitfalls.

Losing sight of team or client needs

AI initiatives that prioritise efficiency at the expense of human needs can alienate your team or clients. For example, automating tasks without consulting employees can lead to anxiety about job security, while overly complex AI tools may frustrate customers.

Involve your team and clients early, ensuring they have a voice in the process. Seek their feedback and address concerns as changes are implemented. Choose AI solutions that enhance, rather than replace, the human touch in your business to maintain trust and engagement.

Neglecting proper training and upskilling

Assuming your team will adapt to AI tools without structured support can lead to low adoption rates and inefficiency.

Invest in training programmes that build confidence and skill, ensuring your team feels prepared to work with AI. Provide ongoing support and make resources readily available to address questions and challenges as they arise.

Failing to communicate AI's purpose and benefits

A lack of transparency about why AI is being implemented can erode trust and create resistance. Be clear about the reasons for adopting AI and how it will benefit employees and clients. Share success stories and examples to build excitement and confidence.

Operational challenges

Operational challenges can derail even the best-laid plans if systems are poorly designed or left unchecked. Let's consider common operational pitfalls.

Overcomplicating systems and processes

Adding unnecessary complexity to workflows can make AI tools harder to use and maintain.

Start simple. Focus on implementing AI solutions that address clear pain points without adding excessive features. Regularly review and streamline processes to ensure efficiency.

Failing to monitor and iterate AI implementations

Treating AI as a 'set and forget' tool can lead to stagnation or unforeseen issues over time. Schedule regular reviews to assess AI performance and adapt as needed. Use data and feedback to refine and improve your AI systems continually.

Overrelying on AI without human oversight

Relying solely on AI without maintaining human checks and balances can result in unchecked errors or unintended outcomes. Design processes where AI supports rather than replaces human decision-making, and assign team members to monitor and validate AI outputs regularly.

Strategic challenges

Without a clear strategy, AI adoption can waste resources or fail to deliver meaningful results. Let's examine common strategic challenges.

Expanding too quickly without alignment

Scaling AI initiatives too fast without proper alignment to business goals can lead to inefficiencies and missed opportunities. Test AI solutions on a smaller scale before rolling them out more widely, and ensure every AI initiative ties directly to a specific business objective.

Adopting AI without clear objectives

Implementing AI for the sake of keeping up with trends often results in confusion and wasted effort. Define measurable goals for every AI project, such as increasing efficiency or improving customer experience. Regularly evaluate whether AI tools are meeting those goals, and adjust as needed.

Ethical and compliance challenges

Trust and transparency are vital in AI adoption. Overlooking ethics or compliance can result in reputational damage and legal consequences. Let's look at common ethical and compliance pitfalls.

Ignoring ethical or legal considerations

Failing to comply with data privacy laws or address ethical concerns can erode trust and invite legal action. Stay updated on relevant regulations and ensure your AI systems comply, and conduct regular audits to evaluate the ethical implications of your AI initiatives.

Underestimating bias in AI models

Using biased data or algorithms can result in unfair outcomes, alienating certain groups and damaging your reputation. Test AI models for bias regularly and involve diverse perspectives in the evaluation process. Use inclusive data sets and consult with experts to identify potential biases early.

Take AI action: anticipating and avoiding pitfalls

To ensure your AI journey stays on track, take a moment to reflect on the common pitfalls and how they might apply to your business. Use these prompts to identify potential gaps and outline strategies to address them:

- **People:** Identify areas where team members or clients may feel overlooked during AI implementation. Improve communication, training, and support to keep them engaged.
- **Operational:** Assess whether AI tools are complicating workflows. Establish a system for ongoing monitoring and refinement to ensure they continue delivering value.
- **Strategic:** Ensure AI initiatives align with business goals. Develop a clear plan to pilot-test implementations before scaling.
- **Ethics and compliance:** Evaluate the ethical and legal implications of AI usage. Implement processes to identify and mitigate risks like bias or data privacy concerns.

Action steps

- Write down one potential pitfall you feel your business is most vulnerable to in each category.
- For each, outline a specific action or resource you'll use to address it.
- Bring together your team or discuss it with your AI guide for feedback and accountability.

By actively reflecting on these issues, you can bridge the gaps in your AI evolution and set your business up for long-term success.

How a Darwin graphic designer REIMAGINED success

For Amira, a Darwin-based graphic designer, running her small business meant juggling multiple roles – designer, project manager, marketer, and client liaison. She collaborated with remote contractors across multiple time zones and managed a roster of diverse clients, each with their own unique demands.

While Amira loved her design work, the inefficiencies in her business operations were draining her creativity and holding her back from scaling. Amira accepted my challenge to reimagine her business using the REIMAGINE Framework. Here's how she transformed her operations step by step, turning a chaotic workload into a streamlined, scalable creative studio.

Relationships: building stronger collaboration

Amira focused on strengthening relationships with her clients and contractors, recognising that communication gaps were causing delays and misunderstandings. To improve collaboration, she introduced weekly check-ins with contractors and developed transparent timelines for clients. These changes built trust, reduced revisions, and made clients feel more connected to her process.

Evaluate: pinpointing problem areas

Assessing her workflows, Amira identified inefficiencies caused by using too many disconnected tools – emails for feedback, spreadsheets for tracking, and messaging apps for updates. By taking stock of her systems and listing redundant tools, she gained a clear understanding of where time was being wasted and where improvements could be made.

Identify: finding the right solution

Recognising the need for a more integrated approach, Amira chose a unified project management system to streamline workflows and improve visibility. This new platform combined task tracking, file sharing, and client communication in one place, reducing complexity and creating a single source of truth for her business.

Mapping: creating a streamlined project lifecycle

Amira mapped out how the new system would fit into her business processes, designing a structured project lifecycle. She documented workflows, standardised steps, and created templates for recurring tasks, ensuring a consistent and efficient process for both contractors and clients.

Activate: training and implementing changes

To ensure a smooth transition, Amira trained her contractors and updated her clients on the new system. She hosted video walkthroughs and provided a simple onboarding guide with a Q&A section. This proactive approach led to quick adoption with minimal disruption to ongoing projects.

Gather: listening and refining

As the new processes rolled out, Amira collected feedback from contractors and clients to identify areas for improvement. Regular check-ins and surveys provided valuable insights, allowing her to address small issues before they became larger problems.

Iterate: tweaking for real-world results

Based on feedback, Amira fine-tuned her workflows and adjusted platform settings to better meet her team's needs. She simplified task assignments and added automated reminders, leading to increased efficiency and fewer missed deadlines.

Narrow: focusing on what works

Amira evaluated her tech stack, eliminating tools that weren't adding value and doubling down on high-performing systems. By consolidating subscriptions, she reduced distractions, saved money, and maintained a lean, focused setup that supported her business without overcomplicating it.

Evolve: scaling with purpose

With her operations running smoothly, Amira shifted her focus to growth. She invested in expanding her expertise in client management systems and developed a pilot programme for scalable projects. As a result, she increased revenue, reduced stress, and created a clear path to long-term success.

Amira's success started with focusing on relationships and listening to her team and clients. Consolidating tools and creating streamlined workflows set the foundation for growth, and small, continuous improvements made the changes manageable and impactful.

Take AI action: a moment to reflect

What inefficiencies in your business could you eliminate with a more streamlined approach? How might a clearer process empower you to scale with confidence?

No more excuses: conquering objections to AI

Adopting AI can feel like a monumental shift, and everything we've done up to this point may feel like a lot of effort. The prospect of integrating new tools, learning new workflows, and adapting to unfamiliar technologies often sparks hesitation, even fear.

Over the years working with clients, I've seen the same concerns arise again and again – whether it's the cost of implementation, the perceived complexity of AI, or doubts about how it fits into their existing business model. These fears are entirely natural. Change is daunting, especially when it feels like the ground beneath your business is shifting faster than you can keep up.

But these objections, while valid, can also be challenged and reframed as opportunities. By addressing these concerns head-on, you can clear the path for growth, innovation, and a future where AI enhances rather than overwhelms your business. Here are the top fears and objections I've encountered and how to tackle them with clarity and confidence.

'Can't I just keep doing what I've always done?'

It's tempting to stick with what works, especially when your current methods seem to meet your needs. But the entire reason we're REIMAGINING your business is because you know that business is shifting. AI adoption isn't about replacing what's working – it's about future-proofing your business. AI isn't a threat to your success; it's a tool to help you scale and stay competitive in a rapidly changing world.

What happens if your competitors embrace AI and gain an edge in efficiency, customer experience, or cost savings? How much time and energy could you save by automating repetitive tasks, freeing you to focus on what you love most?

Think of AI as a way to amplify what you're already doing well, not to replace it. By adopting AI incrementally, you can stay relevant without abandoning your proven methods.

'AI feels too big and complex for my business.'

Many of my clients still see AI as the domain of big corporations with complicated systems and massive budgets. But as I've shown you throughout the book, AI tools today are more accessible, affordable, and user-friendly than ever before, designed to meet the needs of businesses of all sizes.

Have you explored entry-level tools like AI-powered email responders, marketing assistants, or scheduling apps? What if the right tool could help you achieve more with less effort?

AI doesn't have to be overwhelming. Start small with one tool that solves a specific problem, like managing client inquiries or generating content. Over time, you'll grow more confident in integrating AI into your operations.

'I don't have the time or resources to figure this out.'

Many of us are already feeling stretched thin, and the idea of learning something new or adding another system can feel like one task too many. But the right AI tools can reduce your workload and free up time for higher-value activities.

How much time do you currently spend on repetitive or low-value tasks? Could a short-term investment in learning save you hours every week?

View AI as an investment in reclaiming your time. Start with tools that require minimal setup, or seek out affordable training to get started quickly.

'What if AI replaces my value or my team's jobs?'

There's been a lot of media hype that AI will devalue the human element of business or replace roles entirely. But AI works best when it complements our human skills rather than competing with them.

Could AI handle the repetitive tasks you dislike, allowing you or your team to focus on creative, strategic, or client-facing work? How might AI enhance your ability to personalise services or solve client problems?

AI is a partner, not a competitor. It frees you to do the work that only humans can – building relationships, innovating, and adding a personal touch.

'How can I trust that AI won't cause problems?'

Worries about errors, data breaches, or unintended consequences are valid, especially for businesses new to AI. Trusting AI starts with understanding its limitations and ensuring proper safeguards are in place.

Are you considering tools with good reputations, secure systems, and proven results? Do you have processes to monitor AI performance and catch issues early?

Think of AI as part of your broader systems, not a standalone solution. With proper oversight, it can become a reliable and safe addition to your business.

'My clients or industry don't use AI – why should I?'

In industries where AI adoption is slow, it might feel like jumping ahead isn't necessary. But being an early adopter can position your business as a leader and give you a competitive advantage.

What could you learn about your clients' needs or preferences by using AI for analytics or personalisation? How might being first in your industry set you apart as a forward-thinking innovator?

Think of AI as a secret weapon – adopting early helps you build a foundation before it becomes standard in your industry.

'What happens if the AI stops working or makes a mistake?'

Fear of tech failures is common, especially for small businesses where every mistake feels – and can be – costly. But AI is only as good as the systems and people managing it.

Do you have backup processes in place for when tech fails? How can you minimise risks by starting small and scaling gradually?

No system is perfect, and neither are humans. If we combine our powers of human oversight and careful implementation, we can catch and correct mistakes quickly.

'I'm not tech-savvy enough to manage AI.'

Feeling unprepared or intimidated by technology is a common concern, but many modern AI tools are designed to be user-friendly and require no technical expertise.

Could you explore tools with free trials or tutorials to build confidence? Can you find an AI guide who could help you implement AI tools?

You don't have to be an expert to get started. Most AI tools are as intuitive as the apps you already use daily – and help is available if you need it.

Take AI action: AI evolution audit

Before moving on to the next chapter of the book, it's important to evaluate your business's readiness. This audit pulls together everything from this chapter to help you identify your strengths, gaps, and opportunities for growth. Use the prompts below and the scoring system to evaluate where you stand today and create a simple action plan for moving forward.

Step 1: Reflect on your paradigm shifts

Which of the paradigm shifts resonates most with your business? Are there areas where your mindset or approach needs to evolve? What steps can you take to begin adopting these shifts?

For example, if shifting from 'Can AI do this?' to 'Should AI do this?' resonates, identify one area where ethical considerations could impact your decisions – such as data collection practices or customer interactions.

Step 2: Assess your current state

Assess your current state using the scoring system below.

Area	Score (1–5)	Notes/Actions
Relationships		Improve team communication through AI tools
Operations		Streamline workflows with automation
Strategy		Align AI initiatives with key business goals
Ethics and compliance		Evaluate AI vendors for privacy compliance

Scoring guide:

1: Needs significant work.

2: Minor progress has been made.

3: On track but with room to improve.

4: Well prepared, but still refining.

5: Fully optimised and aligned.

Step 3: Overcome your objections

Which of the previous objections feels most relevant to you? What perspective or strategy can help you move past it?

For example, if AI feels too complex, research simple tools like chatbots or scheduling assistants that are user-friendly and low-cost.

Step 4: Take action

Identify your strengths and priorities

- **Identify one strength to build on.** For example, strong client relationships could be enhanced with personalisation tools.
- **Identify one area to prioritise improving.** For example, streamline internal workflows to save time.

Create an action plan

- **Identify one small action to take this week.** For example, explore free trials for AI tools that could solve a specific problem.
- **Identify one longer-term goal for the next 90 days.** For example, streamline client onboarding with AI automation by next quarter.

Reflection

As you complete your audit, reflect on this question: what's the first, most impactful step I can take to make AI a tool for growth and trust in my business?

Not the end, just a smarter beginning

Remember, even though it's the last step in the framework, AI evolution is not a destination – it's a journey. The fact that you're taking the time to reflect, assess, and plan already puts you ahead of many businesses. Change can feel overwhelming, but every small, intentional step you take brings you closer to building a business that is more innovative, adaptable, and resilient. As you've learned throughout the book, REIMAGINING your business is not about mastering AI overnight or transforming everything at once. It's about starting where you are, using the tools and insights available to you, and evolving at a pace that aligns with your goals and values.

Each decision you make – whether it's implementing a new tool, refining a process, or strengthening your relationships – sets the foundation for a future where AI enhances what you do best. This journey isn't just about staying competitive; it's about leading with purpose, embracing progress responsibly, and shaping a future that works for your business, your team, and your clients. As you move forward, keep asking yourself: 'How can I use AI to make my business stronger, smarter, and more human?'

The answers will keep you aligned to your business values and guide you as you take the next steps on this exciting path.

CHAPTER 10

Embracing your AI future

'REIMAGINING your business isn't about reaching a destination – it's about recognising the progress you've made and using it to inspire what comes next. Every step forward is worth celebrating.'

Tracy Sheen

REIMAGINING: a moment to reflect

Congratulations! You've reached a pivotal moment in your AI journey. By working through the REIMAGINE Framework, you're well on your way to creating a business that is not only more efficient and future-ready but also deeply aligned with your values and relationships.

Take a moment to pause and reflect on the steps you've taken. REIMAGINING your business was never about instant transformations – it was about consistent, thoughtful progress. It was about giving you the tools, the confidence, and the permission to reimagine how your business could look. Every decision, every action, and every lesson has brought you closer to your vision for the future.

Take AI action: celebrate progress

You've achieved a lot. Let's take time to celebrate and capture the progress you've made through the REIMAGINE Framework.

Time commitment: 30 to 60 minutes.

Purpose: Celebrate your progress while identifying key insights to guide your next steps.

Step 1: Reflect on Your REIMAGINE journey

For each step in the REIMAGINE Framework, consider:

- **Relationships:** How have your connections with customers, your team, or your community evolved?
- **Evaluate:** What tools or systems have you improved or reimagined?
- **Identify:** Which quick wins made the most impact, and why?
- **Mapping:** How has creating a roadmap clarified your goals?
- **Activate:** What changes have you successfully implemented?

- **Gather:** What insights have you uncovered from your AI experiments?
- **Iterate:** How have you refined your approach to make it more effective?
- **Narrow:** What priorities have you focused on, and what results have emerged?
- **Evolve:** How has your mindset and business adapted for the future?

Step 2: Before and after snapshot

Think about where your business started versus where it is now:

- **Operations:** What processes feel more streamlined or efficient?
- **Customers:** How have you improved their experience?
- **Team:** How has your team benefited or changed?
- **You:** How has your perspective or confidence as a leader grown?

Step 3: Visualise your success

Create a visual representation of your progress and goals:

- **Timeline:** Chart your major milestones from the start of your REIMAGINE journey to today.
- **Mind map:** Illustrate key changes in operations, customer experience, and team dynamics.
- **Future vision:** Use your insights to map out the next step – what's one goal you'd like to achieve in the next phase?

Step 4: Celebrate and share

Share your reflection with your team or a trusted peer group:

- Host a small team workshop or meeting to highlight progress.
- Discuss how the lessons learned can be applied to future projects.
- Use this as an opportunity to gather feedback and ideas.

Building momentum for the future

This reflection isn't the end of your journey – it's a springboard to what comes next. You've built clarity, confidence, and a stronger foundation for your business.

Start this exercise solo to refine your vision, then consider bringing your team into the process. Their insights and shared celebration can amplify your progress and fuel your collective drive. As you celebrate your progress and reflect on your journey so far, it's essential to acknowledge one critical truth: the pace of change isn't just fast – it's *accelerating*. The next phase of your journey isn't solely about what you've achieved; it's about how you'll adapt and thrive in a world defined by rapid, constant evolution. Embracing change isn't optional – it's your greatest strength. This leads us to an essential mindset shift: the age of constant evolution.

The age of constant evolution

Think about how far technology has come in just a few years. In our lifetime, we've gone from landline phones to pagers and then to mobile phones. Dot matrix printers gave way to fax machines, which ultimately evolved into cloud computing. Emails transformed into text messages, MySpace paved the way for Facebook and YouTube, and social media revolutionised how we connect and communicate.

Cast your mind back to the early 1970s, when Patagonia began. At the time, many of us were still earning our pen licences in school. Imagining the way we communicate and do business today would have seemed as far-fetched as teleportation. And yet, here we are. Looking back over the last few years, it feels as though time itself is speeding up. Every week, something new demands our attention. Technology is evolving at an unprecedented pace, reshaping the world we live in, the way we work, and the expectations of our customers.

And this progress? It's only the beginning. Amy Webb, a renowned futurist, describes this period as a 'technology supercycle'. She explains that we are living through a constant wave of advancements – interlinked breakthroughs that fuel one another – creating a flywheel effect that's accelerating every year. From biotechnology and AI to smart devices and renewable energy, each leap forward sparks investment and innovation in the others.[9]

> *'The wave of innovation that's coming is so intense, and so potent, and so pervasive, it will literally reshape our human existence in ways that are exciting, good, and absolutely terrifying.'*
>
> Amy Webb[10]

For small businesses, this supercycle means one thing: staying static is no longer an option. Businesses that resist change are being left behind.

Thriving in the supercycle

The truth about thriving in today's relentless wave of technological evolution is this: you don't need to start by turning your business inside out. Success comes from taking focused, intentional steps

---

9 If the idea of the 'technology supercycle' resonates with you, you might enjoy exploring Amy Webb's work. Her insights into how technological advancements interconnect – and what that means for the future – can inspire fresh ways to think about your business. For a deeper dive, check out her book *The Signals Are Talking* or visit her website for more resources. I've added more details on Amy in the resources section of the book.

10 https://sunnewsaustin.com/2024/03/16/amy-webb-this-is-an-exhilarating-time-to-be-alive/

that align with your core mission while creating immediate, tangible results.

Consider the case studies shared throughout this book. Each business didn't begin their journey with grand overhauls or unlimited budgets. They started with curiosity, asking a simple question: 'What if?' Then, using the REIMAGINE Framework, they found one area where a small win was possible and drilled down until it became a reality.

Here's what thriving in the supercycle looks like:

- **Focused evolution:** Thriving in this supercycle isn't about chasing every new trend. It's about identifying one meaningful area to improve, where technology can create a ripple effect of efficiency and innovation. Start small, but dream big.
- **Accessible wins:** Each example shared in this book proves that small changes can yield big results. A simple scheduling tool, a chatbot for customer service, or AI to streamline inventory – these aren't expensive, but their impact can transform your operations.
- **Empowered teams:** Every project highlighted in this book also freed up valuable time for teams. Whether through automation or smarter tools, staff were empowered to focus on creative, customer-facing, or strategic tasks that drive growth.

And here's how to get your business thriving in the supercycle:

- **Pick your quick win:** Reflect on your business. What's the one task or process that drives you or your team crazy? That's often your gateway to thriving.
- **Commit to intentional growth:** Thriving doesn't mean doing it all. It's about focusing your energy where it matters most. As one business discovered, automating customer reminders saved hours and improved cash flow – a small step with big returns.

- **Test, learn, and refine:** Remember, thriving isn't about perfection. It's about iteration. You might need to tweak your approach, and that's okay. The key is to keep moving forward with purpose.

Ask 'What if?' and embrace possibility

The businesses that will thrive in this supercycle will all share one commonality. They will simply take the first step: they will ask, 'What if?' They will explore how technology could complement their existing business to solve a single challenge, and from there, they will build momentum.

What if AI could give you back 10 hours a week? What if automation meant you would never have to worry about missed appointments? What if technology allowed your team to focus on creativity and strategy instead of admin? Thriving will begin with curiosity – and it will be powered by action.

Take AI action: where do you need to evolve?

Take a moment to reflect on your own business:

- What part of your operations feels stuck in the past?
- Are there bottlenecks, repetitive tasks, or customer frustrations you can address with technology?
- How can you use AI, automation, or other tools to save time and deliver more value?

Start small. Focus on one area that can have a ripple effect.

Adaptability is about staying open, curious, and intentional – ready to reimagine what's possible and turn opportunities into advantages. Every decision you make today to evolve your business brings you closer to reimagining your operations and creating something truly impactful.

Sustainability and AI

When we think about AI, sustainability isn't usually the first thing that comes to mind. Most of us focus on what AI can do – increase efficiencies, save time, or streamline processes. But there's a much bigger conversation to be had.

What does sustainability in AI mean?

Sustainability isn't just a buzzword – today it's a business imperative. While AI can streamline operations and unlock efficiencies, its environmental impact is a conversation every business owner needs to engage with. By understanding the hidden costs of AI and making conscious choices, you can align your technological adoption with your values.

Sustainability in AI means ensuring that the development, deployment, and operation of AI systems minimise their environmental footprint. While this might not be the first thing you think about when adopting AI, it's crucial to consider how the tools you use affect the planet.

'I'm just a small business – what difference can I make?'

For many of us, being a small business doesn't mean we think small. We often have strong ethics and a moral compass guiding everything we do. From the suppliers we choose to the practices we adopt, we strive to make decisions that align with our values – and environmental impact is often high on that list. But when it comes to AI, this consideration might bring up new questions that we haven't yet thought about.

Our choices matter

As a small business owner, the tools you select, how you use them, and the companies you partner with all contribute to the environmental impact of AI. Even small decisions, like choosing energy-efficient software or optimising your tool usage, can make a big difference.

Consider these questions:

- Are the AI tools you're using optimised for energy and water efficiency?
- Do your providers rely on renewable energy to power their operations?
- Are they transparent about their carbon and water footprints?

The answers to these questions can help ensure that your business continues to reflect the values you care about most – whether it's sustainability, community responsibility, or ethical innovation.

How this relates to your business

You've worked hard to ensure your business reflects your values – sourcing sustainable products, reducing waste, or giving back to your community. Now think about your digital operations. Could the AI tools you're using align better with those same values?

Consider these questions:

- Do you need a data-heavy AI tool running constantly, or can you schedule it to operate only during key business hours?
- Are your AI providers transparent about their energy use or efforts to offset their environmental impact?
- Could you prioritise tools designed to minimise energy consumption, or work with companies committed to renewable energy and water-efficient practices?

The hidden costs of AI

I'm the first to sing the praises of the many benefits AI offers business owners. After all, that's the entire premise of this book – to help you reimagine what's possible for your business. But it would be remiss of me to focus only on the shiny, positive side without scratching beneath the surface to explore its environmental impact.

We all have a responsibility to be informed, to understand not just the benefits but also the challenges and the compromises. The environmental footprint of AI systems can be significant. For example:

- Training a single AI model can emit as much carbon as five cars over their entire lifetimes.[11]
- Data centres, the backbone of AI, consume about 1 to 1.5% of global electricity – a number that is growing rapidly.[12]
- Data centres can use millions of litres of water annually to keep servers cool, often in regions where water scarcity is already a concern.[13]

Take AI action: your sustainable AI strategy

Take 10 minutes to review your current tools and providers:

- List the AI tools you're using.
- Research each provider's energy and water policies.
- Identify one action you can take to reduce your AI footprint – whether it's choosing a greener provider, optimising usage, or offsetting emissions.

---

11 https://www.technologyreview.com/2019/06/06/239031/training-a-single-ai-model-can-emit-as-much-carbon-as-five-cars-in-their-lifetimes

12 https://www.iea.org/energy-system/buildings/data-centres-and-data-transmission-networks

13 https://davidmytton.blog/how-much-water-do-data-centers-use

Three steps to reduce your AI footprint

Sustainability doesn't mean sacrificing innovation. Instead, it's about adopting smarter, more responsible practices. Here are three ways you can reduce the environmental impact of your AI tools:

- **Choose energy- and water-efficient tools:** Partner with providers who prioritise sustainability, using renewable energy, transparent carbon and water reporting, and optimised systems.
- **Offset your carbon footprint:** Explore built-in or third-party offset programmes to mitigate AI's environmental impact.
- **Optimise usage:** Reduce resource consumption by scheduling AI processes during off-peak hours, using lightweight algorithms, and running tools only when necessary.

Where businesses go wrong

Here's where I've seen businesses put too much trust in AI, leading to preventable pitfalls.

Blind trust in automation

AI is a powerful tool, but trusting it blindly can lead to costly mistakes. When automation runs without monitoring or review, errors go unnoticed until they escalate, causing inefficiencies and customer dissatisfaction. The key is to regularly evaluate your AI tools – test their outputs, ensure they align with your business needs, and refine them as necessary. AI should support decision-making, not replace oversight.

Forgetting the human touch

AI can streamline processes, but in areas where relationships matter most, overreliance on automation can make clients feel undervalued or ignored. This weakens trust, loyalty, and long-term engagement. Go back to step one of the framework and use AI to enhance, not replace, human connection. Whether it's customer service, sales, or brand interactions, AI should free up time for deeper, more meaningful personal engagement.

Over-automating creativity

AI can generate ideas and optimise workflows, but when teams depend on it too much for creative tasks, results become bland and repetitive. This can cause content, campaigns, or product ideas to lose their spark, leading to customer disengagement. Instead, revisit the Iterate step of the framework – use AI as a brainstorming partner, not the sole creator. Keeping humans at the helm ensures originality, innovation, and a creative edge.

The costs of overreliance on AI

Any business that places too much faith in AI risks:

- **Alienating clients:** Impersonal AI interactions can weaken relationships.
- **Eroding trust:** Mistakes made by AI can make customers question your reliability.
- **Stifling innovation:** Overusing AI for problem-solving can dull your team's creative edge.

How to balance AI with human judgment

Here are three simple ways to keep AI working *with* you, not *for* you:

- **Check outputs:** Review AI decisions regularly. Are they accurate? Do they align with your values?

- **Define roles:** Decide what tasks AI can handle and what needs human involvement.
- **Train your team:** The true power of AI isn't in the tools themselves – it's in the people who use them.

The big opportunity: train your team

If we are truly REIMAGINING our business with relationships at the centre, there are clear opportunities to empower your team from the start. By equipping them with knowledge, confidence, and clarity, you ensure AI enhances collaboration, not replaces it.

Here are six steps to embed AI effectively with your team:

1. **Educate on the role of AI:** Ensure your team understands AI enhances, rather than replaces, their expertise. Host a short workshop to explain its capabilities and limitations.
2. **Establish clear guidelines:** Define roles for AI and your team. Create a simple 'AI Do's and Don'ts' guide to clarify when AI should assist and when human oversight is needed.
3. **Encourage feedback loops:** Gather team insights on AI performance. Set up regular review sessions to identify inefficiencies and refine processes.
4. **Provide role-specific training:** Tailor AI training to each role so team members see its direct benefits. Quick-start guides or tutorials can support adoption.
5. **Foster a culture of collaboration:** Reinforce that AI supports human creativity and judgment. Celebrate successes where AI and human effort work together.
6. **Tie everything back to the REIMAGINE Framework:** Use the framework to refine AI's role, adjust workflows, and keep customer relationships a priority.

Take AI action: key tips for training your team

- Host a workshop to introduce AI tools and address team concerns.
- Create clear guidelines with an 'AI Do's and Don'ts' document.
- Celebrate successes that combine AI and human ingenuity.

With great data comes great responsibility

There's another critical piece of the AI puzzle we need to address: data. Data isn't just the fuel for AI; in my opinion, it's the most valuable business resource in the world. Every organisation is on the hunt for more of it, and they'll do whatever it takes to get it. They'll purchase it, solicit it, partner for it – and sometimes even steal it. Remember Cambridge Analytica?

Every interaction, every transaction, every click – it all generates data. This data powers the personalised experiences your customers love. It's the key to making smarter decisions, running efficient operations, and staying competitive. But with great data comes great responsibility. How you manage and protect it isn't just about compliance; it's about trust – the trust of your clients, your team, and your community.

So here's the big question: what are we trading in exchange for convenience? How much of our data, or our customers' data, are we willing to hand over for tools that make our lives a little easier? And perhaps most importantly, do these choices align with our values and priorities as business owners? Let's take a closer look at what it means to trade data for convenience – and how we can do so thoughtfully and responsibly.

Trading data for convenience

We're about to explore what happens when you trade a little data for convenience – and it's probably going to freak you out. A lot. But stick with me, because this isn't just about giving you the heebie-jeebies. This is about helping you understand the world we're already living in, where data is currency and AI is becoming part of our daily reality. So, grab a coffee – or maybe something stronger – and prepare yourself for a 'holy crap' moment or two.

Let's start with something relatable – because this is a choice we've all made, knowingly or not.

I've just come home from picking up a few groceries. These days, I like to use the self-checkout where possible. Part of that process is always scanning your loyalty card – whether it's Flybuys, Everyday Rewards, or another programme. I mean, why not, right? Last Christmas, Pete and I 'banked' around $100 towards our Christmas shop. With the rising cost of living, saving a few dollars off your groceries or earning points towards a future discount feels like a no-brainer.

But have you ever stopped to think about what you're giving away in exchange for that small convenience? That one harmless interaction provides businesses with a flood of information about you – what you buy, where you shop, how often you visit, and even how you pay. Now, multiply that across other stores linked to these grocery chains – Target, Kmart, Big W, Myer – and suddenly they have a comprehensive profile of you: the brands you prefer, the types of products you buy, and even insights into your lifestyle. With sophisticated data analytics, companies can predict your age group, gender, income level, and even approximate your home address based on your shopping habits.

This level of insight isn't limited to supermarkets. Think about Starbucks. Their loyalty cards and mobile apps track everything:

what coffee you drink, where you buy it, and when. With this data, they predict your purchasing behaviour and tailor their marketing efforts accordingly. It's impressive, yes, but also a little unsettling. You might be thinking, *Okay, that's freaky, but these are the big guys. They have money to burn, so of course they're doing whatever it takes to gain access to this kind of information. As a small business, I don't have that kind of reach or power.*

And this is where we need to pause. Because while you might not be tracking your customers' every move like Starbucks or Amazon, you're already engaging with powerful data tools every day, such as Facebook, Instagram, Google, and LinkedIn. These platforms aren't just where you scroll as a user; they're also where you reach and engage your audience as a business owner.

You may not have the resources of a giant retailer, but how you collect and handle customer data matters. Misusing or mishandling data can break trust, damage your reputation, and even land you in legal trouble. By being aware of what's happening in the wider world of data collection, you can ensure your own business stays ethical, transparent, and on the right side of both your customers and the law.

Data as a commodity

User data has become a highly profitable commodity, with companies buying, selling, and trading it – often without explicit consent. This commodification of personal information raises serious ethical concerns. Third-party cookies track users across websites, allowing platforms to sell targeted ad space based on collected data. Most users are unaware that their information is being monetised, which can lead to feelings of exploitation when they find out. For businesses, engaging in questionable data practices can result in regulatory fines, loss of customer trust, and reputational damage. When data collection crosses the line from questionable to harmful, it can get ugly. Privacy breaches, manipulative tactics, and unethical surveillance expose customers to significant risks. The 2017 Equifax breach, for example, compromised the personal data of 147 million people, while Facebook's 2019 data leak exposed phone numbers and account details of 419 million users.

Beyond breaches, platforms increasingly use algorithms to influence user behaviour – whether to keep them scrolling, nudge them towards certain purchases, or even shape their opinions. Social media algorithms amplify emotionally charged content to maximise engagement, while 'dark patterns' in e-commerce trick users into spending more through false urgency timers or hard-to-find unsubscribe buttons. This kind of behavioural manipulation undermines user autonomy and can make customers feel deceived.

Then there's surveillance capitalism – the commodification of personal data to predict and influence behaviour at scale. Apps that track location data even when not in use, or AI-driven surveillance systems that monitor individuals without their knowledge, highlight the ethical concerns of consent and power in the digital age. Many users feel powerless against these practices, as opting out often means disconnecting entirely from essential digital services.

Take AI action: a data checklist for small business owners

This checklist is built around the REIMAGINE Framework. This approach will help you guide your data practices with intention, transparency, and purpose. Use it to align your business with ethical and forward-thinking data strategies.

Relationships

How does your data collection strengthen or weaken relationships with customers, employees, and partners?

- Are you transparent with customers about what data you collect and why?
- Do you communicate the value customers receive in exchange for their data?
- Are your employees trained in ethical data handling and customer trust?

Include a clear and concise data policy on your website, and make it easy for customers to access.

Evaluate

Assess your current data practices to ensure they align with your goals and values.

- Have you audited the data you collect, including its purpose and storage?
- Are you only collecting data that is truly necessary for your operations?
- Have you reviewed third-party tools and platforms to ensure they align with your ethical standards?

Create a simple data inventory that tracks what you collect, why you collect it, and how it's used.

Identify

Recognise opportunities for improvement and innovation in your data practices.

- Have you identified gaps in transparency or compliance with data regulations?
- Are there areas where you can better educate customers about data use?

- Have you pinpointed opportunities to improve customer experiences with better data insights?

Use customer feedback to identify weak points in your data practices and develop solutions.

Mapping

Create a roadmap for responsible data collection and usage.

- Have you outlined a plan for how data flows through your business?
- Do you have clear steps for obtaining customer consent for data collection?
- Have you mapped out potential risks and mitigation strategies?

Develop a simple flowchart showing how data is collected, processed, and used in your business.

Activate

Take action to implement transparent and ethical data strategies.

- Have you updated privacy policies to reflect current practices?
- Have you communicated with customers about how their data benefits them?
- Have you trained your team to handle data responsibly and securely?

Host a team workshop to review data policies and ensure everyone understands their role in maintaining trust.

Gather

Collect feedback and insights to refine your approach.

- Are you gathering feedback from customers about their data concerns and expectations?
- Do you monitor how well your current data strategies are working?
- Are you using analytics to identify trends and opportunities for improvement?

Set up a quarterly review to gather insights from both customers and team members on data practices.

Iterate

Brainstorm ways to innovate using data while prioritising transparency and trust.

- Have you explored new ways to use data to enhance customer experiences?
- Are you considering how transparency could be a competitive advantage?
- Have you looked for ways to simplify your data practices to reduce complexity?

Schedule a brainstorming session with your team to ideate creative but ethical data-driven initiatives.

Narrow

Focus on the most impactful data practices to streamline efforts.

- Have you prioritised which data practices add the most value to your business and customers?
- Are you eliminating unnecessary or redundant data collection methods?
- Do you focus on quality over quantity in your data collection?

Identify one area of your business where simplifying data practices would create immediate benefits.

Evolve

Adapt your data strategies to stay ahead of changes in technology, regulations, and customer expectations.

- Are you staying informed about data privacy laws and trends?
- Do you have a plan to regularly update your data practices as technology evolves?

- Are you prepared to integrate AI tools responsibly as they become more common?

Schedule an annual review of your data policies and strategies to ensure they're current and effective.

By integrating the REIMAGINE Framework into your data practices, you position your business as a leader in transparency, ethics, and trust. Use this checklist as your guide to navigate the evolving digital landscape while staying true to your values.

Data as a foundation for your REIMAGINED future

We've explored the intricate web of data – what's collected, how it's gathered, and the profound implications it has for our clients and our business. Data is more than just information; it's the lifeblood of AI and the fuel that drives digital innovation. As you've discovered throughout your journey along the REIMAGINE Framework, the power of data lies not in its collection but in how you use it to create meaningful outcomes for your business and customers.

Data is actionable. By integrating data insights into your strategy, you've already taken steps to reimagine your business for an AI-driven future. Ethical, transparent data practices set you apart, building trust with customers and reinforcing your brand's values. Each step of the REIMAGINE Framework – whether it's evaluating your current practices or gathering customer insights – has equipped you with the tools to use data responsibly and effectively.

CHAPTER 11

What's your übermorgen?

'REIMAGINING your business means actively creating the future you want – with relationships at the core and technology as your support partner. It's about staying curious, embracing change, and leaning in with purpose.'

Tracy Sheen

What's your übermorgen?

In 2023, South by Southwest (SXSW), a global event renowned for its leading-edge exploration of creativity, innovation, and technology, came to Sydney. Originating in Austin, Texas, SXSW has long been the meeting ground for visionaries from every field, blending music, film, and interactive technology into a week-long festival of ideas. From the opening keynote by futurist Amy Webb, I was hooked. These were my people, and this was my playground. In 2024, the line-up included another futurist, Brian David Johnson. Brian (or BJ, as he calls himself) is known for his work helping companies imagine and prepare for their futures. During his keynote, he introduced a concept that's stuck with me ever since: *übermorgen*. This German word translates literally to 'the day after tomorrow', but Brian framed it differently.

In the context of business, übermorgen asks, 'What's the thing after the thing?'

It's not just about planning for your next big move but envisioning the step beyond that – what comes *after* AI, *after* automation, *after* your business embraces its next transformation.

I couldn't help but think of Atlassian, the Australian software giant that seems to live in the realm of übermorgen. From reshaping team collaboration with Jira and Confluence to acquiring Trello for non-technical teams, they've mastered the art of anticipating what's next. Today, Atlassian is embedding AI into its products with tools like Atlassian Intelligence and their acquisitions of Loom and Rewatch, but their sights are clearly set on the hybrid, AI-first future where real-time simulations and asynchronous communication define work.

Reimagining the day after tomorrow

Übermorgen. Apart from possibly being the coolest word I've ever come across, it's also a challenge – a mindset that pushes us to think beyond the immediate application of AI or any other new technology. It asks, 'Once we've mastered today's tools, what's next?'

And here's the thing: übermorgen isn't reserved for big corporations with think tanks and deep pockets. It's an ethos – a way of thinking I've embedded into my own business conversations. I believe it's something you can (and should) weave into your own approach to future planning. In this chapter, I'll guide you through the trends shaping the future of business and help you begin charting your own übermorgen. Whether it's new technologies like AI agents or multimodal systems, or cultural shifts like ethical AI governance, this is your chance to embrace the day after tomorrow with clarity, curiosity, and purpose.

Emerging technologies

If we're going to embrace this style of thinking, it's essential to understand the key technologies and shifts already emerging on the horizon. And here's the important part: these innovations aren't reserved for big corporations. They're tools and ideas that small businesses, like yours and mine, can harness to stay ahead. (Oh, and just a quick note on timing … The thing about discussing technology in print is how quickly it can become outdated. You'll notice I've avoided diving into specific tools, platforms, or software. That's intentional. I don't want this book to feel obsolete the moment it's published. By focusing on the concept of reimagining and using the REIMAGINE Framework, you'll have a systematic and structured way to assess and adopt whatever tools or software best suit your needs.)

If you were hoping to find a list of the latest and greatest tech, don't worry – you can still get that! Just join my community or find your own circle of trusted advisers to stay on top of the latest trends.

Around the corner: what's coming in the next 12 months

That said, let's take a look at some technologies and trends already available (not all – we'd be here for years if I included everything) which I believe will play an even bigger role for small businesses in the very near future.

AI agents: autonomous efficiency

AI agents manage entire processes, handling tasks like scheduling, inventory updates, and customer service. They reduce manual work, allowing businesses to focus on strategy and innovation.

Companies already using it

Amazon's AI agents power fulfilment operations, from payment processing to delivery scheduling. Uber leverages AI for ride matching, surge pricing, and route optimisation.

How small businesses can use it

AI agents can streamline operations across industries:

- **Hospitality:** Manage guest bookings, send check-in details, and offer personalised recommendations. This reduces staff workload, enhances the guest experience, and increases upsells.
- **E-commerce:** Monitor stock, reorder inventory, and provide product recommendations. This prevents stockouts, reduces administrative time, and improves customer satisfaction.

- **Professional services (such as accountants and consultants):** Automate appointment reminders and routine paperwork. This saves time, prevents missed deadlines, and strengthens client relationships.
- **Brick-and-mortar retailers:** Analyse sales trends and suggest pricing or promotions. This increases revenue through data-driven strategies while reducing manual analysis.

Potential pitfalls

While AI agents provide significant advantages, businesses should consider these challenges:

- **Overreliance on automation:** AI agents can make interactions feel robotic, leading to a less personal experience.
- **Integration:** Implementing AI systems requires investment and technical expertise.
- **Customer experience risks:** Poorly designed AI may misinterpret complex queries, causing frustration.

Outlook

AI agents will integrate with voice assistants, Internet of Things (IoT), and Augmented Reality (AR), enabling more seamless automation. Expect advancements in predictive decision-making and workflow management.

Multimodal AI: enhanced interactions

Multimodal AI integrates text, visuals, and audio to create seamless, context-aware interactions. This enhances engagement by providing richer, more adaptive customer experiences.

Companies already using it

Google's multimodal AI delivers search results with text, images, and videos. Canva uses it to suggest design elements based on user prompts.

How small businesses can use it

Multimodal AI can enhance customer interactions in several ways:

- **Travel agents:** Offer interactive trip previews with videos, itineraries, and recommendations. This increases bookings by giving customers a preview of their trip.
- **Financial planners:** Build dashboards with charts, summaries, and interactive tools. This simplifies complex financial concepts and improves client understanding.
- **Professional services:** Create tutorials combining written guides, visuals, and voiceovers. This improves client comprehension and engagement.

Potential pitfalls

Despite its advantages, multimodal AI presents some challenges:

- **Data overload:** Excessive information can overwhelm small teams.
- **Cost barriers:** Advanced implementations may require significant investment.

Outlook

Expect further integration with voice assistants, wearable devices, and Virtual Reality (VR), enabling interactive product demos and immersive learning experiences.

Hyper-personalisation: bespoke experiences

Hyper-personalisation uses AI to tailor customer interactions based on behavioural, demographic, and transactional data, delivering bespoke experiences.

Companies already using it

Netflix, Spotify, and Amazon personalise recommendations and shopping experiences based on user habits.

How small businesses can use it

AI-driven personalisation can boost engagement and sales:

- **E-commerce:** Customise email campaigns based on browsing and purchase behaviour. This boosts click-through rates and increases sales.
- **Hospitality:** Offer personalised upgrades or dining experiences based on past preferences. This enhances the guest experience and drives revenue.
- **Franchises:** Run hyper-localised promotions tailored to specific regions. This attracts more foot traffic by offering relevant deals.

Potential pitfalls

Businesses should consider the following risks:

- **Privacy concerns:** Customers may be wary of extensive data collection.
- **Complex implementation:** Requires strong data analytics capabilities to execute effectively.

Outlook

Real-time AI personalisation will evolve, allowing businesses to adjust offers dynamically based on live customer behaviour.

Ethical AI governance: building trust

Ethical AI governance ensures transparency, fairness, and responsible data use, helping businesses maintain trust and compliance.

Companies already using it

Apple processes AI requests on devices rather than in the cloud to enhance user privacy.

How small businesses can use it

Businesses can strengthen trust through responsible AI practices:

- **Accountants:** Ensure compliance with GDPR when using AI analytics. This avoids legal risks and builds client trust.
- **Retailers:** Provide transparent explanations of how loyalty programme data is used. This fosters customer confidence and engagement.
- **Consultants:** Develop policies for AI-enabled tools used with clients. This enhances credibility and reinforces ethical integrity.

Potential pitfalls

Despite its importance, ethical AI governance presents challenges:

- **Complex implementation:** Governance frameworks take time and resources to establish.
- **Lack of awareness:** Employees may need training on responsible AI use.

Outlook

As AI regulations tighten, businesses that prioritise ethical AI practices will gain a competitive advantage in privacy-conscious markets.

Green AI and sustainability technologies: minimising environmental impact

Green AI minimises environmental impact by improving energy efficiency and reducing waste, making sustainability more accessible.

Companies already using it

UPS's AI-driven ORION system optimises delivery routes, reducing fuel consumption. Google uses AI to improve data centre energy efficiency.

How small businesses can use it

Sustainability-focused AI applications can lower costs and improve efficiency:

- **Hospitality:** AI monitors energy use in rooms, adjusting lighting and temperature based on occupancy. This reduces operational costs and demonstrates sustainability commitment.
- **Retailers:** AI optimises delivery routes for local shipments. This cuts down on fuel costs and improves delivery times.
- **Agribusiness:** Sensors and AI reduce water waste in irrigation. This saves resources while improving crop yields.

Potential pitfalls

Businesses should be aware of these challenges:

- **Implementation costs:** Initial setup may require investment.
- **Limited awareness:** Employees may need training to maximise impact.

Outlook

Green AI will integrate with IoT, allowing businesses to automate energy-efficient operations and track sustainability efforts.

Blockchain for business: enhancing transparency and security

Blockchain provides a decentralised, secure way to record transactions, enhancing transparency and security across industries.

Companies already using it

IBM's Food Trust tracks food supply chains, while Walmart uses blockchain for produce traceability.

How small businesses can use it

Blockchain applications can improve security and trust:

- **Retailers:** Use blockchain to verify ethically sourced products. This builds customer trust and enhances brand reputation.
- **Accountants:** Automate and secure financial records. This reduces errors and improves audit readiness.
- **E-commerce:** Implement blockchain-based payment systems. This minimises fraud and streamlines transactions.

Potential pitfalls

Businesses should consider these blockchain challenges:

- **Complexity:** Understanding and implementing blockchain requires technical expertise.
- **Cost:** Early adoption can be expensive and resource-intensive.

Outlook

Blockchain will expand into customer loyalty programmes and supply chain management, with more affordable solutions emerging for small businesses.

Take AI action: find your quick win

Identify one repetitive task or area of inefficiency within your business and explore one of the emerging technology solutions, such as an AI agent or IoT-enabled sensor, that you could use to address it.

How long it takes

One to two hours to brainstorm and research.

Who to include

Solo business owners: Complete independently.

Small teams: Involve one or two team members familiar with the task to share insights.

Remote teams: Use collaborative tools (for example, Zoom or Google Docs) for input.

Steps

1. Review the REIMAGINE Framework.
2. Work through the first four steps of the REIMAGINE Framework with your chosen technology in mind:

   Relationships: Identify which team or client relationship would benefit most from solving this inefficiency. Consider how improving this task would affect collaboration, productivity, or customer satisfaction.

   Evaluate: Assess what tools you're already using. Could they be upgraded or adapted to include the identified technology? Research which tools or platforms are likely to integrate your chosen technology in the near future. Evaluate the return on investment (ROI) by estimating the time or costs saved.

   Identify: Consider the costs, ease of implementation, and the expected impact on your operations. Ask yourself: will this solution save time, improve accuracy, or enhance the customer experience?

Mapping: Using the mapping exercise from chapter 4, outline a basic plan to activate your chosen opportunity. Include steps for research, testing, and evaluating success.

Conduct a quick pilot (optional)

If feasible, trial a low-risk version of the chosen solution for a week or month to gather real-world insights before a full rollout.

This exercise demonstrates how identifying and addressing inefficiencies with emerging technology can improve relationships, reduce costs, and set the stage for a more innovative business. It's a small but powerful first step towards reimagining your business for the future.

Mid-range: what's coming in the next one to two years

3D printing: additive manufacturing

Additive manufacturing creates products layer by layer using materials such as plastics, metals, or composites. It is ideal for rapid prototyping, small-batch production, and highly customised items.

Companies already using it

Boeing uses 3D printing to produce lightweight aircraft components, while Adidas manufactures customisable soles for running shoes.

How small businesses can use it

Small manufacturers can use 3D printing to improve production efficiency and customisation:

- **Prototyping:** Quickly create prototypes without expensive moulds or tooling. This reduces time to market and lowers research and development costs.

- **Customisation:** Offer bespoke products or small-batch production runs for clients. This increases customer satisfaction and diversifies revenue streams.
- **Spare parts:** Print replacement parts on demand instead of maintaining large inventories. This cuts storage costs and reduces downtime.

Outlook

Advancements in 3D printing will introduce stronger and more versatile materials. AI integration will enable optimised designs, while blockchain will enhance secure production authentication.

Cobots: collaborative robots

Cobots are designed to work alongside humans, assisting with repetitive or physically demanding tasks while maintaining safety in shared workspaces.

Companies already using it

Universal Robots supplies cobots used in assembly lines, packaging, and quality control, particularly for small and medium-sized enterprises.

How small businesses can use it

Cobots can enhance productivity in manufacturing and logistics:

- **Assembly:** Assist workers with repetitive tasks such as screwing, welding, or sorting. This increases productivity without replacing human roles.
- **Packaging:** Automate packing and palletising to meet higher demand efficiently. This reduces labour costs and speeds up operations.

- **Quality control:** Use AI-powered vision systems to inspect products for defects. This ensures consistent quality and reduces waste.

Outlook

Cobots are becoming more affordable and adaptable for smaller operations. Future developments will incorporate advanced AI for greater decision-making autonomy and predictive maintenance through IoT integration.

Internet of Things (IoT): improve efficiency and decision-making

IoT connects smart devices to automate and optimise business operations. In the future, IoT will revolutionise how businesses monitor, analyse, and respond to real-time data.

Companies already using it

Amazon's Alexa ecosystem connects smart devices, while John Deere uses IoT-enabled tractors to monitor field conditions in real time.

How small businesses can use it

IoT can improve efficiency and decision-making in various industries:

- **Hospitality:** Install smart thermostats and lighting systems that adjust automatically based on guest occupancy. This reduces energy waste and enhances guest comfort.
- **Brick-and-mortar retailers:** Use IoT sensors to monitor foot traffic and optimise store layouts. This improves sales by maximising high-traffic areas.
- **Agribusiness:** Deploy IoT sensors to track soil moisture, weather, and crop conditions. This boosts yield and reduces resource use.

Potential pitfalls

Despite its benefits, IoT presents challenges:

- **Security risks:** IoT devices can be vulnerable to cyberattacks.
- **Integration complexity:** Ensuring all devices communicate effectively can be a challenge.

Outlook

IoT will continue to integrate with AI for predictive maintenance and dynamic decision-making. Small businesses may soon use IoT for automated inventory reordering and customer demand forecasting.

Biometric technologies: identification and security

Biometric technology uses physical and behavioural characteristics, such as fingerprints, voice, and facial recognition, for identification and security.

Companies already using it

Apple's Face ID and Touch ID are widely used biometric tools, while Delta Airlines uses facial recognition at select airports for check-in and boarding.

How small businesses can use it

Biometrics can enhance security and personalisation:

- **Retailers:** Use facial recognition for personalised in-store experiences, such as greeting customers by name. This improves customer engagement and loyalty.
- **Hospitality:** Implement voice recognition for room controls or concierge services. This enhances guest convenience.
- **Accountants:** Add biometric authentication for secure access to client data. This strengthens security and builds trust.

Potential pitfalls

Businesses should consider the following risks:

- **Privacy concerns:** Customers may be hesitant to share biometric data.
- **Technical barriers:** Implementing biometrics requires a robust infrastructure.

Outlook

Biometrics will evolve to include multi-factor systems, combining physical recognition with behavioural data for enhanced security and personalisation.

AGO systems: autonomous goal-oriented intelligence

AGO (autonomous goal-oriented) systems use AI to set, pursue, and achieve complex goals with minimal human intervention, continuously learning and adapting.

Companies already using it

OpenAI has integrated AGO-like capabilities into its advanced models for automating complex problem-solving. Microsoft incorporates AGO intelligence into its Azure platform for workflow management.

How small businesses can use it

AGO systems can automate decision-making in various industries:

- **Financial planners:** Manage entire client portfolios, automatically rebalancing investments based on market trends. This saves time and improves client outcomes.
- **Franchises:** Automate and optimise local marketing campaigns, adjusting strategies based on performance data. This increases campaign return on investment with minimal oversight.

- **Manufacturing:** Autonomously schedule production workflows, monitor machine performance, and order replacement parts before failures occur. This reduces downtime and improves operational efficiency.

Potential pitfalls

Businesses should consider these challenges:

- **Overreliance:** Human oversight is needed to ensure AI aligns with broader business goals.
- **Complexity:** Implementing AGO systems requires a clear understanding of objectives and sufficient data for training.

Outlook

AGO systems will expand into workflow management and IoT integration. Retailers may use AGO to adjust store layouts dynamically based on foot traffic patterns.

Digital twins: virtual simulations for real-world success

Digital twins are virtual replicas of physical objects, processes, or systems, enabling businesses to simulate, test, and optimise operations before making real-world changes.

Companies already using it

BMW simulates and refines production line workflows using digital twins, while GE monitors industrial equipment performance with the technology.

How small businesses can use it

Digital twins can drive innovation in various industries:

- **Agribusiness:** Simulate crop growth under different conditions to optimise planting schedules. This maximises yield and reduces waste.
- **Hospitality:** Test new restaurant layouts virtually to improve customer flow and reduce wait times before making physical changes. This saves costs and improves customer satisfaction.
- **Manufacturing:** Simulate production line changes to identify bottlenecks. This minimises downtime and improves scalability.

Potential pitfalls

While digital twins offer significant benefits, challenges include the following:

- **High initial costs:** Developing a digital twin requires significant investment in software and expertise.
- **Data dependency:** Accurate digital twins require high-quality sensor data.

Outlook

Digital twins will integrate with AI and IoT, allowing for real-time updates. Retailers may soon use digital twins to test inventory placement strategies based on live sales data.

Decentralised autonomous organisations (DAOs): distributed decision-making

DAOs are organisations run by blockchain-based smart contracts, allowing decentralised decision-making without traditional hierarchies.

Companies already using it

ConstitutionDAO raised funds to bid on a rare copy of the US Constitution, showcasing the power of decentralised collective action.

How small businesses can use it

DAOs can improve transparency and collaboration in various sectors:

- **Franchises:** Create a DAO for franchisees to vote on marketing strategies or operational changes. This promotes transparency and empowers franchise owners.
- **Professional services:** Use a DAO to manage shared resources or investments. This reduces administrative overhead and enhances trust.
- **E-commerce:** Build a DAO for community-driven product development, where customers vote on new features or designs. This strengthens customer loyalty.

Outlook

As blockchain technology matures, DAOs could become a standard for managing partnerships and community-driven initiatives, with simplified platforms making them accessible to small businesses.

Synthetic data: making innovation more accessible

Synthetic data is artificially generated information that mimics real-world data while maintaining privacy. It is used to train AI models, perform simulations, and analyse trends without exposing sensitive information.

Companies already using it

Meta (which owns Facebook, Instagram and WhatsApp) uses synthetic data to train AI models without violating user privacy.

Healthcare organisations use synthetic patient data for research while ensuring compliance with privacy laws.

How small businesses can use it

Synthetic data can support AI development, analysis, and decision-making across industries:

- **E-commerce:** Generate synthetic customer profiles to test marketing strategies. This enables experimentation without compromising real customer data.
- **Professional services:** Train AI tools for sentiment analysis using synthetic client communications. This improves AI accuracy without risking confidentiality.
- **Retailers:** Use synthetic transaction data to forecast sales trends and optimise inventory. This reduces reliance on limited historical data.

Potential pitfalls

While synthetic data offers advantages, there are challenges to consider:

- **Accuracy limits:** Synthetic data may not fully capture the nuances of real-world behaviour.
- **Data complexity:** Creating high-quality synthetic data requires technical expertise.

Outlook

As privacy regulations tighten, synthetic data will play a larger role in AI training and business analytics. Small businesses may soon access ready-made synthetic datasets tailored to their industries, making innovation more accessible while ensuring compliance with data protection laws.

Take AI action: explore the next-level opportunity

Identify a mid-term technology, such as cobots, additive manufacturing, or IoT, that aligns with your business goals, and create a roadmap for gradual integration.

How long it takes

Allocate three to four **hours** for brainstorming, mapping, and initial research.

Who to include

- **Solo business owners:** Complete the exercise independently, but consider consulting industry peers or advisers for external perspectives.
- **Small teams:** Engage team leaders or tech-savvy members to contribute insights and help shape the roadmap.
- **Remote teams:** Use collaborative tools like Miro, Microsoft Teams, or Asana to gather input and build consensus virtually.

Steps

1. Review the REIMAGINE Framework. Use the framework to evaluate the potential of your chosen mid-term technology and begin planning for its adoption:
   - **Assess relationships:** Identify who will benefit most from this technology – team members, customers, or suppliers – and evaluate how its adoption could impact these relationships positively or negatively.
   - **Evaluate feasibility:** Consider costs, required skills, and available resources. Research case studies of businesses in your sector that have successfully implemented similar technology.
   - **Identify key focus areas:** Determine which part of your business would benefit most and define clear outcomes,

  such as increased productivity, reduced costs, or improved accuracy.
  - **Map an adoption plan:** Develop a phased roadmap for implementation, including steps like team training, vendor selection, and pilot testing.
2. Create two scenarios for how this technology might transform your business in the next one to two years:
   - **Best case:** What's the ideal outcome if the integration goes smoothly?
   - **Worst case:** What challenges might arise, and how would you mitigate them?
3. Engage your team:
   - Hold a brainstorming session to gather ideas and feedback on how this technology could be integrated into your workflows.
   - Assign a champion within your team to lead the research or pilot phase.

This exercise empowers businesses to explore mid-term technologies strategically while minimising risk. By using the REIMAGINE Framework, you ensure that your approach is grounded in relationships, thoughtful evaluation, clear priorities, and actionable mapping.

Robotics × AI: revolutionising automation

The combination of robotics and AI is revolutionising automation. Robotics handles physical tasks, while AI provides intelligence, enabling machines to learn, adapt, and make decisions. This synergy is reducing costs, improving precision, and increasing scalability across industries.

Companies already using it

Domino's Pizza is testing autonomous delivery robots that navigate streets and deliver orders. Amazon's fulfilment centres use AI-powered robots to retrieve and sort items, streamlining warehouse operations.

How small businesses can use it

Robotics × AI can automate tasks across industries:

- **Agribusiness:** Deploy AI-enabled drones to monitor crops, detect diseases, and optimise irrigation. This reduces labour costs and improves yields by acting proactively.
- **Brick-and-mortar retailers:** Use robotic assistants to restock shelves, track inventory, and assist customers. This enhances efficiency and customer experience.
- **Hospitality:** Implement robotic waitstaff for order delivery, table clearing, and room service. This reduces staff pressure while maintaining service standards.

Potential pitfalls

While robotics × AI offers efficiency, there are challenges to consider:

- **High initial costs:** Implementing robotics requires significant investment.
- **Integration challenges:** Adapting workflows and retraining staff may cause disruptions.
- **Employee concerns:** Workers may feel threatened by automation, requiring clear communication about its role.

Outlook

AI-enabled robots will expand into sectors such as aged care, manufacturing, and logistics. As technology advances, robots will perform tasks and make real-time decisions, seamlessly integrating into business operations.

Edge AI: smarter, faster decisions

Edge AI processes data locally on devices rather than relying on cloud servers, enabling faster decision-making and reducing dependence on internet connectivity.

Companies already using it

Tesla's self-driving cars use edge AI to process data from sensors in real time, allowing split-second decision-making.

How small businesses can use it

Edge AI can enhance responsiveness across industries:

- **Fitness studios:** Use edge AI in wearable devices to provide real-time feedback during workouts. This enhances the customer experience by delivering immediate insights.
- **Retailers:** Implement AI-enabled checkout systems that process transactions and track inventory simultaneously. This speeds up transactions and reduces delays.
- **Hospitality:** Use edge AI to personalise guest services, such as adjusting room settings based on preferences. This improves guest comfort and satisfaction.

Potential pitfalls

Businesses should be aware of the following risks:

- **Device limitations:** Local devices may lack the power for complex AI tasks.
- **Security risks:** Local data processing can be vulnerable to breaches.

Outlook

As devices become more powerful, edge AI will enable real-time language translation, augmented reality displays, and dynamic in-store pricing adjustments.

Autonomous vehicles: reshaping logistics and transportation

Autonomous vehicles, including self-driving cars, drones, and delivery robots, use AI to navigate and make decisions without human intervention. They are reshaping logistics, transportation, and delivery services.

Companies already using it

Waymo, Google's self-driving car division, leads in autonomous taxi development. FedEx is trialling delivery robots and drones for last-mile deliveries.

How small businesses can use it

Autonomous vehicles can transform transportation and delivery services:

- **Travel and tourism:** Offer autonomous shuttle services between attractions or airports. This provides cost-effective and consistent transport options.
- **Hospitality:** Use delivery robots for room service or luggage transport. This enhances guest convenience and reduces staff workload.
- **Retailers:** Implement autonomous drones or robots for local deliveries. This reduces delivery times and costs, increasing customer satisfaction.

Potential pitfalls

Despite their benefits, autonomous vehicles face challenges:

- **Infrastructure barriers:** They require supportive infrastructure such as charging stations and delivery zones.
- **Regulatory challenges:** Governments are still developing rules for autonomous transportation.
- **Public perception:** Consumers may take time to trust fully autonomous vehicles.

Outlook

Autonomous vehicles will expand into long-haul logistics, cutting costs and improving supply chain efficiency. For small businesses, these technologies will make once-unaffordable delivery options more accessible.

Quantum computing: the power to solve the impossible

Quantum computing uses quantum mechanics to process information exponentially faster than traditional computers. It enables solutions for complex problems such as logistics optimisation, molecular modelling, and cybersecurity.

Companies already using it

Google, IBM, and D-Wave are at the forefront of quantum computing. Pharmaceutical companies like Roche are using it to accelerate drug discovery.

How small businesses can use it

Although still emerging, quantum computing has significant future applications:

- **E-commerce:** Optimise delivery routes and inventory allocation at scale. This reduces operational costs and improves customer satisfaction.
- **Financial planners:** Use quantum computing to analyse vast datasets and identify market trends. This provides unparalleled precision in financial planning.
- **Agribusiness:** Model climate scenarios and optimise crop planting schedules. This helps businesses adapt to environmental changes and maximise efficiency.

Potential pitfalls

Quantum computing is still in its early stages, presenting challenges:

- **Limited accessibility:** The technology requires specialised infrastructure.
- **High costs:** Development and maintenance are expensive.
- **Skill gap:** Quantum computing requires expertise in quantum mechanics.

Outlook

Cloud-based quantum computing services (such as IBM Quantum and Microsoft Azure Quantum) will make this technology more accessible to businesses. Early adopters will benefit from optimised logistics, enhanced financial predictions, and more efficient supply chain models.

Holographic technology: immersive communication

Holographic technology creates 3D visuals that appear to float in space, enabling immersive communication, marketing, and training experiences.

Companies already using it

Coachella famously used holograms to bring Tupac Shakur to life on stage. Microsoft's HoloLens allows businesses to visualise designs and conduct holographic meetings.

How small businesses can use it

Holography can enhance customer engagement and presentations:

- **Retailers:** Use 3D holograms to showcase products in-store. This enhances customer engagement and reduces reliance on physical inventory.
- **Travel agencies:** Offer immersive holographic previews of destinations. This increases bookings by giving clients a vivid sense of their trips.
- **Event planners:** Use holograms for virtual guest appearances or immersive storytelling. This creates memorable experiences that set events apart.

Potential pitfalls

While promising, holographic technology has limitations:

- **High costs:** Advanced holographic displays remain expensive.
- **Technology limitations:** Current systems are often bulky and require controlled conditions.

Outlook

As holographic technology becomes more affordable and portable, it will integrate into everyday business tools. Virtual meetings may soon feature 3D holograms of participants, and product launches could include immersive holographic demonstrations.

The AGI revolution: hype, hope, and an honest opinion

I couldn't possibly write a section on emerging technology without talking about Artificial General Intelligence (AGI). It seems like it's all anyone wants to talk about, and boy, does it have the camps divided.

On one side we have people clutching their pearls, saying this is the moment that Sarah Connor (cue Terminator reference) was fighting against. On the other side we have the optimists, those who think AGI will lead to shorter working weeks and a Star Trek–style existence focusing on our creative passions and doing meaningful work.

My opinion? Well, technology itself is neither inherently good nor bad. It's the humans and the corporations behind the deployment and usage of the technology that make the difference. Either way, I do believe it's coming … and probably faster than we care to admit.

So, let's take a look at what it is, what you need to know, and how you can prepare your business for the inevitable impacts.

What is AGI?

Artificial General Intelligence is the next frontier of Artificial Intelligence. Unlike the AI we know today (often referred to in the industry as 'narrow intelligence'), which excels at specific tasks (like ChatGPT generating content or a recommendation engine suggesting your next Netflix binge), AGI would have the capacity to think, learn, and reason like a human – across any domain. It's about creating machines with generalised intelligence, capable of understanding and solving complex, multifaceted problems without explicit programming.

How is AGI different from current AI?

Today's AI, including models like ChatGPT, is classified as 'narrow' or 'weak' AI, meaning it is designed to handle specific tasks and lacks general cognitive abilities. In contrast, AGI would have the capacity to generalise learning across diverse domains, adapting to new situations without explicit programming.

Futurist Ray Kurzweil has long predicted the emergence of AGI by 2029, suggesting that machines will achieve human-level intelligence by that year. OpenAI CEO Sam Altman has expressed confidence in achieving AGI sooner, stating, 'We are now confident we know how to build AGI as we have traditionally understood it,' and anticipates that by 2025, AI agents may begin to 'join the workforce' and significantly impact company outputs.

The potential impacts of AGI

Potential positive AGI impacts include the following:

- **Enhanced productivity:** AGI could automate complex tasks, leading to increased efficiency and allowing humans to focus on creative and strategic endeavours.
- **Advancements in healthcare:** With its ability to process vast amounts of data, AGI could revolutionise diagnostics, personalised medicine, and treatment plans.
- **Economic growth:** By driving innovation, AGI has the potential to create new industries and job opportunities, contributing to economic expansion.

Potential negative AGI impacts include the following:

- **Job displacement:** The automation of tasks traditionally performed by humans could lead to significant employment challenges across various sectors.

- **Ethical concerns:** The development and deployment of AGI raise questions about decision-making authority, privacy, and the potential for misuse.
- **Security risks:** Advanced AI systems could be exploited for malicious purposes, including cyberattacks or the creation of autonomous weapons.

Implications for teams and clients

Workforce dynamics will shift as teams adapt to working alongside AGI systems, requiring new skills that emphasise emotional intelligence, creativity, and complex problem-solving. Client interactions could also evolve, with businesses leveraging AGI to deliver more personalised and efficient services. While this enhances customer satisfaction, it also demands transparency about AI involvement to maintain trust.

AGI presents both opportunities and challenges. It enables businesses to develop innovative products and services that were previously inconceivable, gaining competitive advantages, while also streamlining operations to reduce costs and improve quality. However, implementation comes with substantial expenses, requiring investment in infrastructure and training. Additionally, ongoing maintenance, including continuous updates and ethical oversight, is essential to ensure AGI systems function effectively and responsibly.

Preparing for AGI

Build AGI awareness

Educating yourself and your team on AGI – what it is and how it differs from current AI – will help you prepare for its potential impact. Taking proactive steps now ensures you stay informed and ready to adapt.

To stay ahead of AGI developments, engage with reliable sources and participate in industry discussions:

- **Follow key thought leaders:** Join my community and subscribe to updates from credible sources like OpenAI, *MIT Technology Review*, or AI-focused newsletters.
- **Attend webinars or events:** Look for accessible talks or forums on AGI developments.
- **Read industry-specific AGI predictions:** Focus on how AGI might impact your sector.

Identify potential impacts

Understanding how AGI might affect your business – including opportunities, risks, and disruptions – will help you plan ahead. Assessing where AGI could integrate into your operations can give you a competitive edge.

Here's how to evaluate impact, analyse your current workflows and anticipate AGI's role in improving or disrupting key areas:

- **Review core processes:** Map out workflows and identify tasks involving complex decision-making or repetitive manual processes.
- **List AGI-driven changes:** Consider how AGI could enhance client insights, supply chain optimisation, or customer service.
- **Consider team and client impacts:** Evaluate how AGI might reshape team roles and customer expectations.

Upskill your team

Preparing your team for an AGI-driven future means focusing on skills that complement AI rather than compete with it. Training in these areas will ensure employees remain valuable as technology advances.

Help your team develop capabilities that enhance collaboration with AGI rather than being replaced by it:

- **Train in critical thinking and creativity:** Encourage team members to develop skills AGI can't easily replicate, such as strategic planning, empathy, and innovation.
- **Provide basic AI literacy:** Offer resources that explain AI and AGI fundamentals to build confidence in working alongside these tools.
- **Create a culture of adaptability:** Reward experimentation and learning to help your team embrace technological change.

Pilot narrow AI tools

Since AGI isn't available yet, leveraging narrow AI tools can introduce your business to automation and help gauge its potential impact. Testing AI solutions now will ease future transitions.

Use current AI-driven solutions as a foundation for future AGI integration:

- **Identify immediate needs:** Pinpoint challenges – such as customer queries or inventory tracking – that could benefit from automation.
- **Trial AI solutions:** Implement tools like chatbots, AI-powered analytics, or process automation to simulate AGI-like functions.
- **Measure results:** Assess ROI, time savings, and team feedback to understand how AGI could be integrated at scale.

Stay agile and proactive

Keeping a flexible and forward-thinking approach will ensure you're prepared for AGI advancements. Regular evaluations will help you adjust strategies as the technology evolves.

Monitor industry trends and keep your business strategy adaptable as AGI evolves:

- **Set quarterly check-ins:** Regularly reassess AGI developments and their relevance to your business.
- **Monitor competitors and peers:** Observe how similar businesses are engaging with AI to identify early opportunities.
- **Create a technology contingency plan:** Outline steps for integrating AGI when viable, including budgeting and team training.

AGI has transformative potential, but its arrival and impact on businesses remain uncertain. What is clear is the importance of staying informed and integrating AI thoughtfully. Preparing for AGI isn't about making drastic changes now – it's about building a flexible foundation for the future. By fostering awareness, experimenting with AI tools, and cultivating adaptability, your business will be well-positioned to evolve as AGI becomes a reality.

Take AI action: build your AGI readiness matrix

Prepare your business for the potential emergence of Artificial General Intelligence (AGI) by evaluating opportunities, risks, and readiness steps.

How long it takes

Allocate three to four hours over one or two sessions for brainstorming, research, and planning.

Who to include

- **Solo business owners:** Complete this exercise independently with an external sounding board (for example, a mentor or trusted adviser).

- **Small teams:** Involve team leaders or those in strategic roles to brainstorm and shape the plan.
- **Remote teams:** Use tools like Zoom, Miro, or Google Docs to facilitate discussion and collaboration.

Steps

1. Understand AGI's potential:

   Spend 30 to 60 minutes researching how AGI is likely to impact your industry. Focus on:

   - tasks or processes AGI could automate or enhance
   - examples from other sectors that highlight its possibilities.

   Reflect on the good, bad, and ugly aspects: how might AGI improve efficiency, create risks, or disrupt your operations?

2. Create your AGI readiness matrix:

   Divide a page into four quadrants labelled as follows:

   - **Current state:** Where is your business technologically today?
   - **AGI impacts:** What opportunities or disruptions could AGI create for you?
   - **Priority areas:** What should you focus on first (e.g. team skills, client relationships, infrastructure)?
   - **Next steps:** What immediate actions can you take to prepare for AGI?

   Complete each quadrant with input from your team or advisers.

Current state	AGI impacts
Priority areas	**Next steps**

3. Review and prioritise the matrix:

   Spend 20 to 30 minutes reviewing each quadrant. Ask:
   - **Current state:** Are there critical gaps in your technology readiness?
   - **AGI Impacts:** Which opportunities excite you most? Which risks concern you most?
   - **Priority areas:** Are your identified focus areas realistic and achievable?
   - **Next steps:** Which immediate actions will deliver the biggest impact? Highlight the top three priorities from the matrix to tackle first. These should align with your business's goals and capacity.
4. Develop an AGI monitoring plan:

   Set up a system to track AGI developments and their relevance to your industry. Actions could include:
   - subscribing to newsletters, podcasts, or blogs from AI thought leaders like OpenAI, *MIT Technology Review*, or AI ethics forums
   - joining my community for regular updates
   - checking if your industry or association has an AI lead
   - scheduling quarterly 'AGI Updates' with your team to discuss new tools, trends, and potential use cases.
5. Revisit the matrix quarterly:

   Reflect on progress:
   - Has your current state improved?
   - Have new AGI impacts emerged?
   - Are your priority areas still relevant?
   - Update the next steps quadrant to ensure continuous progress.

Preparing for AGI, like REIMAGINING your business, isn't about overhauling everything overnight – it's about taking thoughtful, incremental steps towards readiness. By reflecting on where you are today, identifying opportunities and challenges, and setting actionable priorities, you position your business to thrive in an AGI-driven future.

The goal isn't to predict every outcome but to stay agile, informed, and proactive as this transformative technology evolves. Start small, stay curious, and let your AGI action plan guide you towards new possibilities.

The AI arms race

In 2008, Pete and I stepped off the corporate treadmill and into the unknown. After countless conversations and thousands of kilometres on the road – we'd packed up our sedan and hit the road for an eight-week escape to clear our heads – we landed on an idea for our first business: coffee.

Now, we knew nothing about the industry. We knew we liked coffee, we loved visiting cafés, and, well, how hard could it be … right?

Turns out: hard. We discovered the coffee market isn't the laid-back, artisanal dream we imagined. Café pricing wars are brutal, and a few big players dominate the industry, dictating the terms for small operators like us. At every turn, we were undercut. Larger suppliers were throwing in 'free' equipment with their contracts, making it almost impossible to get a foot in the door.

It didn't take long to realise we couldn't beat the big guys at their own game. So, we did what every scrappy small business owner does when the odds are stacked against them – we changed the game. Having worked in corporate offices across the country, we reflected on one universal pain point: the impossibility of getting a decent latte without a café run. The numbers started adding up: lost productivity as half the office disappears to a local café, and the disruption of mid-morning caffeine fixes.

That's when it hit us. What if we could bring the café experience to corporate offices and the resource sector? That decision allowed us to carve out a fabulous little lifestyle business that thrived for 12 years. We built strong relationships, tailored our service to meet specific customer needs, and stayed independent – all while side-stepping the café market's relentless pricing wars.

Okay, but what has that got to do with AI? On the surface, not much. But step back and take a look 'who' are the players creating the rules? Think Google, Microsoft, and OpenAI. These are the companies that are defining the game, which, as a knock-on effect, makes it difficult for small businesses to keep up.

As Pete and I did in our coffee business, you don't have to compete with them on their terms. With a little reimagining, there's room to carve out opportunities and thrive.

Just as Pete and I needed to understand the coffee industry to find our niche, you need a basic understanding of AI to navigate its opportunities and risks. This doesn't mean becoming an expert – it's about knowing enough to spot the openings, avoid pitfalls, and make confident choices.

Let's start by demystifying some key AI concepts that will empower you to take on the AI 'arms race'. Understanding these concepts isn't about becoming an AI expert – it's about empowerment. Once you 'know' something, you gain the tools to:

- recognise tools that suit your needs and budget
- spot hidden costs, biases, or vendor lock-in risks before they become issues
- ask the right questions and know you're making informed decisions.

My goal in familiarising you with these terms is to give you just enough knowledge to leave you prepared to navigate the AI landscape with confidence.

Barista coffee vs pod machines: open AI, closed AI, and the power struggle

While we're on the coffee analogy, let's continue to milk it (sorry …). We can use the idea of different types of coffee machines when we think about the AI tools and the companies that are building them.

Open AI (the concept, not the company) is like a traditional espresso machine. You can see how it works, tweak the settings, and customise it for the perfect espresso (25 to 30 seconds is how long the perfect pour should take). It takes some effort to learn and master, but the freedom and flexibility mean you can always tailor your coffee to your exact taste.

Closed AI is like a coffee pod machine. You open the box, pop in a pod, press a button, and voilà – you've got coffee. It's quick and convenient, but you have no control over the pour or the settings, or any ability to customise it. And you're locked into buying pods from the same supplier – at their price, on their terms.

Got it? Now, let's layer in the concept of democratisation and monopolisation of AI …

Democratisation is like having espresso machines available for everyone. Anyone can own one, learn how to use it, and buy beans from wherever they like. You have complete control over the quality, the cost, and how it fits your needs. It's freedom, and it levels the playing field for small businesses who don't want to rely on the giants.

Monopolisation is when the pod machine companies take over. Imagine if pod machines became the only coffee option, and every café, office, or home had to use their system. The pods get more expensive, the flavours you love disappear, and you're stuck paying their prices because switching to another system would cost too much.

Why you should care ...

For small businesses, democratisation is about access – making AI tools affordable and available to everyone, not just big players. Open source, on the other hand, is about control – letting you customise tools to fit your needs.

While democratised tools are often open source, and monopolised tools are often closed, they don't always have to be. **Democratised AI gives you freedom of choice, while open AI gives you freedom to adapt.**

Choosing democratised tools (like open-source platforms) gives you the control and flexibility to customise, innovate, and scale – just like sticking with a traditional espresso machine. Relying on monopolised platforms is convenient at first, but over time, you might lose control, paying more while missing out on better opportunities. If the provider raises prices or limits access, you're stuck with fewer options.

By understanding these dynamics, you can make informed decisions: choose tools that empower you, avoid overreliance on big providers, and keep your business in control.

Demystifying AI terms

Before diving deeper into democratisation and monopolisation, let's quickly cover a few key AI terms that will help you navigate this 'arms race'. Don't worry – this isn't a deep dive into jargon. Think of it as your AI starter pack, designed to help you make confident decisions. And remember, if you want more detail, you'll find a glossary at the back of the book.

Democratised AI

These are tools that are accessible and affordable to businesses of any size – not just tech giants.

- **Why it matters:** Democratised tools level the playing field, allowing small businesses to experiment, innovate, and grow without massive investment.
- **Example tools:** Canva (AI-powered design), ChatGPT (free tier).
- **Pro:** Affordable and empowering.
- **Con:** Free tools may lack advanced features.

Monopolised AI

These are tools or platforms controlled by a few major players, often with restrictions that limit flexibility.

- **Why it matters:** Monopolised tools can lead to dependence on big providers, making it harder to switch if prices rise or terms change.
- **Example tools:** Google Bard, Microsoft Copilot.
- **Pro:** Polished, user-friendly, and often cutting-edge.
- **Con:** Higher costs and limited control.

Open AI (the concept, not the company)

Open AI tools are like DIY kits – you get full access to the code, so you can customise it to your needs.

- **Why it matters:** Open tools give you freedom and flexibility, reducing reliance on big providers.
- **Example tools:** Hugging Face, TensorFlow.
- **Pro:** Customisable and transparent.
- **Con:** They require some technical skills.

Closed AI

Closed AI tools are pre-packaged systems – ready to use but not customisable.

- **Why it matters:** These tools are easy to implement but can lock you into their ecosystem.
- **Example tools:** OpenAI's ChatGPT (Pro), Google Bard.
- **Pro:** User-friendly and polished.
- **Con:** Limited flexibility and potential vendor lock-in.

Black box AI

These tools give you results without showing how they work – like getting the answer without the workings.

- **Why it matters:** They're efficient but can hide biases or errors, making them harder to trust.
- **Example tools:** Many off-the-shelf chatbots or analytics tools.
- **Pro:** Convenient for quick results.
- **Con:** Lack of transparency can lead to unexpected risks.

Sandbox AI

Sandboxes provide a safe space to test AI tools without affecting your actual systems.

- **Why it matters:** Sandboxes let you experiment risk-free, helping you decide if a tool fits your needs.
- **Example tools:** Free trials or open-source environments for testing.
- **Pro:** Safe experimentation.
- **Con:** May not reflect full functionality in live use.

Understanding these terms helps you make smarter choices about which tools to adopt. Democratised AI offers freedom and opportunity, while monopolised AI can create risk and reliance. By recognising these dynamics, you'll be better prepared to choose tools that empower your business to innovate, scale, and stay in control – on your terms.

Monopolised tools: friend or foe?

Around 85% of the tools I use in my business are owned by big players. I work on Apple devices, and use Google for my email and calendar, Microsoft when needed for clients, and ChatGPT on a daily basis. Most likely, the tools you'll use in your business will also be part of the 'monopoly'. And that's okay! We choose these tools for their reliability, ongoing support, and frequent upgrades. The key is to approach them with intention:

- **Use them strategically:** Leverage their strengths while balancing them with other options.
- **Avoid overreliance:** Don't let one tool or platform dominate your operations.
- **Build flexibility:** Keep your options open by using tools that integrate easily or allow you to switch providers if needed.

You just have to know when to rely on the big players and when to keep things under your own control. I think of it like this: I'll always choose a barista-style coffee machine for home – but I'm still happy to shop at Woolies or Coles when I need to stock up on essentials.

What's next in the AI arms race?

The big players – Google, Microsoft, OpenAI, and others – are not just competing to develop the best AI. They're also competing to lock you into their ecosystems. You can expect these companies to roll out more incentives, free tools, and exclusive features to keep you tied to their platforms. On the surface, this might seem like a win for small businesses – but there are catches:

- These incentives often come with hidden costs, like vendor lock-in, rising subscription fees, or limited flexibility.
- Smaller companies and democratised tools may struggle to get a foothold, which could reduce your future choices.

The AI arms race will continue to shape the tools available to your business. As the big players compete, your job is to stay strategic, adaptable, and in control. Here's how:

- **Stay aware of incentives:** Free trials and discounted tiers can be tempting, but consider the long-term impact – what happens when the price increases? Can you leave if needed?
- **Support democratised tools when you can:** Choosing tools that promote accessibility and innovation helps create a more balanced AI ecosystem.
- **Balance big players with flexibility:** Leverage the reliability of monopolised tools for critical functions but keep alternatives in place to avoid being locked in.

The AI arms race will undoubtedly shape the future of your business tools. But by staying informed, asking the right questions, and choosing tools that fit your needs – not just the ones with the flashiest incentives – you'll be ready to thrive no matter how the landscape shifts.

How to build your winning team

In every great story, the hero needs a strong team to succeed. Whether it's The Avengers, a pit crew at the Grand Prix, or a small business owner like you, the right team makes all the difference.

When it comes to AI, your 'team' is made up of the tools and providers you choose to work with – and picking the wrong ones can cost you time, money, and flexibility. Now that we've explored the AI arms race and the dynamics of democratisation vs monopolisation, it's time to focus on how to build your AI lineup. This isn't about becoming an expert; it's about asking the right questions to find tools that empower your business without locking you in.

Take AI action: AI provider questionnaire

This questionnaire is part of the Identify phase of your REIMAGINE Framework. It helps you pinpoint the right AI tools and providers to match your business's unique needs. Not every question will apply to your situation, but use it as a guide to make confident, informed decisions.

Step 1: Key questions to ask about AI providers

Question	Why it matters	Answer
Does it fit your budget?	Start with what you can afford today, but also consider future costs as your business grows.	
Who owns the data?	Retaining control of your data is critical to avoid being locked in. Check if you can easily export it.	

Question	Why it matters	Answer
Is it transparent?	Look for clear explanations of how the tool works, what happens to your data, and all associated costs.	
Is it flexible?	Can it integrate with your current tools? Can you easily move to another provider if needed?	
Does it align with your values?	Ethical AI is becoming a priority. Ensure the provider's practices match your business's standards.	
What kind of support is available?	Responsive customer service ensures problems don't derail your operations.	
Is it scalable?	Will this tool grow with your business, or will you outgrow it in a year?	
Are there hidden fees?	Check for additional charges for extra users, integrations, or premium features.	
How long is the contract?	Avoid long-term contracts where possible – month-to-month allows for greater flexibility as technology evolves.	
Can I test it before committing?	Free trials or demo periods let you evaluate the tool's fit for your business without financial risk.	

Step 2: Evaluate and score

Give your answer to each question a score from 1 (poor) to 5 (excellent), and add up the scores for each provider:

- **20 to 25 points:** This provider is a strong match for your business.
- **15 to 19 points:** There are areas of concern. Review carefully before committing.
- **Less than 15 points:** Look for alternatives. This provider may not be the best fit for your business.

Step 3: Make a strategic decision

Once you've completed the questionnaire for each provider you are considering, reflect on your notes and scores:

- Does this provider give you the flexibility to adapt as your business grows?
- Are there better alternatives that align with your needs?

Avoid 12-month contracts

When possible, avoid locking yourself into 12-month contracts. Yes, month-to-month plans might cost a little more upfront, but they give you the freedom to jump, change, or grow as technology evolves. This flexibility is invaluable in a world where the pace of innovation is only speeding up. Of course, for essential tools like email or accounting software, longer commitments might make sense. But for everything else? Stay nimble – your business will thank you.

CHAPTER 12

The mindset shift: from reactionary to reimagined

'"Business as usual" is a relic of the past. In today's world, the ability to reimagine what's possible isn't just an asset – it's your lifeline. The ability to evolve isn't optional; it's essential.'

Tracy Sheen

The REIMAGINE Framework isn't just about picking tools or providers; it's about stepping into a new way of thinking. Small business owners have always thrived on resourcefulness and adaptability, but the speed at which AI is evolving means that sticking to old habits – like relying on gut instincts or waiting for the 'right time' – no longer cuts it.

The 'hold position and wait' philosophy feels a lot like shaking a Magic 8-Ball and hoping for a clear answer. It might give you something to act on, but it's no substitute for a deliberate, well-informed strategy. To stay competitive, you need to move beyond guesswork and reactive decisions. It's time to embrace a mindset that's forward-thinking, experimental, and ready to turn uncertainty into opportunity.

This means reimagining your relationship with technology. AI isn't just a set of tools; it's a collaborator that can amplify your strengths, free up your time, and give you the edge you need in a constantly shifting landscape. But to unlock its full potential, you'll need to start thinking differently – not just about AI, but about your business's future.

The final step in REIMAGINING your business is as much about mindset as it is about the practicalities of day-to-day life in an AI-driven world. Some of the concepts we're going to discuss may feel strange, and some may even make you feel uncomfortable. That's good. Discomfort is often a signal that you're on the edge of growth. Lean into it – it might be the key to uncovering your next breakthrough. Remind yourself, you're just reading right now; nothing needs to change yet. When you're ready, you'll decide what parts of this vision align with your REIMAGINED business.

In the coming pages, we'll explore mindsets and practical tools to shift your business from reactionary to REIMAGINED. These ideas are designed to challenge you, not because change is easy, but because it's necessary for those ready to thrive in this AI-driven world. Okay … with that said, let's dive in.

Reimagining success in an AI world

For decades, success in small business has been measured in familiar terms: profit margins, growth rates, customer retention, and operational efficiency. But in an AI-augmented world, these measures only tell part of the story. Success now includes how well your business can adapt to change, leverage technology to create unique value, and preserve what makes your brand authentically human. AI introduces opportunities to streamline processes, anticipate customer needs, and make data-driven decisions, but it also brings the risk of losing personal connections or becoming overly reliant on automation. To navigate this shift, we must redefine what success means in a landscape where technology and humanity are partners, not adversaries.

Success in an AI-augmented world isn't about doing more or keeping up with the latest technology for its own sake. It's about doing the right things smarter, preserving what makes your business unique, and embracing new opportunities as they arise. For small businesses, this means balancing operational efficiency with authenticity, staying deeply connected to your community, listening to what they're telling you, and using AI to amplify – not replace – what you already do best.

When Pete and I first went into business together back in 2008, he asked me one very important question: 'What does success look like to you?' You see, Pete is a phenomenal business coach in his own right, balancing an in-depth understanding of the technology landscape with an engineering mindset built on processes and procedures. As we discussed the concept of success, I realised it's a question we need to ask ourselves every year. Why? Because our idea of success morphs and grows with our age, our lifestyle, and our stage of business. With that in mind, the following concepts are here to inspire you as you design your REIMAGINED business. Not all will apply – or maybe they will. That's the beauty of creating your future. You get to choose.

Success as community connection

Many business owners are deeply connected to their local communities, not just running businesses but also volunteering and supporting local initiatives. AI can help strengthen these connections by enabling smarter outreach and more personalised engagement. A café, for example, could use AI-driven tools to remind local customers about special offers, seasonal products, or community events, reinforcing its role as a neighbourhood hub.

Ethical and responsible AI usage

Incorporating AI responsibly is more than a technical choice – it's a value-driven decision. Prioritising ethical AI use can differentiate your business, strengthen customer trust, and reinforce your role in the community. A small accounting firm, for instance, could use AI tools that prioritise data security while streamlining tax preparation. Communicating this commitment to ethical AI could also serve as a market differentiator.

Measuring emotional and cultural impact

Beyond profits, many business owners measure success by the relationships they build and the cultural value they add. AI can support these efforts by revealing customer satisfaction, engagement, and opportunities for growth. A yoga studio, for example, could use AI to anonymously survey clients, helping to make classes more inclusive and community-focused, strengthening loyalty and relationships.

Empowering employees

AI doesn't just transform customer experiences; it redefines success internally by allowing employees to work to their strengths. Whether automating tasks or streamlining processes, AI can create a more inclusive work environment. For instance, an employee with neurodiverse needs could use AI to create processes tailored to their strengths, enabling them to contribute fully to the business's success.

Scalability without losing personalisation

Small business owners juggle multiple responsibilities, making growth challenging. AI enables businesses to scale while maintaining their unique, personalised approach. An e-commerce store, for example, could use AI to send personalised emails recommending products based on past purchases, keeping interactions relevant and engaging even as the business grows.

Learning and adapting to stay competitive

Success in an AI-driven world requires continuous learning and adaptability. AI allows businesses to test ideas, gather feedback, and pivot quickly to remain competitive. A business coach, for example, could use AI to analyse industry trends, refining offerings and creating new opportunities to support clients in more meaningful ways.

Reducing stress and overwhelm

Balancing responsibilities to staff, family, and clients can be overwhelming. AI can simplify operations, freeing up time for business growth or personal well-being. An electrician, for example, could automate appointment scheduling and payment collection, saving hours each week to focus on expanding the business or spending time with family.

Environmental and social impact

Many small businesses prioritise sustainability and social responsibility. AI can help align operations with these values by providing actionable insights. A restaurant, for instance, might use AI to predict demand, reducing food waste and adjusting sourcing based on environmental impact.

Bridging digital divides

Technology should enhance accessibility rather than create barriers. AI should simplify customer interactions and improve accessibility for all users. A hair salon, for example, could implement an AI-powered booking system that's intuitive for all clients, whether they prefer online or in-person scheduling.

Affordability and ROI

Small businesses don't have corporate-sized budgets, making ROI a key measure of AI success. AI tools should deliver tangible value within defined budgets. A mortgage broker, for example, might invest in AI-powered proposal templates, saving time and allowing them to offer competitive pricing without compromising quality.

Reimagine success for your business

Success in an AI-augmented world is no longer defined solely by traditional metrics like profit and efficiency. It's about creating a future where your business thrives by amplifying its core strengths, empowering its people, and embracing the community it serves. AI isn't just a tool; it's a catalyst that enables small businesses to scale with purpose, adapt with confidence, and maintain the personal touch that customers value most.

The question isn't whether AI will change the way small businesses operate – it already has. The real question is in what ways you need to shift your mindset in order to leverage this powerful opportunity to redefine what success means for your business and the people it serves.

Mindset reset: from survival to futurist mode

For many small business owners, survival mode is a default position. Juggling multiple roles, putting out daily fires, and navigating an unpredictable landscape has become so ingrained that there is often little room to think about growing the business, what we really want, or even what our ultimate goal is. If our plan is to thrive in an AI-augmented world, you need to shift gears – from reacting to what's in front of you to proactively building the future you want. This shift takes us into the world of futurist thinking. So, what is a futurist, and why is their mindset so crucial for small businesses right now? A futurist is someone who explores possibilities and prepares for what's coming, rather than waiting for change to happen. They don't predict the future; they shape it by recognising trends, embracing curiosity, and making informed decisions today that lay the groundwork for tomorrow. Futurists see uncertainty not as a threat but as an opportunity – a chance to innovate, adapt, and grow.

In the words of Australia's leading futurist, Dr Catherine Ball, 'The future is already here; we just need to listen to it'.

For small business owners, this mindset is no longer optional. The speed of change driven by AI and other technologies means that holding your ground is the same as falling behind. You don't have to abandon the uniqueness that made your business, but you do need to listen to what the future is telling you. Pairing those qualities with the ability to think like a futurist can turn uncertainty into a competitive advantage.

By adopting a futurist mindset, you can:

- **Stay ahead of trends:** Spotting opportunities within your industry early allows you to act before the competition does.
- **Build resilience:** Planning for multiple scenarios equips you to adapt, no matter what the future holds.
- **Unlock innovation:** A futurist approach encourages creative thinking, helping you see how AI can transform your business in ways you might not have imagined.
- **Thrive in change:** Instead of resisting or fearing disruption, you'll be positioned to harness it.

The good news? You don't need a crystal ball or a team of data scientists to make this shift. Futurists aren't defined by the resources they have but by the habits they cultivate. With a curious mindset and a willingness to experiment, you can take small, consistent steps that lead to exponential growth.

First, you need to understand the difference between surviving and shaping your future. Tell me if this sounds like you: you're juggling competing demands, addressing urgent issues, and navigating the day-to-day chaos. By the end of the day, your 'to do' list is often longer than when you started. You find yourself working late into the evening or giving up your weekends just to catch up on the tasks that didn't get done while you were busy putting out fires. I know this landscape well. It's familiar, and it can work in the short term, but it rarely leaves room for long-term growth or innovation. Futurist mode, by contrast, is about stepping back, reimagining possibilities, and planning strategically. It doesn't mean you stop being resourceful – that's one of your greatest strengths. Instead, it means using that resourcefulness to move beyond reacting, towards proactively designing the future of your business. Here's how the two mindsets look side by side:

Survival mode	Futurist mode
Reacting to immediate problems	Anticipating challenges and trends
Focused on maintaining the status quo	Actively seeking ways to innovate
Overwhelmed by the day-to-day	Carving out time for strategic thinking
Hesitant to try new tools or methods	Embracing experimentation and learning
Reluctant to invest in change	Viewing change as a growth opportunity

Do any of these sound familiar?

- You're jumping from one fire to the next and struggling to find time to focus on the big picture.
- You avoid adopting new technology because it feels overwhelming or risky.
- You find yourself saying, 'That's the way we've always done it,' even when things feel inefficient.
- Your energy is spent maintaining what you already have, leaving no capacity for growth or innovation.

Survival mode isn't inherently bad – every business, not just small ones, ends up there at times. The key is recognising when survival mode becomes a habit rather than a temporary state. If your default is simply getting through the day, it's time to reimagine how things could look.

What futurist thinking could look like for you

Like the rest of this book, I'm not asking you to burn what you have to the ground. It's not about massive overhauls or complete disruption. It's about small shifts that prioritise progress over perfection.

Here's what it might look like in action:

- **Proactive planning:** You dedicate time to exploring emerging trends – like AI – to address challenges and uncover new opportunities. Even 15 to 30 minutes a day reading, listening to a podcast, or watching updates can have a significant long-term impact.
- **Experimentation:** You remain open to trying new tools and processes instead of dismissing them due to time constraints. By testing small-scale changes, you discover what works and continuously refine your approach.
- **Big-picture thinking:** Every decision is made with a long-term perspective. You consider how today's choices will shape the business in one, three, or five years, ensuring sustainability and growth.
- **Collaborative mindset:** You engage your team in reimagining how things get done. By encouraging brainstorming and diverse perspectives, you create an environment where innovation thrives.

Thinking like a futurist isn't about discarding the things that work. It's about using the inherent strengths of your business to think ahead, embrace change, and unlock new possibilities. I promise you, if you make this shift, you will be better equipped to:

- navigate any business uncertainty with confidence
- adapt to new technologies like AI without feeling overwhelmed
- identify and act on the right opportunities at the right time
- build resilience for whatever the future looks like.

Take AI action: a moment to reflect

Take a moment and be completely honest with yourself about where your business stands right now:

- Are you spending more time reacting or planning?
- When was the last time you tried something new in your business?
- If you could fast-forward five years, what do you wish you'd started today?

After reflecting on these prompts, choose one action – whether it's setting aside 15 minutes a day for learning, testing a new tool, or brainstorming with your team – and commit to it this week.

Building futurist habits

Shifting from survival to futurist thinking doesn't happen overnight. It's a process of adopting small, intentional habits that align with the vision of your REIMAGINED business. These habits aren't about complexity – they're about consistency. They help you stay curious, innovative, and ready to adapt to change before it happens.

If you want to dive deeper into habit building, there are some fantastic resources to explore. Books like *Atomic Habits* by James Clear and *The Power of Habit* by Charles Duhigg offer proven strategies for creating habits that stick. These authors show how small, consistent actions compound over time to create meaningful change – a concept that's directly aligned with adopting a futurist mindset.

It's not an exhaustive list, and some won't apply, but here are a few key habits to start building your futurist mindset.

Dedicate time for curiosity

Curiosity is the foundation of futurist thinking. By intentionally exploring new tools, trends, or technologies, you'll stay informed and spot opportunities early. Carve out 15 to 30 minutes a day or week to explore emerging ideas. Listen to podcasts like *News From The Future*, read blogs such as *TechCrunch*, or attend webinars. Experimenting with tools like ChatGPT can spark ideas. And of course, I'm going to suggest you connect to my community.

Schedule regular 'daydreaming' time

We spend so much time in 'doing' mode that reflection often takes a back seat. Allocating time to step back and think is critical for strategic planning. Set aside 30 minutes a week to evaluate progress, assess challenges, and brainstorm opportunities. Use this time to look at business data, review customer feedback, or consider how AI might solve a recurring issue.

Hold quarterly (or regular) innovation sessions

Innovation thrives in a collaborative environment. Involving your team or trusted advisers can uncover fresh ideas and solutions. Dedicate a quarterly meeting to identify one process, product, or customer experience that could benefit from AI or new technology. Ask your team, 'What's one thing we could improve with technology right now?' Encourage brainstorming with sticky notes or digital whiteboards.

Lean into the REIMAGINE Framework

Progress comes from small, deliberate actions. By observing challenges, experimenting with solutions, and reflecting on outcomes, you create a cycle of continuous improvement. Identify pain points or inefficiencies in your business. Test one tool, process, or strategy each quarter. Evaluate results – what worked, what didn't, and how to improve.

Build a learning culture

Continuous learning is essential for staying ahead of the curve. Surrounding yourself with diverse sources of knowledge keeps you inspired and informed. Set up a mix of learning tools, such as newsletters, LinkedIn groups, and webinars. Bookmark three to five trusted resources for AI trends or small business innovations. Commit to reading or listening to one new insight per week.

Engage in scenario planning

Futurists prepare for multiple possibilities. Scenario planning allows you to act with confidence, no matter what the future holds. Map out potential challenges and opportunities quarterly. Ask questions like, 'What happens if my customer demand doubles?' or 'What if a competitor integrates AI tools next year?'

Focus on progress, not perfection

Waiting for perfection can paralyse progress. A futurist mindset embraces learning through action. Launch initiatives in beta mode and refine them over time. Test an AI-powered scheduling tool with a small subset of customers before scaling it business-wide.

Collaborate with your broader team

Innovation doesn't happen in isolation. Engaging your network can reveal shared challenges and fresh solutions. Host a roundtable with local businesses or join a digital community to exchange AI adoption insights. Collaborate with neighbouring businesses on shared AI tools, like a regional delivery optimisation platform.

Track and celebrate progress

Recognising small wins reinforces positive habits and builds confidence in your ability to embrace change. Create a dashboard or log to track improvements. Note time saved by automating tasks or increased customer satisfaction from personalised interactions.

Take AI action: your futurist habit plan

To get started, choose one habit from the list in the previous section and plan how to integrate it into your routine:

- **What you'll do:** Which habit resonates most with you?
- **How you'll start:** What's the first small step you can take this week?
- **Who will support you:** Can you involve your team or a trusted colleague to help stay accountable?

By adopting small, consistent habits, you'll cultivate the mindset needed to REIMAGINE your business in an AI-enabled world. Each step you take builds momentum, helping you stay curious, innovative, and resilient in the face of change.

So, what's your first habit going to be?

Applying the habits: turning thought into action with the REIMAGINE Framework

It's time to take our mindset shifts and ground them with the REIMAGINE Framework. When I was reverse-engineering my process of working with clients, I realised that the success of any client was based on equal measures of a step-by-step process and a willingness to embrace a significant mindset shift.

What's exciting – well, for me, anyway – is that as I was pulling this all together, a light-bulb moment hit me: futurist thinking overlays with each of the stages of the REIMAGINE Framework.

This means that as you work through the framework, you get to embed and enhance your ability to navigate change, adapt, and innovate. By applying the habits of a futurist, you can approach each step of the framework with curiosity, strategic insight, and a readiness to embrace new possibilities.

Let's take a closer look at how futurist thinking aligns with the REIMAGINE Framework and enhances your journey.

Relationships

Building strong relationships is the foundation of your business, and futurist thinking ensures these relationships evolve with the times. By observing trends and engaging in proactive planning, you can anticipate customer needs and strengthen trust. Setting aside time for exploration helps uncover new ways AI can enhance customer interactions, such as personalised emails or chatbots for instant support.

Evaluate

Evaluation is about understanding what's working and what needs improvement. The futurist mindset ensures you don't just assess today's needs but consider how tools and strategies will perform in the future. Engaging in scenario planning can help determine whether your current technology aligns with future trends and potential disruptions.

Identify

Identifying opportunities is at the heart of futurist thinking. By observing challenges and experimenting with solutions, you can pinpoint areas where AI can have the biggest impact. Using the futurist habit loop – observe, experiment, reflect – allows you to test quick wins, such as automating appointment scheduling or improving inventory management.

Mapping

Mapping your strategy is about turning insights into action. A futurist mindset helps visualise how today's decisions shape tomorrow's outcomes. Applying big-picture thinking when creating a roadmap ensures that each step aligns with long-term goals, whether they span one, three, or five years.

Activate

Activation is about moving from planning to doing. The futurist mindset encourages starting small and building momentum through iterative progress. Focusing on progress, rather than perfection, allows you to launch initiatives in beta mode and refine them based on real-world feedback.

Gather

Gathering feedback and data is critical for understanding the impact of your changes. A futurist mindset ensures this information is viewed through the lens of improvement and adaptation. Turning learning into a team sport by involving employees in gathering insights and sharing ideas helps foster continuous improvement.

Iterate

Iteration thrives on curiosity and collaboration, which are core elements of futurist thinking. Innovation sessions with your team can reveal how AI might solve challenges or create new opportunities, helping push your business forward.

Narrow

Narrowing your focus is about making strategic choices. A futurist mindset ensures you prioritise efforts that align with long-term vision while remaining flexible enough to adapt. Proactive planning helps evaluate which opportunities will have the greatest long-term impact on your business.

Evolve

Evolution is the ultimate goal of futurist thinking. By staying curious, resilient, and adaptable, you can ensure your business remains relevant and competitive in an AI-driven world. Tracking and celebrating progress reinforces a commitment to growth and innovation.

Take AI action: where does futurist thinking fit for you?

Take a moment to reflect on how futurist thinking aligns with the REIMAGINE Framework for your business:

- Which stage of the framework resonates most with your current challenges?
- What futurist habit could you adopt to enhance that stage?
- How can you involve your team or network to amplify the impact?

By integrating futurist habits into the REIMAGINE Framework, you create a structured yet flexible approach to building your AI-driven future. This combination ensures you're not only prepared for what's next but are actively shaping it.

'What if I can't keep up?'

Shifting into a futurist mindset is as much about your beliefs as it is about your habits. While the practical fears of AI adoption – such as cost or complexity – are often addressed with tools and strategies, the deeper, internal fears can feel harder to tackle. These are the quiet doubts that whisper, 'I'm not ready', or, 'I'll never be able to keep up'.

But here's the truth: futurist thinking isn't about doing everything perfectly or being the first to innovate. It's about staying curious, taking small, intentional steps, and building the confidence to navigate change.

Let's tackle the most common fears and show you how to reframe them as opportunities.

'What if I fail?'

Failure is feedback – an essential part of the learning process. Every experiment provides valuable insight, even when things don't go as planned. The key is to shift your perspective and focus on what you can learn rather than what went wrong. Failure is simply a step towards growth.

'I don't have the skills'

You don't need to be a tech expert to integrate AI into your business. Today's tools are designed to be user-friendly, and learning them is often simpler than it seems. Embrace learning as part of the process by dedicating just 15 to 30 minutes a week to exploring new tools, tutorials, or resources.

'I'm not an innovator'

Innovation isn't about creating something entirely new – it's about improving what already exists. Small businesses innovate every day by refining how they serve customers. Recognise that your resourcefulness is innovation in action. Start small by asking, 'What's one process I could make easier?'

'I don't have the vision to think like a futurist'

Thinking like a futurist isn't about predicting the future – it's about staying curious and asking the right questions. Start with simple prompts like, 'What if this could be easier?' or 'What do my customers need next?' The answers will naturally guide your next steps.

'I'm too set in my ways to change'

Change doesn't mean discarding what makes your business unique – it means evolving to keep it relevant. You're not starting over; you're building on your strengths. Adaptation isn't about losing your business's identity – it's what ensures its longevity.

'I don't know where to start'

You don't need to have a perfect plan before you begin. The most important step is simply starting, even if it's small. Focus on progress rather than perfection by asking, 'What's one small action I can take today?' and building from there.

'Uncertainty feels overwhelming'

Uncertainty isn't something to fear – it's where growth happens. It's about being adaptable and open to possibilities rather than controlling every outcome. Remind yourself that you've navigated change before and can do it again. Start by focusing on what you can control, such as learning, testing, or experimenting.

Fears aren't roadblocks – they're signposts pointing you towards growth. By reframing doubts and taking small, intentional actions, you'll build the confidence and resilience to thrive in an AI-driven world.

Take AI action: your fear reframe plan

Take a moment to reflect on any fears or doubts you've been carrying. Write them down and ask yourself:

- Is this fear based on fact or assumption?
- How can I reframe it as an opportunity?
- What's one small action I can take to challenge this fear today?

Spotting the next trend in your business

You've spent time working on your mindset – shifting from survival mode to forward thinking, embracing habits that keep you curious, and reframing the fears that hold you back. Now, it's time to learn how to spot the trends that will shape your business's future. Trends don't appear out of nowhere – they begin as small signals.

In fact, futurist Amy Webb wrote an entire book called *The Signals Are Talking*, which I highly recommend you read. These signals might be subtle changes in customer behaviour, shifts within your industry, or even broader cultural movements. The ability to spot and act on these signals is one of the most valuable skills for any small business owner. This isn't about chasing every shiny new idea. It's about finding the opportunities that align with your business's strengths, values, and goals. The exercise opposite will guide you through a simple, repeatable process to identify trends that matter and turn them into action.

Take AI action: spotting the next trend

Step 1: Tune into the signals

Trends often reveal themselves through small signals. Start by exploring sources that are already available to you:

- **Customer feedback:** What are your customers consistently asking for or complaining about?
- **Competitors:** What changes or innovations are your competitors adopting?
- **Industry news:** Read blogs, listen to podcasts, or attend webinars to stay informed about your industry.
- **Adjacent industries:** Are there trends in related fields that could cross over to yours?
- **Social media:** What topics are trending in your niche on platforms like LinkedIn, Instagram, or X?

Step 2: Observe patterns

Once you've collected insights, look for recurring themes or ideas. Ask yourself:

- Are there common customer pain points that keep coming up?
- Do multiple competitors seem to be adopting the same type of solution or tool?
- Are there societal or cultural shifts influencing your industry (such as sustainability, personalisation or convenience)?

Step 3: Test the trend

Not every trend is the right fit for your business. Before investing time or money, test the idea on a small scale to gauge interest:

- **Pilot programme:** Launch the trend as a limited-time offer or trial.
- **Customer feedback:** Ask for feedback through surveys, polls, or direct conversations.

- **Measure impact:** Track metrics like sales, engagement, or operational efficiency to evaluate success.

Step 4: Reflect and decide

After testing, evaluate whether the trend aligns with your business goals and values. Ask yourself:

- Did the test improve customer satisfaction or solve a key challenge?
- Is this scalable for your business?
- Does it align with your business values?

If the answers are *yes*, consider integrating the trend more broadly into your operations. If not, take the lessons learned and move on to the next idea.

Choose trends, not fads

Remember the fidget spinner?

It hit like a plastic tsunami – everywhere one day, gone the next. Fads come and go, but trends have staying power because they're rooted in solving real problems or addressing genuine customer needs. Spotting and acting on trends isn't about jumping on every bandwagon. It's about finding the opportunities that align with your goals, serve your customers, and help your business grow sustainably. With this framework, you'll feel confident navigating what's next without the overwhelm. The key is simple: stay curious, stay intentional, and take one step at a time. The future of your business isn't something that happens to you – it's something you shape, starting today.

Reimagining a day five years from now

You may remember way back at the start of the book I walked you through what a 'typical' day looked like for me as I embed more and more AI into every aspect of my life.

As we wrap up this section on future thinking, I thought it could be fun to circle back to our day in the life … but with a little crystal ball–gazing.

It's five years from today. My sleep tracker, which has been monitoring my biometrics throughout the night, gently brings me out of REM sleep at the optimal time. The blinds in my bedroom transition from blackout to daytime, allowing the optimal amount of sunlight through while blocking any UV. The air sits at a comfortable temperature based on my biometric readings. My AI-enabled assistant selects a morning meditation based on the events of the day's calendar, and my day officially begins.

While I'm still not a huge fan of mornings, I manage to rally for my latte, which fortunately is still brought to me each morning by Pete, and the puppies wander closer for morning cuddles.

Instead of having to scroll through my phone, my AI-enabled assistant transitions from meditation to updating me on selected family news from the day before. Images shared into family albums are projected, and I can see the grandkids headed to school and funny memes friends have shared. It then segues into an update of what the day ahead is looking like.

My calendar has shifted a little overnight as clients have rescheduled, or pressing matters have taken priority. The day has been optimised to ensure I'm maintaining focus on the projects I have in place. The AI has already advised clients of any updates to schedules and handled the email and messaging minutiae that did not require my attention.

The device turns my attention to sharing a cliff notes version of several websites and companies I follow on a daily basis. At any point, I can interrupt and ask for additional detail, to have the article read to me or shared to a device for me to read. Any resources or data relevant to clients, books, or presentations are automatically clipped, anodised, and stored in a folder ready for use as needed.

As Pete and I prepare to take Obi and Lando for a walk, we hear the auto feeder for Watson scheduling a delivery of his preferred crunchies because they have come on sale. We pop the leads on the dogs and head off for our morning wander.

Our trackers tell the optimal time to pause and when the kids need to break for water.

When we return home, my office has been prepared, lighting, temperature, and so on ready for my first client session. As I set myself up, the assistant reminds me of where our last call finished, the work the client was focused on, and the progress they have made since our last call.

Throughout the day, as I chat with clients, the AI is taking notes, setting follow-up events, applying tasks to the project manager and calendar as required, and organising any travel that is identified off the back of emails or calls. As my preferred accommodation and travel partners are in the system, the AI can seamlessly select flights based on cost, arrival, and client requirements, as well as organising specific requests with hotels or transfers in between. Updates are immediately shared with clients to ensure transparency and effective communication.

An on-tap water feature keeps me hydrated, and I'm reminded based on my health inputs of the best times to stand to work, or sit, and the best times to walk away for a break and to step away for a longer period to brainstorm, eat, or play with the dogs.

As my house is completely AI-enabled, groceries are ordered and delivered based on my preferred brands, with awareness of specials and selecting options for reduced environmental impact. My fridge is able to automatically order based on the change in weights within cartons, and my pantry is scanned on a daily basis to ensure everything remains in date and stocked.

My utilities are connected to monitor for price fluctuations and opportunities to reduce emissions, which means various devices throughout the house and yard are optimised to operate at their most efficient times.

Our car, sadly, remains a plug-in hybrid. Due to the amount of regional travel we do, the infrastructure to support fully electric vehicles in regional Australia has yet to occur, but there is positive progress continuing as we move towards a hydrogen alternative.

At my preselected time, my office begins its wind-down procedure for the day, updating and backing up files, sending off final updates to contacts based on project dates or work to be concluded. The blinds transition from maximum natural light to the shut-down sequence. I call it a day in the office.

We round the dogs up for their afternoon walk and receive an update to advise Obi has stepped on something that could cause his foot an injury. We resolve this and continue on our evening walk, stopping to throw the ball for Lando to ensure he has expended the energy on his activity counter before returning home.

Around 5 pm each day, I get an automated update from my parents' aged-care facility. I'm advised of how both of them went through the day, any medical issues, outings, concerns, or achievements. It's a great time to reach out for a chat with them as they settle in front of their TV for another evening. They are 'getting used to' the AI-enabled robot that is now coming through to make their beds each day. Dad is amused at how fastidious it is at cleaning floors and dusting, while Mum just finds the whole thing a little overwhelming. What they do appreciate, though, is that the staff are spending more quality time with them, chatting and generally just connecting. This has led to an increased quality of care and, they've managed to pick up a few additional medical declines in Mum that they are able to better monitor because of the additional time spent with her each day.

In the time since we've returned home from our evening walk, our house has transitioned to its nighttime routine. Temperature is adjusted; black-out blinds come into place in the bedroom. Amber lights softly glow, and a scent of lavender is piped in while our lounge shifts to a softer light or glasses transition to a blue tint in preparation for watching our favourite show.

At 10 pm, our house does its final notified security checks before going into monitor mode. We're advised the garage door is ajar, but all other devices are functioning as normal.

As we crawl into bed, our optimised sleeping positions are adjusted, and a meditation to induce melatonin begins.

As I prepare for another night of restful sleep, I'm struck by how seamlessly AI has woven into every corner of my life – not as a replacement for the human touch, but as an amplifier of what matters most: connection, creativity, and impact. Each innovation has freed me to focus on what truly brings joy and meaning – whether that's time with family, exploring bold ideas, or serving clients in ways that were once unimaginable.

Looking back to where this journey started, I see how each step has built towards this future. It didn't happen overnight; it came from clarity of purpose, small, deliberate actions, and a commitment to using AI as a tool to support – not supplant – humanity. Now, as I close my day, I'm reminded that the future isn't something that happens to us. It's something we create.

Now it's your turn.

Take AI action: your day in five years

AI has the power to revolutionise the way we work, live, and connect. But what does that future look like for you? Let's step into your tomorrow and imagine how AI could transform your personal and professional life five years from today.

Visualise your future day

Take a moment to reflect on what your ideal day might look like five years from today, with AI seamlessly integrated into your life. Use the prompts below to guide your vision:

- **Morning rituals:** How does AI support your morning routine? What tasks or decisions are automated, and how do they free up your time or mental space?
- **Your workday:** How does AI enhance your business, work, or creative projects? What roles or processes are simplified, and what areas do you focus on more deeply as a result?
- **Relationships and wellbeing:** How does AI help you stay connected to the people who matter most? What tools or insights support your health and well-being?
- **Evening and reflection:** What does your ideal wind-down look like? How does AI help you celebrate the wins of the day, big or small?

Take it one step further

After writing down your vision, choose one actionable step to start making this future a reality. For example:

- automate a repetitive task to free up time
- explore an AI tool that could improve your customer experience
- delegate a small process to AI so you can focus on a high-value area.

Keep your vision somewhere accessible – whether it's in a journal, on your desk, or even as a voice note. Revisit it periodically to assess your progress and refine your goals. The future isn't just something to dream about; it's something you can start building today.

CHAPTER 13

Turning ideas into impact

'By reimagining your business, you haven't just learned about AI – you've started shaping the future of your business, one bold step at a time. What comes next isn't just about progress; it's transformation that lasts a lifetime.'

Tracy Sheen

Cue the happy dance and crack the champagne – you've made it.

It's no small feat to push aside the nagging doubts and give yourself permission to ask the boldest of questions: *what if?*

What if you reimagined the way you've always done things?

What if you leaned into this brave new world and chose the future of your business by design, not default?

Believe me, I know how challenging this book has been for you. Reimagining isn't easy – it requires courage, curiosity, and no shortage of persistence. So, let me be the first to congratulate you for sticking with it. If you implement even 10% of the mindset shifts and framework steps we've covered, I promise you this: in 12 months, you'll have a business that's more productive, more efficient, and more focused on what you love.

Remember, AI – or any technology – isn't here to compete with you. It's not here to take the jobs of your team. It's here to amplify the things that make your business unique. It's here to partner, not replace.

And now, welcome to the final chapter – where all the puzzle pieces come together. You've explored new ways of thinking, unpacked powerful ideas, and wrestled with what AI means for your business. It's been a big journey, and if you're feeling equal parts inspired and overwhelmed, you're in good company.

This is it. This is where everything we've covered transforms into something tangible. Together, we'll weave all the threads into a practical plan that turns the time and energy you've invested into real-world results.

Think of this as the final step in our REIMAGINE Framework. You've built relationships, evaluated tools, identified opportunities, and activated strategies. Now, we're taking the momentum you've built and creating something enduring. This isn't about cramming in more information; it's about clarity, confidence, and walking away with a plan that works for your business.

The goal? To leave you with a roadmap that grows with you, anchored in what you've learned but flexible enough to adapt to whatever the future holds. After all, reimagining your business isn't about knowing all the answers – it's about having the courage to start, iterate, and evolve.

So, pour the bubbly, raise a glass to your reimagined business, and let's bring this home.

Mindset: the foundation of REIMAGINING

Rethinking decades of 'business as usual' isn't just tough – it's transformative. Many of us have spent years, even decades, building systems and habits that feel comfortable and familiar. Change, especially when it's as monumental as integrating AI, can feel unsettling – even threatening.

But here's the truth: *your mindset is the linchpin of your REIMAGINE journey.*

Throughout this book, you'll have noticed mindset woven into every chapter – not as an afterthought, but as a critical foundation. Why? Because to truly embrace AI and the opportunities it brings, you need to overcome the fear that holds you back. By leaning into curiosity, you shift your perspective: AI stops being a threat and becomes an amplifier of what already makes your business exceptional.

This shift isn't about ignoring challenges or pretending AI is a magic bullet. Instead, it's about equipping yourself with a framework to objectively analyse AI. It's about seeing both the opportunities and the challenges and weighing them against your ethics, relationships, values, and sustainability. AI becomes the tool that magnifies your strengths, eliminates bottlenecks, and forges deeper connections with your customers and team.

Stepping into this future demands confidence – not in AI, but in your ability to guide its use. Technology isn't here to replace the human heart of your business; it's here to support it.

Critical thinking becomes your compass on this journey. Questioning assumptions, staying grounded in your values, and making deliberate choices will help you navigate complexity with clarity. This isn't just about keeping pace; it's about outpacing the toughest competition of all: the version of yourself that fears change. The real question is: will you follow the paths others have forged, or will you reimagine a business future based on your own vision of success?

The only constant is change. Embrace it and you hold the advantage.

While others resist or fear what's ahead, your willingness to adapt and reimagine will set you apart. In a world of constant evolution, your adaptability isn't just a survival tactic – it's your superpower.

Mindset to momentum

With a reimagined mindset as your foundation, you're beginning to see through the matrix of moving parts and understand how everything is connected.

The REIMAGINE Framework isn't just a list of steps – it's a unified system designed to help your business evolve in real time. It's the lens that reveals the threads tying together your relationships, tools, ethics, and decisions into a cohesive whole.

At its core, it's a blueprint for growth, flexibility, and ethical decision-making that places people and purpose at the heart of every action. The framework isn't static – it evolves with you, adapting as your business, your customers, and the world around you change.

Just as change is constant, the REIMAGINE Framework is fluid – a dynamic system that not only builds momentum but keeps it alive. It helps you make sense of complexity, navigate change, and transform it into opportunity.

The nine steps to reimagine your business

Let's walk through the REIMAGINE Framework one last time – not as isolated steps, but as the fluid and interconnected system it is.

Relationships: the heart of transformation

At the centre of every successful change are the people who make it happen, from your customers to your team, suppliers, and community. Relationships are your most valuable asset, as strong connections create trust, and trust forms the foundation for innovation and change. AI doesn't replace relationships – it amplifies them, allowing you to deepen connections and scale trust without losing the human touch.

Evaluate: looking at tools through an ethical lens

In a world full of shiny new tech, it's easy to be distracted by what's possible. But evaluating tools isn't about what's new – it's about what's right for you. This step challenges you to assess every tool against your values, mission, and long-term goals. Ethical, thoughtful evaluation ensures your AI decisions align with your future vision and create lasting value.

Identify: finding the low-hanging fruit

Big transformations start small. Identifying quick wins – the areas where AI can deliver maximum impact with minimal effort – builds confidence and momentum. Just like the 'butterfly effect', sometimes the smallest change creates the biggest ripple across your business.

Mapping: creating a plan with flexibility

Mapping isn't just about laying out steps – it's about building a roadmap that's flexible enough to adapt to change. In today's fast-paced world, your map should be a living document, ready to evolve as new opportunities arise. Success isn't about rigid plans – it's about clarity, direction, and the agility to pivot when needed.

Activate: turning ideas into action

Activation is where everything starts to come to life. It's not about waiting for the perfect moment; it's about starting where you are with what you have. Every bold move begins with one small, deliberate step.

Gather: learning from the journey

Activation isn't the end – it's the beginning of a feedback loop. Gathering insights allows you to refine your efforts, uncover hidden opportunities, and ensure you're heading in the right direction. Insights aren't just numbers; they're stories that guide your next steps.

Iterate: refining and repeating

Business isn't about getting it right the first time – it's about getting better every time. Iteration is the process of refining what works, discarding what doesn't, and continually improving. Think like a boat captain, constantly tacking to meet the wind. Small, consistent adjustments – not giant leaps – being sustainable progress.

Narrow: focusing on what works

Narrowing your focus is a superpower. By doubling down on what delivers value and letting go of what doesn't, you free up resources to grow in the areas that matter most. Success isn't about doing more – it's about doing the right things at the right time.

Evolve: shaping your future business

Reimagining doesn't end – it evolves. As your business grows, so does your ability to anticipate change and create the future you want. Evolution isn't about staying ahead of the game; it's about creating the game you want to play.

The REIMAGINE Framework isn't a rigid process – it's a living, breathing system that grows with you. It's built on leadership, ethics, critical thinking, and a futurist mindset, empowering you to adapt to change while staying grounded in your values.

This is your moment to take everything you've learned and turn it into momentum. With this framework, you're not responding or reacting to the future – you're designing it.

Beyond the framework: the need for critical thinking

As you've seen in the REIMAGINE Framework, every step depends on one thing: your ability to think critically. AI may be a game-changing tool, but it's not a replacement for your judgment, intuition, or values. It's a partner that amplifies your strengths, and it's your critical thinking that ensures you wield it wisely.

In an age when automation is everywhere, critical thinking has become the ultimate superpower. It's what sets your businesses apart, ensuring all decisions are human-centred, ethical, informed and aligned with your goals and values.

In a world driven by automation, critical thinking sets you apart

AI excels at processing data, identifying patterns, and automating repetitive tasks. But, as we identified early in our framework, it lacks one vital ingredient: human judgment.

This is where critical thinking comes in, acting as the filter through which AI tools are selected, deployed, and managed:

- **Asking the right questions:** Every AI tool you evaluate should pass the test of your core values and business goals. Ask yourself:
  - Does this tool solve a real problem?
  - How does it align with our ethics and priorities?
  - What are the potential risks or unintended consequences?
- **Balancing intuition with data:** While AI provides valuable data-driven insights, your intuition and experience remain crucial. Critical thinking allows you to blend both, ensuring decisions are not just logical but also human-centred. Never ignore your 'gut instincts', we get them for a reason.
- **Recognising the need for human oversight:** Even the smartest AI can misstep, misunderstand, or reflect unintended biases. Critical thinking and a human-centred approach to reimagining your business helps you recognise where human oversight is essential to maintain trust, accuracy, and ethical integrity.

Automation may make things faster and easier, but it's your ability to think critically that ensures your business stays true to its vision. By staying curious, asking tough questions, and combining intuition with data, you'll make decisions that aren't just efficient – they're intentional and impactful.

AI may power the future, but critical thinking is the fuel to make that future yours.

Thinking critically and leading boldly

Critical thinking isn't just about making better decisions – it's about designing the type of business you want and the community you want to create. For businesses, this role goes beyond day-to-day operations. You have the unique power to lead by example in your communities, setting a tone that bigger businesses often struggle to match.

Small businesses don't just serve communities – we shape them. Whether it's through the way you connect with customers, the decisions you make about the tools you use, or the values you champion, your leadership resonates far beyond your bottom line.

In the age of AI, small businesses have an extraordinary opportunity that extends well beyond the boundaries of their own operations:

- **Setting the tone for ethical AI adoption:** As a small business owner, you're not tied to the inertia of sprawling systems. You have the ability to integrate AI thoughtfully, ensuring every decision reflects your values. By leading with ethics and communicating with transparency, you set an example that customers, competitors, and your broader industry will notice.
- **Championing sustainability and inclusivity:** You have the agility to innovate in ways that prioritise people and the planet. From sourcing products responsibly to building diverse and inclusive teams, every choice you make sends ripples of positive impact.
- **Fostering trust and connection:** In a world that feels increasingly impersonal, small businesses play an irreplaceable role in creating meaningful connections. While others scale purely for efficiency, you have the power to scale for trust – turning every interaction into an opportunity to build lasting relationships.

Beyond this, I believe we all hold a responsibility to our communities and our people to act as educators and ambassadors for what AI really means. This isn't about fear or resistance – it's about curiosity and understanding. By sharing the true potential of AI and demonstrating how to adopt it thoughtfully and responsibly, you empower those around you to navigate this new world with confidence and purpose.

And if intention really does create reality, then it's in our best interest to have open conversations about everything we're learning – exploring the ways AI is and will continue to impact society at large.

Your leadership shapes not only your business but the culture around you. The decisions you make set a standard, inspiring those who work with you and the community you serve to think differently about what's possible.

By leading with purpose and educating with curiosity, you're not just navigating change – you're defining it. You're creating the kind of society and community where everyone has the opportunity to thrive, together.

Leadership and humanity: our role in an AI-driven world

At the start of our REIMAGINE Framework journey, we explored the role of relationships and the importance of committing to keeping humans at the centre of everything we do.

Technology is an enabler, not a replacement. Remove humanity and relationships and we have no business.

But as AI continues to embed itself across every facet of society, questions emerge: *What does this look like in an AI-driven world? What is our role as humans in this evolving landscape?*

As AI takes on more of the repetitive, time-consuming tasks that often weigh us down, it frees humans to focus on what we do best: creativity, empathy, critical thinking and leadership.

The future isn't a competition between AI and humans – it's a collaboration, with each playing to their strengths to create something better:

- **AI handles the mundane; humans drive the meaningful:** With AI managing routine tasks like scheduling, inventory updates, and data analysis, your time and energy are freed up for innovation, strategy, and building stronger relationships. This shift allows you to focus on the bigger picture – creating, inspiring, and leading with purpose.
- **Emotional intelligence as the key differentiator:** While AI excels at patterns and precision, it lacks the ability to understand emotions or the value of trust, or create meaningful connections. This is where emotional intelligence becomes your differentiator. In customer service, leadership, and collaboration, your ability to empathise, understand, and connect sets you apart in ways no machine can replicate.
- **The rise of human-centric leadership:** In an AI-first world, the role of a leader becomes more human than ever. Guiding your team through change, fostering a culture of curiosity and adaptability, and connecting deeply with your customers will be your edge in a landscape where technology alone is no longer enough.

The future of business isn't AI versus humans – it's AI and humans working together as collaborators. AI's strength lies in efficiency and precision, while humanity's lies in creativity, empathy, and connection. Together, they form a partnership that's not just powerful, it's transformative.

By embracing this collaboration, you're harnessing the best of both worlds to create a business that is smarter, more innovative, more creative, more intuitive, values-driven, and uniquely human.

Collaboration to action: embedding reimagining in your business

Understanding the REIMAGINE Framework means we've recognised that AI and humans aren't competitors – they're collaborators. We've embraced the leadership role we have to play as educators and ambassadors for our communities, and we've recalibrated our mindset to adopt futurist thinking.

This is a powerful step, but the real transformation comes with the final shift – from realisation to a committed decision to embed the REIMAGINE Framework into your business.

Reimagining your business isn't a one-time effort; it's an ongoing process that must become part of your DNA to truly unleash its positive, powerful, and potent potential.

Infusing REIMAGINING into your DNA

Turning what you've learned into action doesn't have to feel overwhelming. The key to consistent and long-term reimagining is starting small, staying consistent, and remaining flexible. Here are some practical steps to make the REIMAGINE Framework a part of your everyday operations:

- **Integrate AI into daily operations with small pilot projects:** Start with something manageable, like automating a repetitive task or improving customer engagement through AI-powered tools. Test it on a small scale, gather feedback, and refine before rolling it out further.
- **Conduct regular reviews of tools and processes:** Schedule regular reviews to evaluate how your tools and systems are performing. Are they still aligned with your goals and values? Do they need fine-tuning, replacing, or scaling?

- **Build flexibility into your roadmap:** No roadmap or plan should be set in stone. Stay open to pivoting based on new opportunities, feedback, or changes in your market. Think of your roadmap as an organic document – designed to evolve as you do.
- **Scale the framework as your business grows:** As your business expands, the framework can scale with you. Use the nine steps of REIMAGINE to guide larger projects or bring new team members into alignment with your vision.
- **Focus on small, consistent steps:** Implementation doesn't have to happen all at once. Start where you are, with what you have, and take small steps. Momentum builds when you take consistent action.

Big results come from small, consistent steps

Reimagining your business isn't about sweeping everything off the desk and starting fresh – it's about making progress one step at a time. By starting small, staying flexible, and committing to consistent action, you'll build the momentum needed to carry your business forward.

It's about adopting a fluid attitude towards the future of business. Like water flowing through a natural watercourse, we must bend, slow down, or speed up to continue our journey. There will be moments of turbulence and moments of stillness. Sometimes we'll solidify around an idea, while at other times, we'll sweep away debris – removing what no longer serves us. Ultimately, we are forever adapting, analysing, and steering our path based on the obstacles or opportunities we encounter.

When you truly instil reimagination into your DNA, you make the powerful decision to actively shape and create the type of business you desire – one that's adaptable, intentional, and built for the future.

Your REIMAGINING starts now

This is it – the moment to turn intention into action. You've come so far on this journey, exploring new ways of thinking, embracing bold ideas, and discovering how AI can help reimagine your business. Now it's time to take the first step forward.

One final truth bomb: *you're never going to have all the answers.*

But here's the good news: you don't need to. Because along the way, you've learned something far more powerful – how to ask the right questions. These questions will guide you to create the best possible results every single time, whether it's learning from something that didn't go to plan or finally solving a problem that's been frustrating your team for ages.

If you're still feeling unsure or hesitant, know this: you don't need to have everything figured out to begin. The most important thing is to take one small step forward. Even the tiniest action creates momentum, and with each step, the path becomes clearer. Trust the process, and trust yourself – you're more ready than you realise.

Reimagining isn't about having every detail figured out in advance. It's about having the curiosity to explore, the confidence to take the first step, and the courage to adapt as you go.

Here's a simple path forward:

- **Start small:** Choose one area of your business where AI can make an immediate impact. Maybe it's automating a repetitive task, improving scheduling, or streamlining your customer service. The key is to pick one thing and take action.
- **Lean into the REIMAGINE mindset:** Think of this as an experiment. Embrace iteration, and be open to what you learn along the way. Small adjustments over time will lead to big results.

- **Commit to regular reflection and refinement:** Set time aside to evaluate what's working, what's not, and what needs tweaking. This process of continual refinement ensures your progress stays aligned with your goals and values.

You've got this

Taking that first step can feel daunting, but remember: you're not starting from scratch. You've already built a foundation of insight, strategy, and confidence. Now, it's about putting it into motion.

With every small step forward, you're creating momentum. You're building a business that's more resilient, innovative, and aligned with the future you want to create.

The key is this: action beats perfection every time. You don't have to get it right on day one. You just need to begin.

From my business to yours

As we come to the end of this journey together, I want to share something personal. The REIMAGINE Framework isn't just something I've written about, and it's not just something that has guided my clients over the years.

It's what I live.

And it took me writing this book to truly realise it.

Embracing emerging technologies and living this mindset has been at the heart of what I've done since I was five years old, sitting on the floor of my parents' factory, pulling electronic scales apart. The REIMAGINE Framework has been the roadmap of my life, shaping how I approach challenges, opportunities, and the unknown.

Danish philosopher Søren Kierkegaard explains what I'm thinking better than I can: 'Life can only be understood backwards; but it must be lived forwards.'

It wasn't until I sat down to write this book that my career and life came into focus. It was only then that I realised how the REIMAGINE Framework was born in my childhood curiosity and matured as I placed the final full stop on this book.

This framework has moulded how I view the future. It has shown me the power of leaning into change with curiosity and purpose, and I'm truly excited for what it can do for you too.

This journey isn't just about adapting to today's challenges – it's about actively designing the future you want for your business. With every step forward, you're building a business that isn't just ready for change but thrives because of it. It won't always be straightforward, but I promise it will be worth it. You've already taken the most important step by committing to reimagine what's possible for your business. From here, it's about taking one small step at a time, staying true to your values, and allowing curiosity to guide your decisions.

I'd love to hear how you go. Whether it's a small win or a major breakthrough, please reach out to me on my socials (just google Tracy Sheen The Digital Guide and find your social platform of choice) and share your progress. If you ever feel stuck or need guidance, I'm here to help.

Most of all, *thank you*. Thank you for trusting me to be your guide as you commit to building a business that's innovative, human-centred, forward-focused, ethical, and uniquely yours.

You've got everything you need to reimagine your business – and I'm cheering for you every step of the way.

With gratitude,

Tracy

Take AI action: the AI leadership pledge

Your commitment to leading with integrity

Start as you mean to continue.

As you take everything you've learned and begin your own reimagining journey, it's important to ground yourself in the values and principles that have guided you this far. This framework and process isn't just about adopting new tools – it's about leading with integrity, ensuring that the choices you make serve your business, your community, and your customers in meaningful ways.

Here's a simple pledge you can adopt to keep your AI journey aligned with your vision and values. Feel free to adapt it in any way that best aligns with your own business.

The AI Leadership Pledge

I pledge to:

- **Commit to transparency:** I will openly communicate how AI is used in my business, ensuring customers, team members, and stakeholders understand its purpose and value.
- **Prioritise relationships over automation:** I will use AI as a tool to amplify human connection, not replace it. Relationships will remain at the heart of my business.
- **Integrate AI thoughtfully:** I will evaluate and integrate AI tools in a way that aligns with my values, ensuring they enhance efficiency without compromising ethics or trust.
- **Regularly reflect and refine:** I will periodically assess the impact of AI on my business and community, making adjustments as needed to ensure it continues to serve the greater good.
- **Lead by example:** I will act as an ambassador for ethical AI adoption, educating my team, customers, and community about its potential and its responsible use.

This pledge is your commitment to lead with integrity, curiosity, and purpose as you navigate the opportunities and challenges AI presents. By anchoring your decisions in these principles, you'll not only build a better business – you'll inspire others to do the same.

Take action now

Your AI Leadership Pledge is more than just words – it's a commitment to lead with purpose, integrity, and intention. Make this pledge a reality today:

- **Write your pledge:** Start by writing out your personalised version of the pledge in a journal or document. Reflect on how each principle aligns with your business's unique values and goals.
- **Share your commitment:** Share your pledge with your team, customers, or community. Or, you can share it with me on any of my social media platforms; I'd love to see what you come up with. This act of transparency will inspire others to join you on this journey.
- **Revisit it regularly:** Keep your pledge visible – pin it to your office wall, make it a part of team discussions, or set a quarterly reminder to revisit it. Use it as a compass to guide your decisions and keep your business aligned with its values.

Remember, this isn't about perfection – it's about progress. Every small step you take reinforces your leadership and sets the tone for your business's future. By acting on your pledge, you're not just imagining change – you're creating it.

FURTHER RESOURCES

Learning beyond the book

'Learning doesn't stop when you put this book down. The most successful business owners aren't those who know it all – they're the ones who stay curious, embrace change, and keep asking, "What's next?"'
Tracy Sheen

Your AI journey doesn't stop here. *AI & U* has equipped you with a foundation to reimagine your business with AI, but staying ahead in this fast-evolving landscape requires continued learning, curiosity, and adaptability. This section offers curated resources to help you deepen your understanding, track emerging trends, and prepare for what's next.

Whether you're looking for books, podcasts, or tools to explore new AI concepts or wanting to monitor future trends, you'll find practical and inspiring guidance here. Use this section as your go-to resource for learning beyond the book.

Recommended reading and learning resources

All resources are grouped into categories, including books, podcasts, YouTube channels, and blogs/websites. Each section provides small business owners with multiple ways to explore and learn.

I'd be silly not to lead with my own community, and I'd love you to stay in touch. If you'd like to connect with me, you'll find me on the following platforms:

The Digital Guide

- **Website:** thedigitalguide.com.au
- **YouTube:** @thedigitalguideau
- **LinkedIn:** /company/thedigitalguide
- **Facebook:** @tracythedigitalguide
- **Instagram:** @thedigitalguide

AI foundations

For understanding the basics of AI and its practical applications.

Books

- *The Singularity Is Nearer.* Ray Kurzweil. An updated exploration of Artificial Intelligence and its trajectory towards reshaping humanity, providing new insights and developments since *The Singularity Is Near.*
- *What You Need to Know About AI: A beginner's guide to what the future holds.* Brian David Johnson. A simple, approachable introduction to AI for non-technical readers.
- *AI Superpowers: China, silicon valley, and the new world order.* Kai-Fu Lee. Explores the global race for AI leadership and how small businesses can tap into emerging opportunities.

Podcasts

- **Lex Fridman Podcast.** Conversations with thought leaders, including discussions on Artificial Intelligence, ethics, and its future.

Websites/blogs

- **Ben's Bites.** A daily, easy-to-digest newsletter summarising the latest AI tools, news, and trends for small businesses and enthusiasts.

Futurism and trends

To stay ahead of emerging trends and think like a futurist.

Books

- *The Signals Are Talking: Why today's fringe is tomorrow's mainstream.* Amy Webb. A framework for identifying early signals of change before they disrupt industries.
- *Converge: A futurist's insights into the potential of our world as technology and humanity collide.* Dr Catherine Ball. Explores how technology and humanity intersect, with actionable insights into building a better future.
- *Non-Obvious Trends.* Rohit Bhargava. Offers insights into global trends and how to prepare for them.

Podcasts

- **News from Tomorrow.** A fresh and thought-provoking podcast exploring emerging technologies, global shifts, and futurist insights.

YouTube Channels

- **Amy Webb's Future Today Institute.** Features talks, interviews, and videos that explore emerging trends and the future of technology.

Websites/blogs

- **World Economic Forum: AI & Machine Learning.** Focuses on global trends and their implications for businesses.
- **Amy Webb's Future Today Institute Blog.** Offers reports and resources on tech trends shaping industries.

Ethics and governance

For adopting AI responsibly and aligning it with human-centred values.

Books

- *Man-Made: How the bias of the past is being built into the future.* Tracey Spicer. Explores how bias and inequality are being perpetuated by AI systems, with practical advice for building a fairer future.
- *Weapons of Math Destruction.* Cathy O'Neil. A compelling look at how algorithms can reinforce inequality – and how to address it.
- *Checkmate Humanity: The how and why of responsible AI.* Sam Kirshner, Richard Vidgen, and Catriona Wallace. Explains the foundations of responsible AI practices and their importance for creating a fairer future.

Websites/blogs

- **Australian AI Principles.** A guide developed by the Australian Government to ensure responsible and ethical use of AI.
- **Australian Human Rights Commission: AI & Human Rights.** A comprehensive resource exploring the ethical and human rights implications of AI in Australia.

Take AI action: get started

Choose just one resource from each section that aligns with your current goals or knowledge gaps. Commit to exploring it within the next 30 days – steady, focused learning will make the biggest impact.

GLOSSARY

AI terms for small business owners

Computer vision: AI that enables machines to interpret and process visual information from the world. *Example: A smartphone camera recognising faces to unlock the phone.*

Conversational AI: AI systems designed to engage in human-like conversations, often through chatbots or voice assistants. *Example: A chatbot handling customer inquiries about shipping and returns.*

Data privacy: The practice of protecting personal or sensitive data from unauthorised access or misuse. *Example: Encrypting customer data stored in a business's systems.*

Data sovereignty: The principle that data is subject to the laws and governance of the country where it is collected or processed. *Example: Ensuring customer data stored in the cloud complies with UK data protection laws.*

Decentralised autonomous organisations (DAOs): Organisations run by smart contracts on blockchain technology, allowing decentralised, transparent decision-making without traditional hierarchies. *Example: Using a DAO to manage shared resources or investments among collaborators.*

Deep learning: A type of machine learning that uses neural networks with many layers to solve complex problems. *Example: AI diagnosing medical conditions from X-ray images.*

Democratised AI: Making AI technologies or resources widely accessible to people, regardless of expertise or resources. *Example: AI tools being available to small businesses at an affordable price, enabling broader adoption.*

Digital transformation: The process of using technology to fundamentally change how a business operates and delivers value. *Example: A small business transitioning from paper-based invoicing to cloud-based systems.*

Digital twin: A virtual replica of a physical object, system, or process used to model and test scenarios. *Example: Simulating changes in a warehouse layout to optimise storage and workflow.*

Disruptive innovation: Innovations that significantly alter or replace existing markets or business models. *Example: AI-powered platforms that enable small businesses to compete with larger competitors in marketing.*

Edge computing: Processing data near the source of generation (such as a device) rather than relying on a centralised location. *Example: A smart thermostat analysing room temperature locally to make adjustments.*

Emerging technologies: New and developing technologies with the potential to disrupt industries and create new opportunities. *Example: AI, blockchain, and quantum computing are emerging technologies reshaping how businesses operate.*

Explainable AI (XAI): AI systems designed to provide clear and understandable explanations for their decisions and actions.

Example: An AI tool used for loan approvals that explains why an application was accepted or rejected.

Fairness in AI: Ensuring AI systems do not unfairly favour or disadvantage any group or individual. *Example: Testing a recruitment AI tool to ensure it evaluates candidates equally, regardless of gender or ethnicity.*

Generative AI: AI that creates new content, such as text, images, or music, based on the data it has been trained on. *Example: Tools like ChatGPT or DALL-E that write articles or design visuals.*

Holographic technology: The creation of 3D, lifelike visuals that appear to float in space, enabling immersive experiences. *Example: The ABBA Voyage virtual concert experience.*

Human-in-the-loop (HITL): An AI system that relies on human intervention to refine, guide, or approve its output. *Example: A content generation AI where a human reviews and edits the generated copy before publishing.*

Hyperautomation: The use of AI and machine learning to automate as many business processes as possible. *Example: A business automating inventory management, customer service, and invoicing with integrated AI tools.*

Hyper-personalisation: AI tailors every interaction to individual customer preferences by analysing behavioural, demographic, and transactional data. *Example: The 'Recommended for You' section on streaming or e-commerce platforms.*

Internet of Things (IoT): A network of interconnected devices that exchange data. *Example: A fitness tracker sending activity data to a smartphone app.*

Innovation stack: The layered combination of tools, technologies, and strategies a business uses to drive innovation. *Example: Combining AI, automation, and analytics to create more efficient workflows.*

Intentionality: The practice of deliberately choosing AI tools and strategies that align with a business's goals and values. *Example: Evaluating AI tools based on their alignment with ethical principles and a company's mission.*

Large language model (LLM): A type of AI trained on vast amounts of text data to understand and generate human-like language. *Example: Tools like ChatGPT that can write emails, generate reports, or answer questions.*

Low-code/no-code platforms: Tools that allow users to build applications or automate tasks without needing extensive coding knowledge. *Example: Automating email workflows using platforms like Zapier or Airtable.*

Machine learning (ML): A subset of AI where computers learn from data to improve their performance over time without being explicitly programmed. *Example: Email spam filters that get better at detecting spam as more emails are analysed.*

Metaverse: A collective virtual space where people interact using digital avatars, often blending VR and AR technologies. *Example: Hosting virtual events or conferences in a metaverse platform.*

Monopolisation: When a technology or market is dominated by a single organisation or a few large players. *Example: Concerns about large corporations controlling access to critical AI platforms.*

Multi-modality: The ability of AI systems to process and integrate information from multiple types of data, such as text, images, video, and audio. *Example: An AI tool analysing customer feedback (text),* *product images (visuals), and recorded customer calls (audio) to identify patterns in satisfaction levels.*

Natural language processing (NLP): AI's ability to understand and generate human language. *Example: Chatbots that answer customer queries on a website.*

Neural networks: A type of machine learning inspired by the human brain, using layers of nodes (like neurons) to process data and make predictions. *Example: Recognising faces in photos on social media platforms.*

Open AI (the concept, not the company): Open AI tools are like DIY kits – you get full access to the code, allowing customisation. *Example: Creating a system tailored to a business without purchasing a pre-built platform.*

Personalisation: Customising products, services, or communications using AI to match individual preferences. *Example: AI recommending tailored products based on a customer's purchase history.*

Predictive analytics: Using historical data and AI to predict future trends or behaviours. *Example: A retailer predicting which products will sell best during the holiday season.*

Predictive maintenance: Using AI to predict when equipment or machinery is likely to fail, allowing for proactive repairs. *Example: A smart coffee machine that alerts the owner when maintenance is needed to avoid breakdowns.*

Quantum computing: A type of computing that uses the principles of quantum mechanics to process information exponentially faster than traditional computers. *Example: Quantum computing could revolutionise supply chain optimisation, cryptography, and AI by solving complex problems that classical computers cannot.*

Tracy Sheen is Australia's #1 Digital & AI Speaker, author of AI & U, and a trusted advisor to governments and corporates navigating AI adoption and governance.

Inspired by the book?
Find out more about Tracy in the following pages.

- **www.tracysheen.com**
- **www.thedigitalguide.com.au**

BRING AI TO LIFE IN YOUR ORGANISATION

From boardroom strategy to team capability and client tools – this is AI that works for your world.

Whether you're:

- Leading a team ready to streamline how things get done
- Shaping policy and need clarity on governance
- Educating others who need confidence, not complexity

Tracy Sheen helps teams make AI work – one smart, strategic step at a time.

For more information on working with Tracy email or scan the code.

info@thedigitalguide.com.au
www.thedigitalguide.com.au

SPEAKING & WORKSHOPS: TRANSFORM AI OVERWHELM INTO OPPORTUNITY

Tracy delivers clear, practical sessions that cut through the jargon and get people thinking differently about AI.

Perfect for:

- Conferences and keynotes
- Leadership offsites
- Boardroom brainstorms
- Industry panels

To book Tracy for your next event email or scan the code.

info@tracysheen.com
www.tracysheen.com

CREATE A LASTING IMPACT: LICENSING, LEARNING & BULK ORDERS

Turn AI insights into action across your team or event.

Options include:

- Bulk book orders with branded inserts
- Companion PDF playbook for continued learning
- Licensing for internal L&D programs
- Co-branded resource kits

Equip your people to keep learning long after the session ends.

To find out more about bulk book purchases or continued learning email Tracy or scan the code.

info@thedigitalguide.com.au

www.thedigitalguide.com.au

IN THE MEDIA

The Daily Telegraph

Looking for someone to cut through the AI noise and connect?

Tracy Sheen is a trusted voice in a sea of hype – calm, clear, and credible.

With 30+ years in the digital space, she's been featured across national media for her expertise on AI adoption, digital tools, and tech literacy.

To talk to Tracy about media appearances email Tracy or scan the code.

info@tracysheen.com
www.tracysheen.com

EXPAND YOUR BRAND REACH

Want to grow brand awareness or improve usage of your product?

Tracy partners with forward thinking brands to deliver:

- Roadshows
- Product reviews (B2B and digital tools)
- Strategic digital education campaigns

To talk to Tracy about brand partnerships email Tracy or scan the code.

info@tracysheen.com
www.tracysheen.com
www.thedigitalguide.com.au

www.ingramcontent.com/pod-product-compliance
Lightning Source LLC
LaVergne TN
LVHW071051260826
846485LV00065B/996

* 9 7 8 1 9 2 3 2 2 5 7 8 7 *